The Art of the Real

POETRY IN ENGLAND AND AMERICA SINCE 1939

To Charlie, who arrived,

and to Maggie, who arrived in time

The Art of the Real

POETRY IN ENGLAND AND AMERICA SINCE 1939

Eric Homberger

Lecturer in American Literature
University of East Anglia

DENT, LONDON AND TORONTO

ROWMAN AND LITTLEFIELD, TOTOWA, N.J.

Made in Great Britain
at Biddles Ltd, Guildford, Surrey
and Bound at the Aldine Press, Letchworth, Herts
for
J.M. DENT & SONS LTD
Aldine House, Albemarle Street, London
First published in the U.K. (Everyman's University Library) 1977

First published in the United States
(Rowman & Littlefield University Library)
by ROWMAN AND LITTLEFIELD, Totowa, New Jersey 1977

This book is set in 10 on 11pt IBM Press Roman

Dent edition
Hardback ISBN 0 460 10084 x
Paperback ISBN 0 460 11084 5

Rowman and Littlefield edition
Hardback ISBN 0-87471-938-0

Contents

angry primitivism arrives, led by Gary Snyder; Galway Kinnell from alienation to primitivism; the loose, baggy monsters of John Berryman and Robert Lowell; the final contention between Geoffrey Hill and Ted Hughes.

Preface

In April 1969 a Museum of Modern Art exhibit entitled 'The Art of the Real: An Aspect of American Painting and Sculpture 1948-1968' was presented at the Tate Gallery. Prominently featured were works by Kenneth Noland, Paul Feeley, Barnett Newman, and Morris Louis. The director of the exhibition, E. C. Goossen, wrote a lucid if negative explanation of the paintings and sculptures he had brought together:

> The 'real' of today as it is posited by this new art has nothing to do with metaphor, or symbolism, or any kind of metaphysics. It is not the ideal Hegelian essence that Hans Hofmann was invoking several decades ago in his essay, 'The Search for the *Real*'. It does not wish to convey the notion that reality is somewhere else. Neither is it related to the *symbolic* reality Malevich thought he had discovered when, in 1913, he first isolated his black square on a white field . . . Today's 'real' . . . makes no direct appeal to the emotions, nor is it involved in uplift. Indeed, it seems to have no desire at all to justify itself, but instead offers itself for whatever its uniqueness is worth — in the form of the simple irreducible object.

The poets personally closest to this art — Frank O'Hara, John Ashbery and Kenneth Koch — saw themselves as a 'school' in the painter's sense of an accepted collective enterprise. By the early 1950s they settled in New York and moved easily in the world of painters, galleries and collectors. Uptown, the New Critics and formalist poets at Columbia University lived in a different world, one dominated by the great literary reviews, the prestigious universities, and which represented the core of an Anglophile literary culture. The tragically early death of Frank O'Hara in 1966, and the emergence of a publicity-conscious school of younger writers in the New York Area who consciously modelled their work after O'Hara, Ashbery and Koch, transformed an aesthetic argument into propaganda and polemics. But the New York school could not claim an exclusive right to the idea of an art of the real, for there are other meanings, other poets, neither tied together by a programme or even necessarily aware of each other's work, for whom the phrase is appropriate. Alun Lewis, Theodore

Roethke and Sylvia Plath were in quite different ways devotees of an art of the real in Goossen's sense, and in D. H. Lawrence's:

> ... the essence of poetry with us in this age of stark and unlovely actualities is a stark directness, without a shadow of a lie, or a shadow of deflection anywhere. Everything can go, but this stark, bare, rocky directness of statement, this alone makes poetry to-day.

In an unpublished lecture delivered in 1933, T. S. Eliot quoted these words of Lawrence's, with the comment that

> This speaks to me of that which I have long aimed, in writing poetry; to write poetry which should be essentially poetry, with nothing poetic about it, poetry standing naked in its bare bones, or poetry so transparent that we should not see the poetry, but that which we are meant to see through the poetry, poetry so transparent that in reading it we are intent on what the poem *points at*, and not on the poetry ...[1]

'Transparency' is Eliot's way of suggesting the self-effacing temperament of the poet, more committed to the real, 'what the poem *points at*', than to the fascinations of the process of poetry itself. This kind of 'art of the real' is quite the opposite, even deeply hostile, to the work of the New York school. It represents a different spirit in poetry — certainly less doctrinaire, less theoretically minded, and suggested a poetry somewhat less satisfied with its own sense of humour.

In the last months of his life, Alun Lewis craved experience which would give 'more and more life'. Roethke found in the greenhouse 'a reality harsher than reality'. Plath grew more and more aware that there are many ways by which we are fobbed off with the tamed or the cultivated (thinking of the meadows outside Grantchester). Travelling in the summer of 1959 in the Mojave Desert and in the Canadian mountain country, she grew hungrier for the real in all its fierceness. An art of the real is not a celebration of what is, nor a grumbling inability to imagine things otherwise; it is not a materialism in search of praise; rather, it represents a process of transformation and renovation of the possibilities of the real world in which we live. That 'real world' has changed immeasurably since 1939, and the adequacy of any art of the real is to be measured by the depth and meaningfulness of the liaison it maintains with that world of everyday cares and preoccupations, with everything that is not poetry. In this sense this is a study of the age itself, and of the ways the relation between poetry and society have been expressed.

This book is not a survey, or even, strictly speaking, a comparison of the whole range of poets who have emerged in England and America. It was necessary at the outset to concede that it was impossible to do justice to the Irish, Scots and Welsh poets, given the size of the book; and that certain convenient categories of poetry, such as poetry by blacks, women, and the various ethnopoetries, would play little or no part in the argument; and that there are writers whom I greatly admire who do not appear in these pages for the same reason. Other schools, traditions, groups, movements, in an increasingly Balkanized literary context, have had to be ignored, if this book was to remain literary criticism instead of a reference book. It is sobering, nevertheless, to discover so vividly the provinciality of an education, of a 'literary tradition'.

A decade ago M. L. Rosenthal wrote that 'poetry can be understood one poem at a time only'.[2] This is a fairly concise indication of the reason why we do not have anything like an adequate history of contemporary poetry. The most intelligent critics, such as Josephine Miles, have been content to work exclusively within the language of poetry, or have written extended formal analyses of a small number of poets. That sixth sense of an historical dimension has often been lacking. Some recent critics have transformed the plodding of the New Critics into something racier, more extravagant and stylish, yet which remains deeply formalist at heart. I have tried to retrieve that dimension of historicity. My literary judgments have often been influenced by my interest in the historical reality of certain kinds of social experience. The publication in English of Walter Benjamin has shaped my own unsystematic and impressionistic inclinations, while at the same time discouraging any attempt to mistake his own waywardness for a method. *Illuminations,* and the study of Baudelaire, remain for me the most exhilarating criticism of our age.

I have assumed throughout that English and American cultures were close enough to be often linked, and not too guardedly. The existence of unique national traditions does not contradict this assumption, any more than the existence of a Southern novel negates the idea of an American novel. The historic openness of England and America, while at the same time remaining openly and ostentatiously contemptuous of each other, seems indisputable. It does not mask the rapid and irreversible change of world roles and national power that took place during the lifetime of someone like Pound who was born in 1885. But in the period covered by this study the changing roles in the world at large has had little consequence on the place poets occupy in either society. Despite the national traditions, such as a line of descent in poetry from Whitman to Pound, Williams and Charles Olson, which do not easily cross the Atlantic in any meaningful form, the Americans and the English have been living out of each other's cultural pocket for a long time. The pickings may have been selective, but they have been plentiful. So much so that it wouldn't be inappropriate now and then to say that it has been, over all, mutually advantageous. As an American who has lived now for a dozen years in England, I might be expected to have a vested interest in this set of cultural relations, as opposed to any other which happen to be available. The shared language, and the financial benefits of shared publication, has made the Atlantic of considerably smaller cultural meaning for those living in England than the Channel.

The organization of the book follows the decades, grouping the 1960s and 1970s together for the sake of convenience. Within each chapter a number of different poets are discussed, with a greater or lesser attempt to indicate the emergent social experience behind the verse. Each chapter is prefaced by a chronology listing some of the individual volumes of poetry published in any given year, as well as a selection of other, related titles: criticism, anthologies, letters, translations. The length at which any particular poet is discussed should not be taken as a judgment on his or her merits. I have written about Louis MacNeice in detail not only because he seems to me the most underrated poet of his generation, but because his development encapsulates the experience of liberal humanism in the inter-war years, and forms the necessary prelude to a discussion of the literature of the war itself.

Parts of this book have appeared in different form in the *Cambridge Review, The New Review,* the *Times Higher Education Supplement,* and *Poetry Nation.* My thanks to the editors for permission to reprint. I have received financial assistance from the Overseas Grants Committee, and from the research funds of the School of English and American Studies, University of East Anglia, as well as a term's study leave to complete the manuscript.

I should like to acknowledge the kindness and interest of Anthony Thwaite. Without his help, certain parts of this book would have been a great deal more difficult to write. And I am also grateful to those who commented on parts of the manuscript, and for the comments and help of others who have amusedly watched this book swell up into shape and finally emerge. It is a traditional author's prerogative to embarrass one's wife or husband, and say 'thank you' in public. So I take the opportunity: thank you, Judy, without whom, etc.

E. H.

1977
University of East Anglia,
Norwich

Chapter 1

The 1940s

MacNeice and the art of the real; his dilemma in *Autumn Journal*;
MacNeice as a war casualty; Auden departs for New York, and rejects his
political poetry; the 'new' Auden and *New Year Letter*; Randall Jarrell
and the end of the Audenesque; literature and society during the war, and
the new *Kulturbolschewismus*; Alun Lewis and the crisis of creativity
during wartime; Roy Fuller and the decline of political commitment in
English poetry.

Selected Chronology

1939

Roy Campbell, *Flowering Rifle*
Roy Fuller, *Poems*
Geoffrey Grigson, *Several Observations*
— ed., *New Verse: An Anthology*
Louis MacNeice, *Autumn Journal*
Delmore Schwartz, *In Dreams Begin Responsibilities*
Stephen Spender, *The Still Centre*
Stephen Spender and J. B. Leishmann, trans., Rilke's *Duino Elegies*
Stephen Spender and John Lehmann, eds., *Poems for Spain*
Dylan Thomas, *The Map of Love*
W. B. Yeats, *Last Poems*

Cleanth Brooks, *Modern Poetry and the Tradition*
Cyril Connolly, *Enemies of Promise*
Gorham B. Munson, *Robert Frost*

1940

W. H. Auden, *Another Time*
Keith Douglas and Alec Hardie, eds., *Augury: An Oxford Miscellany of Verse and Prose*
T. S. Eliot, *East Coker*
William Empson, *The Gathering Storm*
Five Young American Poets (Jarrell, Berryman, etc.)
J. F. Hendry, ed., *The New Apocalypse*
C. Day Lewis, *Poems in Wartime*
Federico Garcia Lorca, *The Poet in New York*, trans. Rolfe Humphries
Louis MacNeice, *The Last Ditch*
Ezra Pound, *Cantos LII-LXXI*

1941

W. H. Auden, *New Year Letter*

T. S. Eliot, *The Dry Salvages*
— *A Choice of Kipling's Verse*
J. F. Hendry and Henry Treece, eds., *The White Horseman*
Louis MacNeice, *Plant and Phantom*
Michael Meyer and Sidney Keyes, eds., *Eight Oxford Poets*
Marianne Moore, *What Are Years?*
Carl Rakosi, *Selected Poems*
Charles Reznikoff, *Going to and Fro and Walking Up and Down*
Theodore Roethke, *Open House*
Delmore Schwartz, *Shenandoah*
Julian Symons, ed., *An Anthology of War Poetry*
John Wheelwright, *Selected Poems*
Louis Zukofsky, *55 Poems*

R. P. Blackmur, *The Expense of Greatness*
Kenneth Burke, *The Philosophy of Literary Form*
Glenn Hughes, *Imagism and the Imagists*
Louis MacNeice, *The Poetry of W. B. Yeats*
J. C. Ransom, *The New Criticism*
Allen Tate, *Reason in Madness*
Edmund Wilson, *The Wound and the Bow*

1942

John Berryman, *Poems*
T. S. Eliot, *Little Gidding*
Robert Frost, *A Witness Tree*
Roy Fuller, *The Middle of a War*
Randall Jarrell, *Blood for a Stranger*
Sidney Keyes, *The Iron Laurel*
Alun Lewis, *Raider's Dawn*
Carl Rakosi, *Two Poems*
Arthur Rimbaud, *Selected Verse Poems*, trans. Norman Cameron
Karl Shapiro, *Person, Place and Thing*
Stephen Spender, *Ruins and Visions*
Wallace Stevens, *Notes Towards a Supreme Fiction*
M. J. Tambimuttu, ed., *Poetry in Wartime*

Horace Gregory and Marya Zaturenska, *A History of American Poetry 1900-1940*
Alfred Kazin, *On Native Grounds*
Allen Tate, ed., *The Language of Poetry*
Lawrance Thompson, *Fire and Ice: The Art and Thought of Robert Frost*

1943

T. S. Eliot, *Four Quartets*

David Gascoyne, *Poems 1937-1942*
Michael Hamburger, trans., *Holderlin: Poems*
Sidney Keyes, *The Cruel Solstice*
C. Day Lewis, *Word Over All*
Delmore Schwartz, *Genesis, Book One*
Selected Poems by Keith Douglas, J. C. Hall and Norman Nicholson

C. M. Bowra, *The Heritage of Symbolism*
Yvor Winters, *The Anatomy of Nonsense*

1944

W. H. Auden, *For the Time Being*
Roy Fuller, *A Lost Season*
Stanley Kunitz, *Passport to the War*
Robert Lowell, *Land of Unlikeness*
Louis MacNeice, *Springboard: Poems 1941-1944*
Marianne Moore, *Nevertheless*
Karl Shapiro, *V-Letter*
Wallace Stevens, *Esthétique du Mal*
Allen Tate, *The Winter Sea*
W. C. Williams, *The Wedge*

The Kenyon Critics, *Gerard Manley Hopkins*

1945

William Bell, ed., *Poetry from Oxford in Wartime*
Patric Dickinson, ed., *Soldier's Verse*
Richard Eberhart and Selden Rodman, eds., *War and the Poet*
Robin Fedden, ed., *Personal Landscape: An Anthology of Poetry*
Robert Frost, *A Masque of Reason*
Randall Jarrell, *Little Friend, Little Friend*
Philip Larkin, *The North Ship*
Alun Lewis, *Ha! Ha! Among the Trumpets*
Vladimir Nabokov, trans., *Three Russian Poets: Verse Translations from Pushkin, Lermontov and Tyutchev*
J. C. Ransom, *Selected Poems*
Karl Shapiro, *Essay on Rime*
Oscar Williams, ed., *The War Poets*

Cyril Connolly, *The Condemned Playground*

1946

Elizabeth Bishop, *North and South*

Sidney Keyes, *Collected Poems*
John Lehmann, ed., *Poems from 'New Writing', 1936-1946*
Denise Levertov, *The Double Image*
Robert Lowell, *Lord Weary's Castle*
Pablo Neruda, *Residence on Earth,* trans., Angel Flores
Kenneth Patchen, *Selected Poems*
Henry Reed, *A Map of Verona*
Stephen Spender, *Poems of Dedication*
Dylan Thomas, *Deaths and Entrances*
R. S. Thomas, *The Stones of the Field*
W. C. Williams, *Paterson, Book One*
Louis Zukofsky, *Anew*

Keith Douglas, *Alamein to Zem Zem*
Alun Lewis, *Letters from India*
Yvor Winters, *Edwin Arlington Robinson*

1947

W. H. Auden, *The Age of Anxiety*
Robert Duncan, *Heavenly City, Earthly City*
Robert Frost, *Steeple Bush*
— *A Masque of Mercy*
Bernard Gutteridge, *Traveller's Eye*
Howard Nemerov, *The Image and the Law*
Edgell Rickword, *Collected Poems*
Karl Shapiro, *Trial of a Poet*
Wallace Stevens, *Transport to Summer*
Allen Tate, *Poems 1920-1945*
Richard Wilbur, *The Beautiful Changes*

Cleanth Brooks, *The Well-Wrought Urn*
Charles Olson, *Call Me Ishmael*
Yvor Winters, *In Defence of Reason*
W. H. Auden edits Yale Series of Younger Poets (1947-1959)

1948

John Berryman, *The Dispossessed*
Robert Graves, *Collected Poems 1914-47*
Gerard Manley Hopkins, *Poems,* ed. W. H. Gardner. 3rd ed.
David Ignatow, *Poems*
Randall Jarrell, *Losses*
C. Day Lewis, *Poems 1943-1947*
Louis MacNeice, *Holes in the Sky: Poems 1944-1947*
Ezra Pound, *The Pisan Cantos*

Theodore Roethke, *The Lost Son*
W. C. Williams, *Paterson, Book Two*

Eric Bentley, ed., *The Importance of Scrutiny*
Stanley Edgar Hyman, *The Armed Vision*
Richard Marsh and Tambimuttu, eds., *T. S. Eliot: A Symposium*
Poets at Work (essays by Arnheim, Auden, Shapiro, Stauffer)
Allen Tate, *On the Limits of Poetry: Selected Essays 1928-1948*
W. C. Williams, 'The Poem as a Field of Action' delivered at the
      University of Washington
Louis Zukofsky, *A Test of Poetry*

1949

Roy Fuller, *Epitaphs and Occasions*
Geoffrey Grigson, ed., *Poetry of the Present*
Louis MacNeice, *Collected Poems 1925-1948*
Kenneth Rexroth, ed., *The New British Poets*
Louis Simpson, *The Arrivistes*
Stephen Spender, *The Edge of Being*
W. C. Williams, *Paterson, Book Three*
— *Selected Poems,* ed. Randall Jarrell
Helen Gardner, *The Art of T. S. Eliot*
Jean-Paul Sartre, *Baudelaire,* trans. Martin Turnell
Allen Tate, *The Hovering Fly*
René Wellek and Austin Warren, *Theory of Literature*

The 1940s

Louis MacNeice wanted a poetry which would be 'conditioned by the poet's life and the world around him' ('Preface', *Modern Poetry*, 1938). The son of the man who became Anglican Bishop of Down, Connor and Dromore, educated at Marlborough and Oxford, a classics don at the University of Birmingham, and a producer and scriptwriter in the B.B.C.: the biography is less that of an individual and more like that of his class. But, along with other members of the intelligentsia in the 1930s, MacNeice began to look more carefully at the society in which he lived. As Maurice Bowra has written on the Labour Party leader, Hugh Gaitskell, the world 'wounded both his feelings and his intelligence. His natural tenderness was outraged by the sordid and brutal conditions in which a large part of the population lived; his sense of order and decency was appalled by the jungle of a competitive system in which the few had too much and the many too little'.[1] This is a plausible account of the growth of the politics of conscience within the élite bourgeoisie. The possibility of a political 'conversion', sped on by the depression, was never far from MacNeice's contemporaries. He himself was converted into politics by a gradual process, not unlike Gaitskell's. But the old values survived within the new commitments of the socialist. When at last the new faith lapsed, as much an historical phenomenon as a result of contradictions within MacNeice's consciousness, he moved towards a position out of politics. The way of looking at the world which led to socialism did not disappear; rather, it remained at the core of the dilemma MacNeice faced in the 1940s. He cannot praise the world too keenly, for the socialist in him knows that it is rotten, unjust and dying. But neither can he condemn it unequivocally. The ambivalent values of the bourgeoisie leave room for manoeuvre, for the flowering of an individualism which, though it may be historically finished, defines the essence of our (bourgeois) notions of humanity.

MacNeice was at Marlborough College from 1921 to 1926, when the reaction was in full swing against the drabness and moral earnestness of the Home Front during the First World War. The atmosphere in cultural circles, in London society, was hedonistic and aesthetic. The arch-aesthete of public schoolboys was Brian Howard, whose *Eton Candle,* published in March 1922, struck a great blow on behalf of avant-garde art, the Sitwells, and the cause of aestheticism. The chief influence on MacNeice at Marlborough was Anthony Blunt, who believed in pure form and entirely discounted 'the representational elements in painting'. Blunt, who also discovered politics in the early 1930s, gave talks to student societies on cubism. He decorated the study he shared with MacNeice with small prints of Picasso and Cézanne. MacNeice enjoyed whatever chance there was to *épater les bourgeois* in Marlborough, reading papers in which he attacked common sense and science. He and Blunt preferred exotic and advanced literature, from *Vathek,* Dunsany's fairy tales and Edward Lear to the newest publications of Aldous Huxley and T. S. Eliot, bestowing a private scheme of blasts and blesses. Blunt 'despised Tennyson, Shakespeare, the Italian High Renaissance and Praxiteles, but was all in favour of the Primitives, of Uccello, of the Byzantine mosaics, of Brueghel and Negro sculpture'.[2] In the age of Lytton Strachey, styles of irony, mockery, po-faced pomposity, and a delight in outrages of every kind were part of the normal equipment of public schoolboys when they went up, as MacNeice did in the Michaelmas term of 1926, to Oxford.

Merton College was little touched by the General Strike of that year. By all accounts the event had been a great lark for the undergraduates, trying their hand at a little strike-breaking. Even Cyril Connolly, having come down from Balliol an extravagant aesthete, signed on as a special constable.[3] At MacNeice's first party at Oxford 'there was no drink but champagne, a young man played by himself with a spotted, stuffed dog on a string and the air was full of the pansy phrase "my dear". I discovered that in Oxford homosexuality and "intelligence", heterosexuality and brawn, were almost inexorably paired. This left me in the cold and I took to drink.' Political concerns were unusual in Oxford. Bowra, a young fellow at Wadham College, had been shaken by the General Strike. He felt that the miners' action was 'ill-judged', but that the strike-breaking undergraduates 'might involve violence'. Dismayed by the intransigence on both sides, he had toured north Oxford, collecting signatures of the distinguished for a petition calling on the government to negotiate with the strikers. Bowra was impressed with Hugh Gaitskell, who had remained in Oxford 'with quiet determination', working for the strike when most undergraduates had gone to London on the other side. But for himself, Bowra felt it was not quite so simple as merely choosing sides. As Auden scathingly put it in 'A Communist to Others', Bowra might be numbered among those who were 'Proud of your nicely balanced view'. For MacNeice and his contemporaries newly arrived at Oxford, the most significant choice presented to them was between brain and brawn, between homo- and heterosexuality, rather than the need to choose between the miners, who remained on strike and were starved back to work, and all that Stanley Baldwin's government stood for. Cambridge was little different. Julian Bell wrote that, 'In the Cambridge that I first knew, in 1929 and 1930, the central subject of ordinary conversation was poetry. As far as I can remember we hardly ever talked or thought about politics...'[4]

MacNeice did not, by some miraculous transformation, become a different person when the depression came. Although he lived in Birmingham, where he was appointed to a lectureship in classics in 1930, he and his wife Mariette were 'living on an island':

> We ignored our Birmingham context as much as possible — Mariette said someone had left the salt out of the Midland accent — and spent most of our free time driving into Shropshire in a Baby Austin...[5]

His marriage caused a nearly complete break in his poetry during the Birmingham years. His first volume of poetry, *Blind Fireworks*, appeared in 1929, but he subsequently discarded most of the collection as juvenilia. The sheer presence of Birmingham could hardly be avoided, and when he came to write of the city in 'Birmingham', published in *New Verse* in February 1934, his loathing is immediately and intensely felt. 'Birmingham' is written in a heightened style, more strained and violent than the imagery of urban life which Eliot, by way of Baudelaire, had gone far towards inventing for the young poets of the early 1930s. The techniques of urban impressionism, complete with flickering gas lamps, fog and the sound of carriages, was too 'soft', too closely associated with the aesthetes of the 1890s, to be adequate for the endless materialism of modern urban life. MacNeice omitted punctuation, transmuting the distinctness of objects in a catalogue into a deliberate verbal jumble: 'Cubical scent-bottles artificial legs arctic foxes and electric mops'. He found an almost surrealistic symbol for the thinness of a way of life in its houses:

> ... half-timbered houses with lips pressed
> So tightly and eyes staring at the traffic through bleary haws
> And only a six-inch grip of the racing earth in their concrete
>   claws ...

There was something grotesque in the faces of shopgirls, 'Diaphanous as green glass, empty as almanacs', and the 'sleep-stupid' faces of the factory workers. 'Birmingham' is a sourly hieratic poem, more marked by contempt than compassion, and not without direct class hostility. But MacNeice is scarcely more sympathetic towards the bourgeoisie, who

11

> . . . as in a dream pursue the Platonic Forms
> With wireless and cairn terriers and gadgets . . .

The poem documents a personal revulsion. At the same time it enacts a social criticism of a particular kind. MacNeice has detached himself from the inhumanity of Birmingham, from the typically urban and industrial. The poem is a response to mass civilization on the part of a fastidious and alienated intelligence. 'Birmingham' is a less penetrating document than F. R. Leavis's *Mass Civilization and Minority Culture* (1930), but one which emerges out of a similar revulsion and sense of cultural decline.

MacNeice's most sustained and doom-laden expression of the early 1930s comes in 'An Eclogue for Christmas', which appeared in *New Verse* in April 1934. The eclogue is in the traditional form of a dialogue between 'analogues' of the self. The poem represents a process of self-communing of which Yeats was the undoubted master. The jazz-weary urban sophisticate, 'A', and a man from the country gentry, 'B', take a perverse pleasure in rehearsing the causes of their impending doom. (Empson's 'Just a Smack at Auden', published in 1938, could just as well have been directed towards this vein of MacNeice's work.) The townsman, reflecting on the bright years of jazz, pomade and nightlife, sees himself as someone dehumanized, turned into an automaton by the modern way of life. The transition of Picasso from the Harlequins of his Blue Period to the radical decreations of the analytical phase of cubism suggests an analogy: the townsman is now nothing other than

> Abstractions scalpelled with a palette-knife
> Without reference to this particular life.

The cubism which turned him into 'pure form' confirmed a process of dehumanization. This is an oblique judgment upon his youthful mentor Anthony Blunt, who had introduced him to modern abstract art. MacNeice is harshly deprecatory: advocates of pure form, and the art which they praised, were symptoms of a corrupt social order. (By this time Blunt was no longer a devotee of 'pure form'.) In the 'Auden Number' of *New Verse* (November 1937) MacNeice misquoted Marx:

> 'Other philosophies have described the world, our business is to change it.' And that if we are not interested in changing it, there is really very little to describe. There is just an assortment of heterogeneous objects to make Pure Form out of.

The figure of the whore, the blind man and proud country types are used in 'An Eclogue for Christmas' to undermine individualism. The townsman attributes individuality to a kind of false consciousness. People may think they are free, but are 'merely the counters of an unknown mind'. The countryman thinks that the country gentry will die 'from angry circumstances and moral self-abuse', poisoned in the end by 'the flotsam of private property, pekinese and polyanthus'. Both are doomed and possessed by the consciousness of their coming destruction. MacNeice concludes the dialogue with a striking flourish, recognizing the manifest truth that classes, however oppressed by the tang of apocalypse in the air do not willingly cast themselves upon the ash-heaps of history. The townsman and the countryman cannot remake themselves in the image of the proletariat. They may be anachronisms, but can at least be consoled by simply being themselves. MacNeice here sees that hedonism is not a real alternative to history, but the first of a series of refuges which people seek out in dark times.

> I will gorge myself to satiety with the oddities
> Of every artiste, official or amateur,
> Who has pleased me in my role of hero-worshipper
> Who has pleased me in my role of individual man —

MacNeice became a 'thirties' poet in 1934. One side of him openly savoured the security of the unproblematic age before the awakening of political consciousness. He would like to

> . . . keep this door for ever
> Closed on the world, its own world closed within it.
>
> ('Trilogy for X')

Remote places such as Iceland and the Hebrides, rather more manifest islands than that which he had been able to create in Birmingham with his first wife, were places where the world of telegrams and anger had not yet reached. They recalled in MacNeice a state of utter passivity:

> We should like to lie alone in a deaf hollow
> Cocoon of self where no person or thing would speak.   ('The Ear')

Of the many enemies of the 'cocoon of self ', the most powerful in MacNeice's imagery is *time*. Characteristically time exists as a force of destruction, whether of love slowly transmuted into painful indifference in 'Les Sylphides', or of the smile of the 'cruel clock' from which he fled to Iceland ('Letter to Graham and Anna'). Time, and its associated images of clocks, ticking and hours clearly had an obsessive personal meaning for MacNeice. 'Sometimes in the nights', he wrote in *The Strings are False,*

> I woke and wondered where we were going, but most of the time I was doped and happy, most of the time except when I thought about time that most of the time is waste but whose is not? When I started again to write poems they were all about time.[6]

Images of the sea attest to the inevitability of loss and destruction. Instead of a classical stoicism, MacNeice is often nostalgic. In 'Les Neiges

D'Antan' the 'squadrons of butlers, valets, grooms and second housemaids' stand for the lost comfort of childhood. It was only when this security was gone (relatively speaking, of course; he was a university lecturer at the time), when he grew up and began to look at the real world, that he could grasp how totally he had been cocooned. He wrote a poem, 'Taken for Granted', to make this point.

In none of the poems of this period does MacNeice seem at all like a socialist, far less a Marxist. The best that one critic, D. E. S. Maxwell, can come up with in his study of the mistaken men of MacNeice's generation is that 'among the attitudes his poems expresses is a sort of reluctant Marxism which accepts the premises but has no enthusiasm for the conclusion'.[7] But even 'reluctant Marxism' is going too far. In the slight poem 'To a Communist', published in 1935, he opened himself to a damaging comparison with Auden's 'A Communist to Others'. MacNeice's poem is a little squib, an ironic riposte; Auden's remains, despite his subsequent reservations, a reckless, clever performance. In truth, politics made MacNeice glum. It was that part of 'the world around him', to use his phrase from the preface to *Modern Poetry* in 1938, which could not be avoided yet to which he responded with the greatest ambivalence where it impinged upon his responsibility as a poet. To whom, after all, was a writer responsible? To accept Stalinist policy would, as he saw, turn him into a propagandist, and MacNeice was naturally against propaganda. In the *New Verse* double number on commitment (Autumn 1938) he published the following statement:

> The world no doubt needs propaganda, but propaganda (unless you use the term, as many do, very, very loosely indeed) is not the poet's job. He is not the loud-speaker of society, but something much more like its still, small voice. At his highest he can be its conscience, its critical faculty, its grievous instinct. He will not serve his world by wearing blinkers. The world today consists of specialists and intransigents. The poet, by contrast, should be synoptic and elastic in his sympathies. It is quite possible therefore that at some period his duty as a poet may conflict with his duty as a man. In that case he can stop writing, but he must not degrade his poetry even in the service of a good cause; for bad poetry won't serve it much anyway. It is still, however, possible to write honestly without feeling that the time for honesty is past.

MacNeice was characteristically sardonic in his presentation of propaganda, all those 'Thousands of posters asserting a monopoly of the good, the beautiful, the true' ('Morning Sun'). He wanted an art which would be the opposite of propaganda, with its inevitable oversimplifications. Life is too complex, there are too many sides to each argument, to act as though it was otherwise. While MacNeice's views constitute a norm, there were enough voices to the contrary in the 1930s for us to understand his statement in *New Verse* as a quite serious intervention. Edward Upward, for one, wrote in *The Mind in Chains* (1937) that 'no modern book can be true to life unless it recognizes, more or less clearly, both the decadence of present-day society and the inevitability of revolution'. The hostility of the bourgeois intelligentsia towards the Stalinist cultural line of the British Communist Party may have been responsible for a quite conscious attempt to avoid the cruder formulations of policy. Thus Christopher Caudwell, distinguishing between the genuine and the false propagandist:

> What, then, is the proper position for a bourgeois poet today who finds himself arrived at the situation of Auden, Spender, and Lewis? To be a revolutionary, certainly, but a real revolutionary, not a freelance agitator; to be a member of a revolutionary party and to carry out a common party line, not his own line; to be a revolutionary not only in blank verse but in every activity, which he can carry out and his party suggests. Agitation is necessary certainly, so is propaganda, but let the poet be a genuine propagandist, not a blank-verse propagandist. Is the proletariat made conscious of its goal by rhymed economics? No, verse is not, and never was, the instrument of propaganda in this sense.[8]

Caudwell takes the 'loose' or 'soft' position on propaganda, but he did not speak for the central Party line. George Orwell, who had a keen nose for new kinds of hypocrisy, wrote in the *New English Weekly* (31 December 1936) of a 'frightful intellectual dishonesty' in propagandist critics, who were

> ... employing a double set of values and dodging from one to the other according as it suits them. They praise or dispraise a book *because* its tendency is Communist, Catholic, Fascist or what-not; but at the same time, they pretend to be judging it on purely aesthetic grounds. Few people have the guts to say outright that art and propaganda are the same thing.[9]

MacNeice, with his still, small voice and his conscience, sets himself squarely within the tradition of bourgeois humanism. He wanted an 'impure poetry', as he wrote in his preface to *Modern Poetry*, as opposed to an autonomous, self-regarding aestheticism. It must be impure, ironic, biting, but not *too* impure, not defiled by overt and vulgar propaganda about the class struggle, the proletariat, fascism, or the awfulness of the capitalists.

Rather, MacNeice saw himself as one who would labour to unmask the illusions and refuges created by those who chose to remain on that island which he had by now deserted. He was speaking clearly and directly to the class which he knew at firsthand (thus creating the need for the qualification of *bourgeois* humanism: MacNeice was intensely alive to the meaning of class), and he set about the task with brimming good spirits. It helped to focus his work, and was a return to the good old days when he stirred up the complacency of his contemporaries at Marlborough. Sometimes this was best achieved by expressing the hedonism of ordinary life and the conscious desire to pursue, wholeheartedly, the pleasures of private life. He well understood this state of mind, and wrote of that peculiarly decent social irresponsibility in 'Bagpipe Music', published in the January 1937 issue of *New Verse*. Auden, a month earlier, defined in a couplet the portentous task before the committed poet:

> Hundreds of trees in the wood are unsound:
> I'm the axe that must cut them down to the ground.[10]

For MacNeice commitment did not necessarily eliminate humour or witty satire. The contrast with Auden is illuminating in 'Bagpipe Music' where MacNeice captures the mood of a witty debunking hedonism, while in the process of debunking that same hedonism:

> It's no go my honey love, it's no go my poppet;
> Work your hands from day to day, the winds will blow the profit.
> The glass is falling hour by hour, the glass will fall forever,
> But if you break the bloody glass you won't hold up the weather.

MacNeice's work at this time is virtually an anatomy of refuge. In 'Museums' he considers the ways in which culture, and the institutions which define its social existence, offer a refuge from the real. A subsequent poem making the same point is 'The British Museum Reading Room', where men hope that

> . . . these walls of books will deaden
> The drumming of the demon in their ears.

Refinement and sophistication, carried to extremes, were no less an evasion, whereas vulgarity, 'healthy vulgarity' as he called it,[11] keeps us in touch with the real world.

For MacNeice religion was an obvious refuge, a way of avoiding the dilemmas of the real world. 'The Preacher' is a type of the man who denies the world:

> Among old iron, cinders, sizzling dumps,
> A world castrated, amputated, trepanned,
> He walked in the lost acres crying 'Repent
> For the Kingdom of Death is at hand'.

He contrasts the world-denying impulse of the religious martyr in 'Stylite' with the 'white Greek god' who keeps his eyes open and fixed on the world. Open eyes generally signify MacNeice's desire to see things as they are, while closed eyes ban the world. The poet, he noted in his statement on poetry and propaganda in *New Verse,* 'will not serve his world by wearing blinkers'. He recalled in his autobiography that when as a child he, his brother and his sister contracted measles, they were all placed in a darkened room, with bandages over their eyes. 'A bandage over your eyes remits your sense of duty.'[12] Whether the bandage was caused by class, religion, or education, by the middle-1930s MacNeice felt that 'sense of duty' intensely enough to want to discard all forms of refuge. He wanted to immerse himself in things as they were — to create an art of the real.

To discard, to rip off, to unmask constituted a critical function. In place of our illusions and wishful thinking MacNeice holds out a distinctively human form of hope: conviviality. It will not save us, he seems to say, but it will make bearable those moments anxiously spent before the arrival of the 'impending thunder'. Conviviality is a conscious exercise, a fiction, cherished because its artificiality reeks of the human. In 'Wolves' (*New Verse,* December 1934) he calls for 'all of you' to

> . . . come closer, form a circle,
> Join hands and make believe that joined
> Hands will keep away the wolves of water
> Who howl along our coast. And be it assumed
> That no one hears them among the talk and laughter.

The 'make believe' world of personal relations suggests what survives for MacNeice of Forsterian liberalism.* Writing in a mood of 'loneliness/and incommunicableness' in 'Postscript to Iceland', he salutes Auden, his companion during their trip to Iceland in the summer of 1936:

> . . . I drink your health before
> The gunbutt raps upon the door.

The precariousness of the conviviality makes it all the more precious, but MacNeice is free from the wishful thinking that conviviality all round might make things different than they are.

The basic MacNeice formulation, then, turns upon his grasp of the dialectics of reality: order is constantly being imposed upon disorder, the anarchic world constantly asserts its independence of the mental sets which men impose upon it.

> For every static world that you or I impose
> Upon the real one must crack at times and new

---

* Forster, more hard-headed and braver than any caricatured liberalism associated with his work, wrote in 'What I Believe' (1939): 'I hate the idea of causes, and if I had to choose between betraying my country and betraying my friend, I hope I should have the guts to betray my country.'

Patterns from new disorders open like a rose... ('Mutations')

There is something 'out there' which he understands to be *other,* to be indifferent or potentially hostile, something which seemingly refuses to sustain the dream of an 'innocent and integral' life of man in nature. MacNeice's view is that we have no choice but to accept that otherness, to accept the existential quality of things, rather than remain content with the philosophical or numinous meanings which we may be tempted to attach to nature: he is prepared to accept, to celebrate:

> But I would cherish existence
> Loving the beast and the bubble
> Loving the rain and the rainbow...   ('Leaving Barra')

A parallel, but ultimately hostile, mode of acceptance in contemporary writing is considered in Orwell's *Inside the Whale* (1940). The subject of Orwell's essay is Henry Miller as a type of the writer who 'watches the Seine flowing past, in a sort of mystical acceptance of the thing-as-it-is'. If we translate this into the political life of the 1930s, to say 'I accept', as Orwell brilliantly catalogues,

> ... is to say that you accept concentration camps, rubber truncheons, Hitler, Stalin, bombs, aeroplanes, tinned food, machine-guns, putsches, purges, slogans, Bedaux belts, gas-masks, submarines, spies, *provocateurs,* press censorship, secret prisons, aspirins, Hollywood films and political murders.[13]

In the conclusion of the essay Orwell endorses the passivity of 'robbing reality of its terrors by simply submitting to it'. Get inside the whale, he says, 'give yourself over to the world process, stop fighting against it or pretending that you control it; simply accept it, endure it, record it'. It is quite clear that this was not Orwell's permanent position. Rather, it was the mood of a moment, the stunned recoil from the disastrous path which connected Munich to Dunkirk. Orwell's advice to accept, endure and record was, in one sense, correct: 'give yourself over'; but nature for MacNeice was simply there and could never replace that which was fundamental to humanity:

> And when I think of you, my dear,
>   Who were so near, so near, so near,
> The barren skies from wall to wall
>   Appal, appal, pall, pall,
> The spray no longer gilds the wave,
> The sea looks nothing more nor less than a grave
>   And the world and the day are grey and that is all.
>   ('Passage Steamer')

A long poem, deliberately discursive yet which avoids the purely colloquial; which embodies the essential MacNeice tone of an educated, curious, honest man, who was sceptical by nature but not cynical; which was not satiric, save in passages; and which was a 'journal' in which the author carefully explained that he had made no alterations with the benefit of hindsight to what he felt or understood, is going to raise critical problems. Many readers have been naggingly dissatisfied with MacNeice's *Autumn Journal.* 'This *Journal* is rambling, facile, prosy at times, never very deep or certain in thought, rather too consciously elaborating the picture of an easy-going but attractive personality.'[14] One agrees that MacNeice was not a 'very deep' thinker, although that is a notoriously subjective judgment; and equally MacNeice was seldom 'certain' in thought. Who was? The spirit of *Autumn Journal* is consciously diffident. One can imagine Pound's Sextus Propertius, who wanted 'a wreath which will not crush my head', finding in MacNeice a congenial soul. The poem does not commit itself, does not lock its readers into its deceptively casual version of the real. There are contingent values, other people, history, which have an existence of their own.

MacNeice was aware of the likely criticisms which *Autumn Journal* would receive, and tried to anticipate them in a 'Note' to the 1939 edition of the poem. The 'Note' was omitted from further reprintings of *Autumn Journal,* but remains pertinent to what is his central achievement. 'Nor am I attempting', he argued,

> . . . to offer what so many people now demand from poets – a final verdict or a balanced judgment. It is the nature of this poem to be neither final nor balanced. I have certain beliefs which, I hope, emerge in the course of it but which I have refused to abstract from their context. For this reason I shall be probably called a trimmer by some and a sentimental extremist by others. But poetry in my opinion must be honest before anything else and I refuse to be 'objective' or clear-cut at the cost of honesty.

He saw *Autumn Journal* as something impure, engaged, committed, with none of the false objectivity of history, nor the false subjectivity of aesthetic impressionism. Most significantly, it makes an explicit statement of MacNeice's social idealism, and in that formulation he reveals the contradictions of his situation at the end of the 1930s. We have here the misty nostalgia for a past in which there were

> . . . roses on a rustic trellis and mulberry trees
> And bacon and eggs in a silver dish for breakfast
> And all the inherited assets of bodily ease . . .   (Canto I)

'Inherited' cuts right through the mood. And this is typical of the way MacNeice treats things or places about which his feelings have changed. He tries to recall the pleasures, not only for their own sake, but as a foil to newer, perhaps less comfortable wisdom. Seen more clearly, Belfast is

> A city built upon mud;
> > A culture built upon profit   (Canto XVI)

The 'code' of the public school is memorably defined:

> The weak must go to the wall
> > But strength implies the system;
> You must lose your soul to be strong, you cannot stand
> > Alone on your own legs or your own ideas;
> The order of the day is complete conformity and
> > An automatic complacence   (Canto X)

This is MacNeice working a long suit. He is not so much the satirist, a man scandalized by 'complete conformity and/An automatic complacence', but the man who sees things clearly. The strength and confidence in his work derives from a clarity of understanding, if not from great penetration or certainty of thought. He returns to the question of evasions and refuges, appropriate enough for the man who feels he is seeing things a little more clearly than his fellow men. I. A. Richards's little essay *Science and Poetry* (1926) might serve as a prolegomenon for MacNeice's work, particularly in view of Richards's acute criticism of the poets of the 1920s. His scientism meant little to MacNeice, but Richards's basic criticism of the refuge-tendency, the desire to create safe little havens in a world in which God is dead and the only consolation is that there is no consolation to be had, was highly relevant. As MacNeice put it:

> And at this hour of the day it is no good saying
> > 'Take away this cup';
> Having helped to fill it ourselves it is only logic
> > That now we should drink it up.   (Canto V)

He sees that the system itself is 'no go':

> > . . . an utterly lost and daft
> System that gives a few at fancy prices
> > Their fancy lives
> While ninety-nine in the hundred who never attend the banquet
> > Must wash the grease of ages off the knives.   (Canto II)

The class relations of MacNeice's childhood have obviously left a determining mark. The relation here between master and servant is by no means an orthodox symbol of the relations between classes in socialist thought. The image is revealingly appropriate for MacNeice: the silver spoon in his mouth turns out to be tarnished, after all. He had to struggle towards such an understanding against his family, class, education, profession and marriage. What he now sees is not systematic or scientific, nor is his political position easily summarized. He was too much the individualist, too sceptical by temperament, to be very much at home in the Labour Party. The Communists were unthinkable, the Tories unspeakable; MacNeice found himself isolated. He did not accept without a struggle, and this gives *Autumn Journal* an intellectual energy, a sense of the pressure of ideas struggling towards realization. In Canto I he suggests that the only meaningful hope lies in 'the human animal's endless courage'; despite their powerlessness, men must exert the 'powers of will and choice' (Canto V). It is only in community that such choice can be realized. MacNeice's statement of the communal and the collective as the realization of the autonomous individual is the moment when liberalism begins to give way to socialism in his thought. 'Why not admit', he asks,

> . . . that other people are always
> Organic to the self, that a monologue
> Is the death of language and that a single lion
> Is less himself, or alive, than a dog and another dog.
> (Canto XVII)

This is forthright enough, but not very subtle or imaginative. The awkwardness of the illustrations and their evident lack of energy reveal something fundamental occurring in MacNeice's work. Along the border of conviction and feeling a gap, a sign of inner strain, appears. He persists, certainly, with his case:

> For each individual then
> Would be fighting a losing battle
> But with life as collective creation
> The rout is rallied, the battle begins again.   (Canto XXI)

'Life as collective creation' runs like a motif through the second half of *Autumn Journal.* MacNeice's training as a classicist emerges potently in the view he holds of community as the reflection of the moderate man:

> All that I would like to be is human, having a share
> In a civilised, articulate and well-adjusted
> Community where the mind is given its due
> But the body is not disturbed.   (Canto XIII)

In Yeats's more extravagant formulation: 'The body is not bruised to pleasure soul.'

Autumn Journal strives toward a utopian vision of community. Coming as it does between Munich and the outbreak of war, the poem was wholly shaped by a unique moment in modern English history when the consciousness of an individual and the history of the society coincided: the political failure it records was personal and communal. It is characteristic of the man, and perhaps of the society, that his response was not coloured by alienation and despair. The buoyant wit of *Autumn Journal* carries the vivid impress of MacNeice's fundamental sensibility. Yet the wit breaks down when he presses home his vision of the organic community. The essence of such an attempt is that it should seem as impossibly remote from the narrow calculations of the immediately political as it does from the distractions of everyday life; and remoteness from the immediate can often be a symptom of paralysing idiosyncrasy or sterility. MacNeice's dilemma was to actualize, to make specific and tactile, something which contradicted the 'reality' of an entire phase of capitalism. One side of MacNeice's response was dominated by a revolutionary nostalgia. Frederic Jameson suggests such a possibility in his brilliant *Marxism and Form*: 'But if nostalgia as a political motivation is most frequently associated with Fascism, there is no reason why a nostalgia conscious of itself, a lucid and remorseless dissatisfaction with the present on the grounds of some remembered plenitude, cannot furnish as adequate a revolutionary stimulus as any other.' Thus we see MacNeice, in one passage in *Autumn Journal,* developing a series of images of empty churches, law courts, barracks, and then drawing a conclusion:

> Things were different when men felt their programme
>   In the bones and pulse, not only in the brain.
> Born to a trade, a belief, a set of affections.   (Canto XVIII)

But this is merely a shorthand. The organic society, the undissociated sensibility, a world without alienation, nibble at the edge of the problem: how to *realize* community. But the self-consciousness of MacNeice, and his curling sense of irony, make an evocation of the organic society seem merely another version of pastoral, the amusement of an educated, leisured, discontented class.

He is more explicit in another passage:

> If it is something feasible, obtainable,
>   Let us dream for it now,
> And pray for a possible land
>   Not of sleep-walkers, not of angry puppets,
> But where both heart and brain can understand
>   The movements of our fellows;   ·
> Where life is a choice of instruments and none
>   Is debarred his natural music,
> Where the waters of life are free of the ice-blockage of hunger
>   And thought is free as the sun,
> Where the altars of sheer power and mere profit
>   Have fallen to disuse,
> Where nobody sees the use
>   Of buying money and blood at the cost of blood and money

Where the individual, no longer squandered
    In self assertion, works with the rest, endowed
    With the split vision of a juggler and the quick lock of a taxi,
      Where the people are more than a crowd.   (Canto XXIV)

MacNeice's formulation in this passage is generalized; the 'waters of life', and 'altars of sheer power', now fallen into disuse, provide the basic symbolism for Roy Fuller's 'End of a City', published in Fuller's *Poems* in 1939; in MacNeice's hands the symbolism generates no resonance of its own, no verbal pressure, or historical sense. It is thin stuff, as though it was MacNeice's imagination which was faltering. He was pre-eminently the poet of the joys of the real world, the celebrant of true conviviality; but he could not imagine a *community* which embodied such values. They were, in the final analysis, too personal. At the point where he should be triumphantly bringing forth his commitment to the idea of community, and fleshing out that vision with his grasp of the content of an unalienated world, nothing occurs. He has not shown a connection between our familiar world of anxiety and contradiction and the ideal of an organic community. He was not, in the literal sense, a *visionary*.

The consequences of this failure reverberate throughout MacNeice's work. After war was declared he continued to write the same kind of socially concerned poem. He was no less radical, as some of his most remarkable poems of the early years of the war demonstrate. But the meaning of community, its power of ennobling the essentially negative work of critical diagnosis, begins to fade. Experience itself became more private, and it would appear that he accepted this distractedly but without deep misgivings. The failure of *Autumn Journal,* the failure to realize community imaginatively, can be seen as the culmination and final defeat of the whole movement of socially committed poetry in the 1930s.

One traces such momentous events in the life of a single poet not so much to urge his (neglected) virtues, but to demonstrate the way those seismic cultural changes are experienced within an individual *oeuvre.* He is not merely a representative, or a type; MacNeice *is* that metamorphosis from the 1930s to the 1940s, and the consequent constriction and loss in poetry, as in so many other areas of cultural life, is defined in his work with great clarity. He shared the eclipse of social idealism. The effect of the war, which for so many people involved an exposure to hierarchical egalitarianism, military-style, and (enforced) communal life, enhanced MacNeice's sense of the meaning and significance of individualism. The effects of war, in terms of social planning and regimentation, meant that at no time after 1939 was it likely that he would have written of 'life as collective creation'. Julian Symons, certainly a more political person than MacNeice, saw something quite remarkable happening in London during the war.

A wretched time, people say. I recall it as one of the happiest periods of my life. I have always desired a society in which everything should be impermanent and in which the possession of property and the inheritance of money should be eliminated . . . I know now that I shall never see such a Utopia, but life in London at this time gave a hint of it, as life in Russia must have done in the months after the Revolution. . . . Living became a matter of the next meal, the next drink. The way in which people behaved to each other relaxed strangely. Barriers of class and circumstance disappeared, so that London was more nearly an equalitarian city than it has ever been in the last quarter of a century. Was it mere romanticism that discovered 'new styles of architecture, a change of heart' in the bombed places? For a few months we lived in the possibility of a different kind of history.[15]

It was ironic, in one sense, that MacNeice was out of the country when war was declared. He was in Ireland, visiting County Clare. He travelled to America in January 1940 to take up a teaching appointment at Cornell. He did not return to England until October, taking several months to recover from peritonitis. Those 'few months', that possibility of 'a different kind of history' fleetingly glimpsed by Symons, had come and gone while he was, like Auden, in America.

MacNeice volunteered at once for the Royal Navy, but was turned down because of poor eyesight. He worked as a firewatcher in London (Spender joined the Auxiliary Fire Service in the Autumn of 1942), before joining the B.B.C. in 1941 as a scriptwriter and producer. The experience of the blitz was central to MacNeice's 'war' poems. His article 'The Morning After the Blitz' in *Picture Post* of 3 May 1941, describing the raid on the night of 16 April, is a superb piece of stiff-upper-lip reportage, very much in the vein of the famous documentary film, *London Can Take It,* made by Humphrey Jennings and Harry Watt the year before. Unflappableness and understatement were 'what the age demanded'.

Another side of his work during the war was more pessimistic. He had always been enough of a sceptic to accept that 'there is no/Road that is right entirely' ('Entirely'). He now came increasingly to see that the odds were stacked against him no matter which way he turned:

> . . . chances
> Are dubious. Fate is stingy, recalcitrant.   ('Refugees')

> Nature is not to be trusted.   ('Evening in Connecticut')

> . . . Nature's laws exploit
> And defeat anarchic men . . .   ('Prospect')

Faced with a hostile nature, and a growing pessimism now that the 'impending thunder' had finally arrived, MacNeice turned back upon a residual humanism, and an affirmation of the uniqueness of man. 'We are unique', he wrote, 'a conscious/Hoping and therefore despairing creature.' Sometimes he seems on the verge of admitting an explicitly religious dimension to his poetry – a manifestation of the general crisis of values ushered in with the war. Materialism was the unquestioned target of the new spiritual revival, but it also encompassed a fundamental rejection of positivistic thought, empiricism and naturalism. When the fruits of science (such as radar) were crucial to the war effort, the *clercs* were dreaming of heavenly spires. In a superb denunciation of 'The New Failure of Nerve', Sidney Hook quoted a sentence by Reinhold Niebuhr with particular scorn: 'Science which is only science cannot be scientifically accurate' (*Partisan Review'*, January-February, 1943). That a secular imagination like MacNeice's could flirt with religion tells us a great deal about the feeling of crisis which dominated the war years.

Writers with weaker minds, such as Francis Scarfe, writing in *Transformation* in 1943, had a familiar story to tell:

> I find myself, in almost one year, passing from a form of materialism to an emotional acceptance of Christ as the pattern of man and human behaviour. Analysing this change, I can only surmise that materialism led me astray; I can see that as a materialist I found life a very empty and unsatisfactory business, and war little more than butchery. Evolving perhaps towards Christian Socialism, seeing Christ as a great revolutionary figure, I find harmony in myself which sings within me in spite of the enforced conditions in which for a year I have tried to live. Life has meaning, love is no longer a personal matter, war is no longer merely 'the bad against the worse', and poetry becomes a sacred rite and implicit duty.

Scarfe was moving towards the position of Eric Gill, whose pamphlet *Christianity and the Machine Age* (1940) is a neglected but valuable statement of the Christian Socialist alternative. It was Auden, among the 'younger' generation of poets, who led the way back to orthodoxy. In any event, MacNeice did not quite reach the point of religious conversion; but a new fund of imagery was made available, perhaps most significantly in 'The Springboard', a thinly-veiled allegory of his own vacillation and self-doubt. The predominant stance of his war poems is that of the dispassionate observer of the social scene, the *flâneur,* the man 'who goes botanizing on the asphalt', as Walter Benjamin wrote of 'The Paris of the Second Empire in Baudelaire'. Benjamin's discussion of the *flâneur* and the great age of the *feuilleton* in the 1830s, connects the emergence of a new literary mode with the changes in society and the dominant forms of social control in the Second Empire. The types of MacNeice's verse equally signify something more than an idiosyncratic whim on the poet's part. The collective bestiary, the catalogue of the deformed and the grotesque in 'The Gardener', 'The Preacher', 'Death of an Actress', 'The Mixer' and 'The Libertine' are often acute, but the general impression is muted. One wonders whether MacNeice was really vicious enough to write satirical verse of the first power. Certainly none of the poems of this period compares with the high camp of William Plomer:

> 'My dear!' he lists, to whom all men are dear,
> 'How perfectly enchanting of you!'; turns
> Towards his guests and twitters, 'Look who's here!
> Do come and help us fiddle while Rome burns!'[16]

MacNeice was anxious to make an affirmation during the dark years of the war. It was justifiable to 'keep the log' of the 'condemned ship', as he wrote in 'The Satirist', but there was something limiting in the end about the man whose primary concern was to 'discover/A selfish motive for anything'. But it proved difficult, if not impossible, to embody an affirmation of community either in the ironic shorter poems or in the longer, discursive mode. He felt the need to deepen the mood, to make his poems adequate for 'thought' of a more serious kind. The minor crisis of form was a mirror of the greater contradictions and uncertainties in MacNeice's ideology. The decision to look for a weightier kind of poetry turned out to be a disastrously wrong turning. After the publication of 'The Kingdom' and 'Plurality' his reputation never quite recovered, and there was little in his subsequent poetry to make the younger critics of the 1950s and 1960s question their dismissal of his work.* MacNeice's poetry of ironic observation, his stance as *flâneur,* and the longer vehicles for a poetry of ideas seem to be independent, even oblivious of each other. What is in effect a failure to connect the two defines MacNeice's artistic dilemma during the war. He could not realize his 'message', that vision of an unalienated organic community, in the world in which he lived. In the past he had gleefully pointed out the cost of alienation and the illusions of individualism, but during the war he began to celebrate precisely what he had ridiculed. It is an uncomfortable poetry, but an instructive instance of the accommodation with the private which characterizes the poetry of the war.

'Plurality' appeared in *Horizon* in January 1941. 'The Kingdom' did

---

* Christopher Levenson (*Gemini,* Spring 1958): 'What MacNeice lacks is directness, poetic directness, . . . a valid symbol. He is manipulating counters, talking in vacuo.' Stephen Wall (*The Review,* 1964): 'His points of reference are extraordinarily miscellaneous, but though life may be merely bits and pieces one expects more from a poem.'

not go into print until MacNeice's *Springboard* of 1944. Both poems
suffer from some of MacNeice's flattest and most turgid writing. The
language lacks energy or precision, and the imagery is uninteresting.
Eliot's *Four Quartets,* the first two of which had been published by 1940,
is clearly some sort of an influence, though at times one would trade the
leaden earnestness of MacNeice for the deliberate parody of Henry Reed's
'Chard Whitlow'.[17] At least Reed was amusing himself, as MacNeice very
obviously was not:

> Man is man in as much as he is not god and yet
> Hankers to see and touch the pantheon and forget
> The means within the end and man is truly man
> In that he would transcend and flout the human span...

This is ponderous, not weighty, sententious without being wholly serious.
As a paean to liberal individualism 'The Kingdom' is an unconscious
parody. MacNeice uses the 'types' of the short satirical poems, but comes
very close to identifying an eccentricity which obscures rather than
enhances true individualism. In 'The Kingdom' he writes in praise of

> The pairs of hands that are peers of hearts, the eyes that marry with
> eyes
> The candid scholar, the unselfish priest, the uncomplaining mothers
> of many,
> The active men who are kind, the contemplative who give,
> The happy-go-lucky saint and the peace-loving buccaneer.

MacNeice reduces individualism to ethics or temperament, forgetting the
understanding of a decade that the age of bourgeois individualism was
historically the age of *laissez-faire* economics, the Empire, cheap
commodity prices, servants, democracy and peace. There could be no
easy resurrection of this world, particularly during the war, unless (as
MacNeice suggests in 'The Kingdom') individualism can be viewed as an
heroic, but ultimately personal sign of character. MacNeice must take
individualism right outside history to preserve it. Perhaps that is the
deeper meaning of his collection of types and grotesques in his wartime
poems: the pressures of the new forms of social organization created by
the war left room, as the intellectuals saw it, only for a marginal, harmless
eccentricity. MacNeice's physiognomies were soothing versions of
individualism, rather than the real thing itself. He was celebrating
something which to a considerable extent had ceased to exist. His praise
of individualism in 'The Kingdom' has a futile ring to it; but neither does
he persuade when he writes of community in *Autumn Journal.* He was
stranded in the problematic situation of one who praises an individualism
in which he no longer fully believes, and who believes in an ideal of
community which he could not plausibly praise. He might be said to be a

type of those poets of the 1930s who failed, as artists, to negotiate their passage through the war and on into the new decade.

Auden's evolution in the 1939-40 climacteric was, if anything, even more dramatic than MacNeice's. He rejected his left-wing political engagement of the preceding decade, experienced a religious reconversion, and left England altogether. A process of self-detachment, separating Auden from England and from his own early brilliant success, was at work. From the middle years of the decade he had spent more and more time out of England. He went to Iceland with Louis MacNeice for three months in 1936. He was in Spain for approximately three months in 1937. This was the year of the Auden double number of *New Verse,* and the King's Gold Medal for Poetry. He was thirty years old. Auden travelled with Christopher Isherwood to China for seven months in 1938, returning to England across the United States. Within five months of his return Auden sailed to New York, more or less permanently. The decision to emigrate (at the head of a small English contingent including Aldous Huxley, Christopher Isherwood, Gerald Heard, Alfred Hitchcock, Ralph Bates, George Barker and, briefly, Louis MacNeice) placed Auden in the midst of that brilliant intellectual migration of European *emigrés* from fascism — the Mann family, Stravinsky, Tillich, Arendt — with whom Auden's relations were so significant. Auden's departure was intensely resented. Sir Hugh Walpole advised John Lehmann that 'I don't think you realize the harm done by Auden, Isherwood, MacNeice fleeing to America. I'm not blaming them but it has *killed* their influence here.'[18] On a memorable occasion in April 1940, Sir Harold Nicolson had dinner with Kenneth Clark, Somerset Maugham, Mrs Winston Churchill and Leslie Howard:

> We discuss the position of those English people who have remained in the United States. The film-stars claim that they have been asked to remain there since they are more useful in Hollywood, but we all regret bitterly that people like Aldous Huxley, Auden and Isherwood should have absented themselves. They want me to write a *Spectator* article attacking them.[19]

Auden was mentioned in the House of Commons on 13 June 1940 by Major Sir Jocelyn Lucas in a question for the Parliamentary Secretary to the Ministry of Labour and National Service. By mistake the Parliamentary Secretary, Ralph Assheton, took the question to refer to a Mr *Austin,* who

> ... gave an undertaking before leaving the country that he would return if called upon to do so; he is outside the age groups so far required to register under the National Service (Armed Forces) Act.

Mr Mathers: On a point of Order. There is no mention of Mr Austin in this Question.

Sir J. Lucas: Is my hon. Friend aware of the indignation caused by young men leaving the country and saying that they will not fight?

. . .

Mr Assheton: No exit permits would be issued by the Home Office now.

Five days later, on 17 June, Orwell noticed a 'considerable throng' at Canada House. 'Apart from mothers', he noted in his diary, 'they are not allowing anyone between 16 and 60 to leave, evidently fearing a panic rush' (*C.E.J.L.*, II, p. 350). Assheton's comment reflected Government policy, and not displeasure at Auden's departure.

In an unsigned editorial in the second number of *Horizon* (February 1940), Cyril Connolly declared himself frankly encouraged by what he took to be the literary implications of Auden's emigration. As 'a symptom of the failure of social realism as an aesthetic doctrine', Connolly rejoiced in what was 'necessary and salutary'. Stephen Spender published a 'Letter to a Colleague in America' in *The New Statesman and Nation* (16 November 1940) in which he tried to look behind the event to its deeper meaning:

> . . . your letter makes me wonder about you, what some of us —
> particularly the poets — were wondering about England before the
> war: whether you really are beginning to think that there are places
> in the world outside this time, and not merely days and months, a
> few islands, to which the conflagration has not yet extended. That
> is really the only question worth asking about Auden, Isherwood,
> Heard, Aldous Huxley, MacNeice, etc: not whether they have run
> away on this particular occasion, but whether they think there is a
> chance of escaping from this history altogether?

'I had many conversations with Auden this autumn,' MacNeice wrote in *Horizon* (February 1941),

> . . . and he still is anti-Fascist, but he is no longer in any way a
> 'fellow-traveller'; since getting off that particular train, he has
> decided — as he told me in March 1939 — that it was not his job to
> be a crusader, that this was a thing everyone must decide for
> himself, but that, in his opinion, most writers falsified their work
> and themselves when they took a direct part in politics, and that the
> political end itself, however good, could not be much assisted by art
> or artists so falsified. Auden, that is, had repudiated propaganda.[20]

There were consequences of Auden's new position, most notably in his rejection of those poems (such as 'A Communist to Others' and 'Spain') which fell into the quasi-category of propaganda. Spender described 'A Communist to Others' as 'an exercise in entering into a point of view not his own'. (Readers of *New Signatures,* Michael Roberts's Marxizing anthology of 1933 where the poem first appeared, may not have grasped the point, so clear with hindsight.) The subject of the poem, of course, is the meeting between bourgeois intellectual and the proletariat. The dominant emotional tone is a nervous embarrassment, though in fairness to Auden the dreadful 'Brothers for whom our bowels yearn' is patently more than his own self-consciousness writ large. One needs to see the poem in terms of the situation of those writers, collected together by Roberts in *New Signatures,* who had been politicized by the depression and the rise of fascism. Their Marxism and allegiance to the working class was uneasily balanced against their status as intellectuals; the situation itself was fraught with awkwardness and uneasy conviction, memorialized in 'A Communist to Others'.

The poem is an exercise in political parody, and the techniques of parody are useful, especially for a writer who is inwardly detached. He can try a mask on, then discard it as 'trash' (Auden later said that 'A Communist to Others' and 'Spain' were 'trash which he is ashamed to have written'[21]), leaving his inner self untouched. By the time Auden published 'Spain' he was at the peak of his influence and reputation in England. In retrospect, Auden's visit to Spain in 1937 was the crucial step in a process of inner self-detachment. Anne Fremantle, a friend from his New York years, recalls the poet's comment that 'when I was in Spain during the Civil War and all the churches were shut, I realized I didn't like it. I wanted them to be open. I didn't at that point want particularly to pray myself, but I wanted people to be able to.'[22]

This is an early sign of that 'retreat into his own work and his own personality' as Spender described it. 'It wasn't exactly that he was an egotist, but that everything had become his world, you see, his own isolated world.'[23] The Spanish Catholic Church was pro-Franco and pro-fascist. At best one might say that Auden's reaction was mildly self-centred and naïve. Cyril Connolly remembered a rather more comic episode from Auden's visit to Spain. Stepping behind a bush for a piss in the gardens of Monjuich, Auden was seized by two members of the militia, alert for every counter-revolutionary manifestation. 'They were very indignant at this abuse of public property and it took several wavings of Harry Pollitt's* letter to set him free.' Connolly goes on: 'I think the incident was important for it revealed the misunderstanding between the revolutionary poet who felt disinhibited by the workers' victory and the new bureaucracy to whom the people's gardens deserved more respect than ever before.'[24] Auden may have laughed off the incident, whose insignificance hardly merits Connolly's silly comment, but the cumulative

---

* General Secretary of the Communist Party of Great Britain from 1929 to 1956.

effect of his experience in Spain undermined his commitment to the left — to politics at all. It was upon his return from Spain that Auden wrote his poem on behalf of the loyalist cause; in other words, when he had inwardly begun to turn away from political engagement, Auden was able to sit down on his return to England and write what is, after all, fairly high-minded propaganda. Auden later felt 'Spain' was dishonest, but he did not allow any of this ambiguity and doubleness of purpose to reveal itself in the poem. In fact, he consciously withheld his doubts. When he visited the Spenders immediately after returning from Spain, Auden refused to speak of his experiences there.[25]

The ruse worked. Orwell described 'Spain' as 'one of the few decent things that have been written about the Spanish War'.[26] Spender said it was 'the best poetic statement in English of the Republican case'.[27] The poem is psychological and individualistic, addressed as it is to the foreign volunteers who 'came to present their lives' and for whom 'fever's menacing shapes are precise and alive'. The rhetorical structure of the poem suggests an inverted dialectic, moving from Yesterday towards Tomorrow through Today, but is designed to heighten that deeper conjunction of history and will which is at stake in Spain. Auden sets out to bring his readers to the point of assent before the proposition that poetic visions, scientific inquiry, the abstract force of History, will not and cannot 'intervene' (needless to say, this was a desperately *political* term in 1937, but Auden does not engage with the issues at this level). There is no historical *deus ex machina*. Individuals must accept this burden for themselves. For Auden, the ultimate significance of the salvation of the Spanish Republic goes beyond merely political considerations. He is saying, as he had often insisted, that we must learn to confront our inner fears, and have greater insight into the way capitalism manipulates our behaviour by appealing to psychological weaknesses. As he writes in a curious passage,

> For the fears which made us respond
> To the medicine ad, and the brochure of winter cruises
> Have become invading battalions . . .

For Auden, Spain symbolizes modern man's great chance to cure his psyche. On the surface at least, it would appear that the psychological frame of reference has wholly come to replace the explicitly political meaning of the civil war. But Auden is trying to maintain some contact between the two, for he writes that it is possible here and now to reconstruct a society based on affection: 'Madrid is the heart. Our moments of tenderness blossom/As the ambulance and the sandbags.' The vision of 'Tomorrow', that cosy, comradely future in which romantic love is rediscovered, hobbies proliferate (photographing ravens, breeding terriers), political life flourishes ('The eager election of chairmen/By a sudden forest of hands'), depends upon the insistence of 'Today', of Spain and the Loyalist cause.

The poem is a notable achievement. Yet there is an ambiguity in Auden's perception of the cost of commitment:

> To-day the deliberate increase in the chances of death,
> The conscious acceptance of guilt in the necessary murder;
> To-day the expending of powers
> On the flat ephemeral pamphlet and boring meeting.

The 'deliberate' increase and 'necessary' murder imply a determinism against which the whole tenor of 'Spain' has been arguing. It is queerly contradictory. 'Death' and 'murder', what is more, positively smother that rather off-hand 'expending of powers' in political activity. The imbalance in the stanza directs attention away from the political towards the psychological, ethical and moral. The poem unequivocally supports the Republic, but the anti-political emphasis which Auden gives it does not require its readers to look more closely at the civil war nor to discriminate among the issues involved. It is just 'there'. One might prefer to call it an *occasional* poem, written for a special purpose; and that is precisely where Auden placed it, beside epitaphs of Yeats, Toller, Freud and 'September 1, 1939', when he collected 'Spain' in *Another Time* (1940).

Auden's subsequent attitude towards 'A Communist to Others' and 'Spain' is familiar enough. E. P. Thompson calls it a process of 'political bowdlerization'.[28] 'A Communist to Others' was cut by six stanzas when he collected it in *Look, Stranger!* (1936), making it a slightly better poem, more pointed and sarcastic. Auden allowed the earlier text to be reprinted as late as 1938 in a Left Book Club anthology of poems, but has rejected it since then. (An exception was made for Robin Skelton's anthology of 1930s poetry.) 'Spain' appeared unchanged in the Spender-Lehmann anthology, *Poems for Spain* (Hogarth Press, 1939), but was revised for collection in 1940; there is an unrecorded reprint of the earlier text as late as Oscar Williams's anthology, *The War Poets,* in 1945. The notorious line 'The conscious acceptance of guilt in the necessary murder' was revised after Auden went to America: 'The conscious acceptance of guilt in the fact of murder.' This is the most striking *volte-face* of Auden's career. That murders might be 'necessary' struck him now as a very wicked idea. But does he mean that it is wicked everywhere and for all time? While any man in our time might be rightly sickened at the idea of a 'necessary murder', a man, secure in America in 1940, could only say such things if he was ignorant of what was happening in Europe. Auden's point would not have been accepted by Bonhoeffer and others in the July plot against

Hitler. Nor by the partisans in the ghettos of Warsaw or Vilna or in the death camps. Auden's revision of 'Spain' constitutes a deliberate act of simplification, doing nothing more than clear the air for his conscience. The flavour of the 'new' Auden was soon evident. 'When a ship catches fire,' he suggested in *The New Republic* (6 September 1939), 'it seems only natural to rush importantly to the pumps, but perhaps one is only adding to the general confusion and panic: to sit still and pray seems selfish and unheroic, but it may be the wisest and most helpful course.' Reviewing a book by Jacques Barzun in *The Nation* (7 October 1939) he wrote: 'Frankly, democracy will only work if as individuals we lead good lives, and we shall only do that if we have faith that it is possible and at the same time an acute awareness of how weak and corrupt we are.' Ursula Niebuhr recalls a lecture which Auden delivered at Smith College on 17 June 1940:

> The statements and theses which were to become so characteristic are all there; particularly those analysing 'the paradoxical dialectic of freedom'. The label of 'romantic', he chose for all those who in one way or another reject 'this understanding of freedom'. The fate of such is the closed society. Conversely, the open society 'believes that logical necessity can be recognized by everybody and that in consequence, the truth is best arrived at by free controversy. But it will recognize that no thinking or voluntary behaviour is possible without making some absolute presuppositions, or acts of faith.'[29]

Auden extended this analysis in a 1941 essay on 'Criticism in Mass Society'. In the early years of the war he familiarly used the Popperian distinction between open versus closed societies. Renaissance individualism was contrasted to the self produced in an organic, undifferentiated community. Romanticism was the convenient label for the overweening heresy of modern man which received ultimate expression in fascism and Hitler. In one sense, Auden was in sympathy with the traditional hostility towards romanticism in modern Anglo-American conservatism (books of the preceding two decades include Paul Elmer More's *The Drift of Romanticism*, 1913; Babbitt's *Rousseau and Romanticism*, 1919; Hulme's *Speculations*, 1924; Eliot's *After Strange Gods*, 1936; Winters's *Primitivism and Decadence*, 1937). By comparison, the enthusiastic rediscovery of romanticism in painting and literature during the war; the substantial influence throughout the 1940s of Dylan Thomas; the emergence of Thomas's disciples in *The White Horseman* (1941); the pervasive influence of Herbert Read, the indefatigable propagandist for surrealism and romanticism; and the depth of Read's influence, as seen in the declaration of young Oxford poets in 1941 that 'we are all . . . *Romantic* writers':[30] all this seems merely a distraction from the direction of Auden's new-found orthodoxy. Mrs

Niebuhr's vivid memoir indicates how deep was Auden's involvement in the theological issues of the day. The scene has shifted from the dying fall of left politics in the late 1930s to the theological turns of reaction in the 1940s. Auden, as clearly as anyone, defines that mood in 'New Year Letter'.

Here he writes feelingly of the tragedy of the 1930s:

> Who, thinking of the last ten years
> Does not hear howling in his ears
> The Asiatic cry of pain,
> The shots of executing Spain . . .
> The Jew wrecked in the German cell,
> Flat Poland frozen into hell . . .   (Part I)

Unlike 'Spain', this brief catalogue is not in the service of a call to action or to personal commitment. Rather, it analyses the temptation to action in a strained metaphor, in order to point out how the end result ('perhaps one is only adding to the general confusion and panic') confounds our expectations. The promise of sweet revenge, that 'grand apocalyptic dream',

> In which the persecutors scream
> As on the evil Aryan lives
> Descends the night of the long knives;
> The bleeding tyrant dragged through all
> The ashes of his capitol . . .   (Part I)

is seen to be inadequate. Auden is now a quietist:

> No words men write can stop the war . . .   (Part I)

The only use he will accept for the 'good offices of verse' is to make its small contribution to the conference between heart and intelligence. There is no place here, in the gentle function of poetry, for the 'outraged mind':

> Art is not life and cannot be
> A midwife to society . . .   (Part I)

Looking back in the second part of 'New Year Letter' to his experience of socialism, Auden writes of a millennial revelation which has failed:

> We hoped; we waited for the day
> The State would wither clean away,
> Expecting the Millennium
> That theory promised us would come,
> It didn't. Specialists must try
> To detail all the reasons why . . .

Other ramifications of the 'theory that failed' were soon apparent. A failed utopianism, Auden urges, should not propel us into the enticing empiricism of Locke. Dualism and the bastard progeny of pluralism and moral relativity in contemporary thought now seem to Auden the blandishments of the 'Devil' — everything which encourages our frantic search for 'half-truths we can synthesize'. Pre-eminent of such half-truths is the idea of organic community:

> If it were easy to be good,
> And cheap, and plain as evil how,
> We all would be its members now:
> How readily would we become
> The seamless live continuum
> Of supple and coherent stuff,
> Whose form is truth, whose content love ...   (Part III)

But the real world is not such:

> But wishes are not horses, this
> *Annus* is not *mirabilis*;
> Day breaks upon the world we know
> Of war and wastefulness and woe ...   (Part III)

Thus the quietism of 'late' Auden. It would be an exaggeration to say that Auden single-handedly discredited the Audenesque. It was the age itself, the torturous experience of the first years of the war, which overwhelmed the style; it had become 'period' seemingly overnight. Auden presided over the change of climate, the general withdrawal from a politically committed poetry. The poets raised in the shadow of Auden's authority, such as Randall Jarrell, in America, were left to find their own voice, to flounder through that characteristic mood of unease and self-absorption in the 1940s, against which the formalism of the succeeding decade emerged with such shattering self-assurance.

In Randall Jarrell's essays the course of the argument is continually being disturbed by voices. The plain man, interrupting a high critical argument, blurts out, 'Why would anybody want to write like that?' Other voices, cultured ones, are frequently heard: Goethe, Samuel Johnson, James, Eliot, Wordsworth. Jarrell summons voices to the aid of his extravagant, painful critical wit: 'The average poem in [Muriel Rukeyser's] *The Green Wave* is all flesh and feeling and fantasy: as if reality were a pure blooming buzz, with the poet murmuring to the poem, "Flow, flow!"' His own poems, so often dramatic monologues, reverberate with a babel of voices, and give Jarrell's verse (the enabling rhetoric of his conversational style, that is) a feeling of density, population, and even of overcrowding. It is hard to pick out any single tone, and say with assurance that *this* is

Jarrell's: surely that is the point. The voices, and the self-dramatization of his wit, serve Jarrell's rhetoric variously — not least in the evasion of a directly intimate voice. The effort was sanctioned by his desire to resist the cultural milieu of the South. As an undergraduate in the early 1930s, he was in occasional contact with the Agrarians and Fugitives, a group of writers who had come together in the preceding decade in an attempt to create a new cultural front against urban, industrial society; the ultimate philosophic orientation of the Fugitives was hostile to rationalism, science or progress. Allen Tate and John Crowe Ransom were the two Fugitives to whom Jarrell was closest, although he came within their orbit in a glancing fashion. Tate was surprised at the strength of Jarrell's independence of mind as an undergraduate: 'If he ever looked at the writings of the Agrarians, he would have thought it all nonsense, or at any rate an irrelevant excursion into history without value to a poet.'[31] He was a friend of Tate's, to whom he dedicated his first volume of poems, *Blood for the Stranger* (1942); but as early as the mid-1930s John Crowe Ransom was undoubtedly the more potent influence. Jarrell's undergraduate degree was in psychology, but he continued at Vanderbilt to complete a Master's degree in English (his thesis was a critical reading of the poems of Housman). When Ransom went to Kenyon College in Gambier, Ohio, in 1937, Jarrell followed as an instructor of English. After a brief spell at the University of Texas, Jarrell enlisted in the Army Air Force. A group of twenty poems, 'The Rage for the Lost Penny', appeared in a New Directions anthology, *Five Young American Poets* in 1940; *Blood for the Stranger,* came out two years later.

The flavour of the Audenesque is unmistakable in Jarrell's early verse: in the titles of poems, in subjects and technique, he was a disciple of Auden. Though the technical debts are clear, Jarrell's scepticism, the dark turn of his sensibility, shows that he was the product as well of the complex, tragic history of the South. His work suggests how much of an influence Auden exerted, but also the difficulties of accommodating the surface characteristics of the Audenesque in a quite different historical and ideological formation. Jarrell's problem is one of focus. In a poem such as 'Money', a dramatic monologue of a nineteenth-century robber baron, Jarrell accumulates the details, the sociological sense of place, without precisely locating the sources of life which would have turned the plutocrat into a human being. It is an exercise in a mode of satire which he was to perfect to a fare-thee-well in a comic novel, *Pictures from an Institution* (1954). In 'Money' he does not create a unique experience, but merely deals with a type as a type. 'The Emancipators' (whose title must have unconsciously reverberated with an ironical reference to the Emancipation Proclamation — an irony not widely felt outside the South) is another poem in which Jarrell reaches out for a specifically social and historical frame of reference for his sceptical view of the claims of rationalism, progress or science:

> . . . the free
> Drag their slight bones from tenements to vote
> To die with their children in your factories.

> Man is born in chains, and everywhere we see him dead.

Jarrell was writing at a time when the traditional agrarian South was feeling the impact of industrialism, and when the Blacks were emigrating north, to New York and Chicago, in unprecedented numbers. There is a particular twist to the way he uses 'free', an irony that comes with the authority of the Fugitives behind it, which prepares us for the punning inversion of Rousseau in the final line quoted. The poem dramatizes a quarrel of ideologies, but the ideas remain sourly external. Another early poem, 'The Winter's Tale', omitted from the *Selected Poems* of 1955, is an example of Jarrell's facility with the generalizing mode of the Audensque:

> A whole economy;
> The fiascoes of the metaphysicians, a theology's disasters,
> The substitutes of the geometer for existence, the observation
> Of the interminable and euphuist's metaphor exploding
> Into use, into breath, into terror; the millennia
> Of patience, of skills, of understanding, the centuries
> Of terms crystallizing into weapons, the private
> And endless means, the catastrophic
> Magnificence of paranoia; are elaborated into
> A few bodies in the torn-up street.

Jarrell's early poems point to the breakdown of the characteristic idiom and style of the 1930s. To use the Audensque ('The Winter's Tale' is a galloping pastiche of Auden) for a poem drenched in the pessimism of the Fugitives, with its covert romantic despair, was to turn the ideological content of the Audensque upside down. Jarrell turns a mode of political intervention into self-parody: the Audensque was a mode of writing which had clearly reached the end of the line.

Jarrell's critical essays and reviews in the 1940s and early 1950s, collected in *Poetry and the Age* (1953), define an approach to a poetry of the real. This can be illustrated, as Jarrell would have done, through quotation. Robert Frost is 'one of the brilliant partial poets who do justice, far more than justice, to a portion of reality'. Whitman commanded 'a language of the calmest and most prosaic reality', and was a poet 'faithful to the feel of things, to reality as it seems'. Walter de la Mare's verse 'assures us that if reality is not necessarily what we should like it to be, it is necessarily what we feel it to be: to be is to be *felt*'. Wallace Stevens in *Auroras of Autumn* was guilty of 'thinking of particulars as primarily illustrations of general truths'. Jarrell praised William Carlos Williams for his 'concrete presentation'. It was Pound, of course, who based an aesthetic upon 'concrete particulars', and the poet's peculiar ability to perceive them and write of them with utter truthfulness and precision. Jarrell turned back to a facet of the modernist legacy and appropriated it for the crucial touchstone of his criticism. As a critic he identified reality with the immediacy of the known, seen, felt and understood. He resisted any temptation to elaborate his taste into doctrine, arguing that the critic had only his taste and intelligence to rely upon. In his verse 'things of the world', obviously, encompass more than the crude externality of materialism: Jarrell's genius was for rendering fugitive experiences, dream-visions, states of mind, interior monologues, adolescent reverie, mental disturbance, and the extreme experiences of war, concentration camps, imprisonment, murder, and death. But his insistence upon the wholeness and tactility of 'reality' remains central. Despite this, the sense of a unique personal voice is often lacking, as though it was too dangerous, too close to the direct expression of sentiment. His description of John Crowe Ransom's poetry has the insight of self-knowledge:

> He is perpetually insisting, by his detached, mock-pedantic, wittily complicated tone, that he is not feeling much at all, not half so much as he really should be feeling — and this rhetoric becomes overmannered, too-protective, where there is not much emotion for him to pretend not to be feeling, and he keeps on out of habit. Ransom developed this rhetorical machinery — tone, phrasing, properties, and all the rest — primarily as a way of handling sentiment or emotion without ever seeming sentimental or over-emotional; as a way of keeping the poem at the proper aesthetic distance from its subject . . . He was writing in an age in which the most natural feeling of tenderness, happiness, or sorrow was likely to be called sentimental . . .
>
> ('John Ransom's Poetry', *Poetry and the Age*)

It is not the least of Jarrell's strengths as a critic to see the creative role of evasion with such clarity. Jarrell's own work suffers from the lack of a dominant creative style, a creative autonomy. To his contemporaries the early poems seemed clever, but somehow anonymous.[32] With the massive complete poems before us, that anonymity seems more a style, a consciously adopted relation to 'everything that is the case', a 'rhetorical machinery' as he remarked of Ransom. It is possible, and undesirable, to exaggerate one's sense of the anonymity of Jarrell's verse. When he encountered Richard Wilbur's early poems Jarrell understood what *real* anonymity was, and disapproved quite emphatically. Equally, to argue that Jarréll's poems posit a kind of aesthetic autonomy does not mean one is describing the self-contained structures much beloved of the New Critics, then sprouting like weeds in English departments throughout America. Jarrell's poems, particularly in the late 1940s, are lavishly textured by history, literary allusion, puns, and the echoing phrases of the subconscious — some read like a poor man's 'The Waste Land' ('An English Garden in Austria', for example). The style he was evolving was wordy, syntactically limp but convoluted; poems about ideas struggling with their own complexity. His prime concern was to heighten the meaning of the scene, emotion, content of the passage:

> They sense with misunderstanding horror, with desire,
> Behind the world their blood sets up in mist
> The brute and geometrical necessity:
> The Leopard waving with a grating purr
> His six-foot tail; the leopard, who looks sleepily —
> Cold, fugitive, secure — at all that he knows,
> And all that he is: the heart of heartlessness.
>
> ('The Snow-Leopard')

A passage like this, so revealing of Jarrell's desire for emotional resonance in his poems, stands for the limits of his achievement as a poet.

He hoped to be a pilot, but was washed out of pilot training, and spent the war on the ground staff at airbases in the States. It is the air force which comes to stand in Jarrell's thought for the moral ambiguity of the war itself. His best war poems are caught between the imperative of 'concrete presentation', and the ultimate meaning of the scene or action before him. In 'Eighth Air Force' he develops a convincing picture of the sheer ordinariness of life in the barracks ('A puppy laps the water from a can/Of flowers . . .'), but can scarcely control a stagy gesture of moral revulsion ('*O murderers . . .*'). That man can be a wolf to man, and yet be in himself not entirely bereft of humanity, is the 'point'; what energy the poem generates lies between the specific observation and the meaning which puts it into perspective. The tactic does not always work. In 'Losses' he tried to personify death, to make it seem a minor matter (with the ironical 'Our casualties were low'), but the enormity of what he is saying — about the 'losses', the pilots, and the cities which they bombed — will not be subdued by the oddly opaque surface of his rhetoric.

In his best war poems he takes a scene, as in 'Transient Barracks', and allows its full weight of meaning to emerge. The poem unfolds through a series of notations:

> Summer. Sunset. Someone is playing
> The ocarina in the latrine:
> You Are My Sunshine.

A man shaving sees the lights of B-24s on the runway as the first flight takes off. A voice is heard on the radio: 'The thing about you is, you're *real.*' The man shaving sees his own face in the mirror: it, too, is real. There are others in the barracks, a boy in underwear hunting for something, voices from the doorway, whose existence is equally certain:

> These are. Are what? Are.

The central figure in the poem, the man shaving before the mirror, hungers for an affirmation of the real. He is home:

> '*I'm back for good. The States, the States!*'
> He puts out his hand to touch it –
> And the thing about it is, it's *real.*

Jarrell seems to be saying that we need the real, need to see and smell it, to feel, as he wrote in impassioned advocacy of W. C. Williams, 'that almost nothing is more important, more of a true delight, than the way things look'. But somehow the process ends right there, in acceptance.

The roots of this feeling of acceptance lie deep in Jarrell's experience. In the early poems, for example, he shows a passivity before history:

> The beings of this world are swept
> By the Strife that moves the stars.   ('The Breath of Night')

> This world holds us more than we can see or say,
> And it stuffs us like a goose before it kills us.   ('The Bad Music')

He shared with the Fugitives a pessimistic attitude towards the meaningfulness of knowledge or understanding:

> . . . all the knowledge

> I wrung from the darkness – that the darkness flung me –
> Is worthless as ignorance: nothing comes from nothing,
> The darkness from the darkness. Pain comes from the darkness.
> And we call it wisdom. It is pain.   ('90 North')

And so we cannot be surprised when Jarrell, like MacNeice, Auden and Alun Lewis, prepares us to *accept*:

> It happens as it does because it does.
> It is unnecessary to understand . . .   ('Siegfried')

> . . . the world is – what it has been . . .
>   ('The Range on the Desert')

Jarrell is quick to see that humanity, in such circumstances, is merely an adjunct to the machines of war:

. . . you are something there are millions of.
How can I care about you much, or pick you out
From all the others other people loved
And sent away to die for them?   ('The Sick Nought')

But in 'Protocols', a poem of great restraint about children being taken to Birkenau and gassed, and in 'A Camp in the Prussian Forest', one of the finest of Jarrell's war poems, he deals with a heartbreaking, indeed stupefying reality, by refusing to solicit the mildly ironic (but not flippant) sensibility of the poet. It is remarkable for what it does not say, as much as for what it does. There are 'corpses, stacked like sodden wood,/[which] Lie barred or galled with blood/by the charred warehouse'. The speaker makes a slight response of his own by building a rough Star of David and implanting it in the ground. He cannot grasp the meaning of the corpses, the fate of the 'breast's star of hope' utterly destroyed by genocide. His own offering, 'this dead white star', has no meaning in that sense:

                    . . . I laugh aloud
Again and again;
The star laughs from its rotting shroud
Of flesh. O star of men!

That final star might be on one of the piled corpses. Jarrell has slowly allowed its meaning to grow and become more complex: it now stands for more than the traditional national and religious symbol, or even the badge of race imposed by Nazi racial law. Jarrell generalizes the meaning of the experience without losing touch of the 'concrete particulars' before him. The final apostrophe confirms an overwhelming sense of numbness at the inexplicability and permanence of evil. It came in the form of a recognition, an acceptance, of a reality which transcended the quotidian experience of men at peace. There was a rough kind of topicality to Jarrell's war poems, but their underlying revelation of reality, and the poet's relationship to that experience, ushers us not so much into the war years but into the decade-long recoil from the buoyant assertiveness of the 1930s.

After the war, Jarrell's work lost something of its contemporaneity. He could be said to have isolated a single subject – women – and to have written powerfully, in 'Seele im Raum' and 'The Night Before the Night Before Christmas', of those moments when his characters are set apart, when a new phase of consciousness is revealed through disturbance, neurosis, dreams, or maturation. These were the poems Jarrell placed at the beginning of his *Selected Poems* in the 1950s, having deleted just under fifty poems from his wartime volumes. It confirmed a direction, but not an unarguable critical judgment. His later work, culminating in the pathos and introspection of *The Lost World* (1965), shows little feel for the dramatic moment, or the full force of the natural speaking voice:

> Is my voice the voice
> Of that skin of being — of what owns, is owned
> In honor or dishonor, that is borne and bears —
> Or of that raw thing, the being inside it
> That has neither a wife, a husband, nor a child
> But goes at last as naked from this world
> As it was born into it —   ('Seele im Raum')

The moment is one of excruciating self-illumination within the reveries of a disturbed consciousness. The woman represents a *clinical* dissociation of sensibility, a mind whose introspection carries within itself the potential for self-destruction. Jarrell's sympathy is infinite, but the voice sounds too much like the dozens of others which reverberate throughout his poems.

In the early phase of the war it was generally felt by the literary intelligentsia in England that they had been ignored in the war effort. Chamberlain's first Minister of Information had been Sir John Reith. A War Artist's Advisory Committee, headed by Kenneth Clark, was funded with ten thousand pounds. In January 1940 the Council for Education in Music and the Arts was set up with a budget of twenty thousand pounds. There was no provision for writers as such. Orwell remarked in the autumn of 1943 that 'the British Government started the present war with the more or less openly declared intention of keeping the literary intelligentsia out of it'.[33] When Churchill came to power in May 1940 he replaced Reith with Duff Cooper at the M. of I., which was the start of a marginally less ramshackle propaganda policy. Duff Cooper put Kenneth Clark at the head of the films division, but it wasn't until 1941 that the first government-financed propaganda feature film (*49th Parallel*) appeared. With promising changes at the M. of I., the idea was floated in *Horizon* (October 1941) for a war writers programme. The manifesto was signed by Arthur Calder-Marshall, Cyril Connolly, Bonamy Dobrée, Tom Harrisson, Arthur Koestler, Alun Lewis, George Orwell and Stephen Spender. The recognition that wartime conditions were making it difficult, or impossible, for writers stood behind their proposal: they were simply asking for time, and the conditions, within which they could write. To persuade politicians and civil servants that this had anything to do with the war effort probably surpassed the powers of persuasion. The manifesto was in that sense a reminder of the widespread feeling of powerlessness and isolation within the literary community.

What is more, dissatisfaction with the war literature that was eventually produced was widely expressed, even by those, like John Lehmann, who were closely identified with wartime literary life: 'this war has still found no writer in prose or verse to interpret it with any thing like ... depth and power'.[34] Reviewing current verse in *Time and Tide* (16 September 1944), Roy Fuller wrote that 'there can never have been a period when young men have devoted less skill to the writing of poetry'. D. J. Enright, who was a frequent contributor to *Scrutiny*, described the situation as 'a heavy-footed imagination stumbling around in a mental void'.[35] Fuller, Lehmann and Enright were sympathetic towards 'serious' poetry — Yeats, Eliot, Auden — but what of those who had steadfastly ignored or opposed the dominant tenor of inter-war writing? It was back to 1915 all over again, as they called for something simple, patriotic and uplifting. The deification of Rupert Brooke early in World War I had crystallized their taste, as had Edward Marsh's Georgian anthologies. There had been no precise American equivalent to Georgian poetry, but there was a similar reaction, well before America actually entered the war, against the avant-garde. Archibald MacLeish attacked the intellectuals as 'The Irresponsibles' for their collective failure to defend 'western culture' against the totalitarian threat (*The Nation,* 18 May 1940). MacLeish's use of phrases such as 'the community of western culture' and 'the inherited culture of the west' reveals how quickly chauvinism replaced the critical radicalism of the 1930s. The 'culture' of capitalism and imperialism, of class privilege, inequality, and the depression, was brushed aside; this was no time to be critical, but to close ranks. The attack on civil liberties, in the name of 'the war effort', was widely applauded. Goebbels had abolished criticism in the arts by decree in 1936: it was all part of 'the war effort' on the cultural front.

In an inaugural lecture at Hunter College in October 1940, Van Wyck Brooks attacked the fashionable despair and pessimism of modern literature.[36] Brooks had for some years been disenchanted with modernist literature. In an article in the *Yale Review* (Summer 1941), entitled 'What is Primary Literature?', and in a second and more pointed lecture, 'Primary Literature and Coterie Literature', delivered at Columbia University that September, matters were brought to a head. The 'coterie' literature of modernism was, according to Brooks, synonymous with the 'death drive' that imperilled the world.[37] The defenders of modernist writing, led by the editors of *Partisan Review,* organized a collective rejoinder to the Brooks-MacLeish thesis. Dwight Macdonald wrote to T. S. Eliot and enlisted his support. Orwell joined in the intellectual-bashing in the early years of the war, but the most prominent spokesman of the new *Kulturbolschewismus* in England was Lord Elton. He voiced the traditional reactionary view that it was the intellectuals who had sapped the morale of the people, and who had contributed to the economic and military weakness of English society.[38] The specific object of his comments was the anti-war literature which appeared in the 1920s, but the point could be applied more generally. A notorious editorial in *The Times* (24 March 1941) entitled 'The Eclipse of the Highbrow' endorsed Lord Elton's position. The ensuing correspondence from Kenneth Clark, Stephen Spender, and Michael Roberts suggests that a sensitive nerve had been touched. The gut feeling of resentment towards the 'highbrow' writers and artists was fairly widespread. The editor of the *Times Literary Supplement* thought something like this was needed:

> This is the war we always knew,
>   When every county keeps her own,
> When Kent stands sentry in the lane,
> And fenland guards her dyke and drain,
>   Cornwall, her cliffs of stone.[39]

All the apparatus of the patriotic pseudo-ballad is here: Drake's drum, the 'conquering Corsican', and that heroic 'single island . . . Ringed with an angry host'. The author, Dorothy L. Sayers, was unusual in her confidence. Rather more characteristic of that first winter of the war was a stoical reluctance, expressed by Anne Ridler:

> War is not simple: in more or less degree
> All are guilty, though some will suffer unjustly,
> Can we say mass to dedicate our bombs?
> Yet those earlier English, for all their psalms
> Were marauders, had less provocation than we,
> And the causes of war were as mixed and as hard to see.
> And since of two evils our victory would be the less,
> And coming soon, leave some strength for peace,
> Hopeful like Minot and the rest, we pray:
> 'Lord, turn us again, confer on us victory'.[40]

This was the mood of many people who grew up in the shadow of 1914-18, who had lost fathers, older brothers, or who knew those who had such losses, and who felt after Hitler's rise to power that the Nazis would have to be stopped, yet to fight was an unmitigated disaster. The urge to close ranks was overwhelming; with many poems it took the form of social reconciliation. Day Lewis's 'Watching Post' is the supreme example. These are war poems of noncombatants, basically out of touch with the experience of the soldiers. Even so, there were fewer patriotic ballads being written after 1942; they were merely the embarrassing reminder of the mood of a brief moment.

By 1941 it was becoming clear that there would be no 'war poetry' as there had been during the 1914-18 war. Robert Graves, in an acute article in *The Listener* (23 October 1941) pointed to obvious differences in the war itself. For a start, there was universal conscription and no need for patriotic hoop-la to spur on volunteers. The army was not yet engaged on a large scale, and the life of soldiers was comparatively safe; nor was it 'the amateur, desperate, happy-go-lucky, ragtime, lousy army of World War I'. Graves thought that the person most likely to become a war poet now 'feels a mist of the colour of khaki blanco rise between him and the world of his imagination'. When the urge to write poems finally comes, it will probably have more to do with the poet's sense of himself as a sensitive outsider, different from his fellow soldiers, than with 'the necessity of the war's continuance'.

Characteristic poems of the early stages of the war were surprising, at least for some readers, because they showed little sense of occasion, or patriotic fervour. The editor of the *Times Literary Supplement* sounded quite dismayed by *Poems of This War*, edited by Patricia Ledward and Colin Strang:

> That they write with complete sincerity is not to be doubted; they say what they wish to say in their own language; and yet, as Mr Blunden in his introduction implies, there is 'no militarism, or personal claim, or study of revenge'. This is a remarkable comment to make. Militarism is no doubt offensive even in professional soldiers, many of the best of whom have been free of it. Personal claims, again, may be sheer egoism. Revenge may be an injurious study. But is there no such thing as righteous indignation? May not a dear homeland be in imminent danger?   (*TLS*, 8 August 1942)

The most interesting poems reflected the day-to-day, humdrum experiences of military life:

> . . . we stretched out, unbuttoning our braces,
> Smoking a Woodbine, darning dirty socks,
> Reading the Sunday papers . . .
> (Alun Lewis, 'All Day It Has Rained . . .')*

Inevitably it was training camp and troopship, and not heroic battlefields, which provided the locale of the first war poems. The political and cultural élites badly misjudged the initial mood of the people. In a diary entry as early as 24 September 1939, Harold Nicolson remarked that 'the Government had not foreseen a situation in which boredom and bewilderment would be the main elements. They concentrated upon coping with panic and have been faced with an anticlimax.'[41] Everywhere one turns in the written documentation of intellectuals and artists in wartime, there is a heartfelt solidarity: they were just as bored as other

* Cf. Auden, Poem XXII, *Poems* (Faber & Faber, second ed., London 1933), p. 75:
  On the sopping esplanade or from our dingy lodgings we
  Stare out dully at the rain which falls for miles into the sea.

men, if not more so. In an essay completed in March 1942, Sidney Keyes tried to generalize his own experience:

> ... in our country conditions are becoming impossible for creative work. We have no canvases, no paper, no colours, no binding materials; and, above all, no *time*. We are never left in one place long enough to achieve the necessary emotional stability; we are kept too busy to register either the outward or the inward world as we should.[42]

Peter Ure noted in his journal in September 1942:

> I get increasingly tired of the way in which I spend my days, increasingly bored with 'community life', its frittering away of time. Meanwhile
> Life slips by like a field-mouse
> Not shaking the grass...
> The war has produced a vast slagheap of days through which we must shovel and burrow in ignorance of our task, like creatures in some sombre bureaucratic Hell. My one ambition, my one desire has been to write poetry, and I come to this important work miserably ill-equipped, my consciousness chopped into useless fragments by the demands of the day, every instrument blunted and stained.[43]

There were many attempts to state or explain the dilemma of creativity during the war; none, I should have thought, surpasses a journal entry of the painter Keith Vaughan:

> 20 June 1944 Cinema tonight: an impressive display of the war material of the Allies. The accumulated wealth and skill from every part of the world. Orderly stacks of food, bombs, medical supplies, locomotives, guns, aircraft. A man checking the row of boxes, a heavy load on to the quayside. The aircraftsman putting the finishing touches to his machine. And on every face the same bright self-satisfied smile of people conscious that they are sharing together in an enormous undertaking.
> Obviously there is no doubt about the achievement in concentrating into the British Isles the war potential of more than half the world. But each man sees only a fraction of the marvellous whole.
> I know what it feels like to stack boxes all day as they come off a rolling belt. One thinks of the size and weight, the need to co-ordinate one's muscles to handling them with the minimum of exertion. Questions of smoothness and roughness are important, textures of wood and the nails at the corners. One is not concerned with the contents or its purpose but appreciates a box as an absolute thing in itself. The way the markings are placed, the raw smell of wood, the way to avoid the corners catching the rollers. One gains a

tactile understanding of a wooden box, and beyond that is simply the framework of the working day. The time you knock off for lunch, or pause to light a cigarette. The soreness of hands and the sense of relaxation in the evenings. But all this has no connection between the contents of the wooden box or its relation to the war effort as a whole.
The only real thing seems to be the personal experience of the thing one is doing. The relation of that thing is purely conjectural. The experience of loading packing cases remains the same irrespective of the contents or its destination.[44]

This might be said to be the dilemma of creativity at any time, not just during war. The 'relations' of experience, which is always lived for itself and in itself, constitute the essence of an art that would be adequate to the real world. Peter Ure's description of 'consciousness chopped into useless fragments', and Sidney Keyes's oppressive feeling of busyness, suggest the form that immediate experience is likely to take. Vaughan ultimately comes down on the side of the immediacy of personal experience, one's 'tactile understanding' of textures and smells. Graves's vivid image of the 'mist the colour of khaki blanco' rising up between the poet and the world of his imagination, states the obvious problem: that immediate experience can never be an end in itself without impoverishing the imagination. To lie doggo and let it wash over you, as Orwell suggested Henry Miller had done, is to be passively at the mercy of the coercive force of manipulation, propaganda, the inevitable distortions of ideology, of class and education, of cosiness and conviviality, of everything, in fact, that might deprive a writer of the ability to see experience with sufficient clarity to know, or imagine, what the contents or destination of those wooden crates does to the effort of spending all day stacking them. It is not so much a question of choice — between a passive acceptance and an aggressive vigilance — but of a tension, a dialectical relation, between the 'personal experience of the thing one is doing' and 'its relation to the war effort as a whole'. Within the work of Alun Lewis, alone of the younger poets who emerged during the war, do we see the full play of these tensions.

Lewis's first book, *Raider's Dawn,* appeared in March 1942. There are examples here of heightened reportage in the manner of 'All Day It Has Rained . . .', as well as more obviously personal and introspective poems such as 'The Soldier' and 'To Edward Thomas'. Polarities of this nature run through the whole of Lewis's experience during the war. His great dilemma as an artist lay in the relations between the levels of experience in his first book. Edgell Rickword argued in 'Poetry and Two Wars' (*Our Time,* April 1941) that we cannot regard concrete experience as something which exists 'in isolation from the complex of social relationships':

> It is a matter of being able to see what is under one's nose, not of any particular manner or approach to the subject; ridicule and indignation equally serve the truth. The only condition is to feel as the people feel, not as the journalists pretend they feel, nor as we abstractedly might like them to feel.

Lewis's strongest feelings were involved with a humble sense of identity with the common soldier; yet he was capable of a cutting irony, as when he writes in 'The Soldier':

> . . . leisurely my fellow soldiers stroll among the trees.
> The cheapest dance-song utters all they feel.

He was an officer, yet felt little but contempt for the hypocrisy of military life, 'the officer-mind and its artificial assumptions, the rigid distinctions of rank which so rarely go with quality and character'.[45] One feels often in Lewis's poems that he cherishes experience for its own sake (whether it was the 'perpetual undercurrent of hostility' which he felt in the natives, or the 'immediate contact with the wild sea'); yet his poems from India are overwhelmed by a disturbing, halluciné feeling of abandonment, that he was leaving the known and the felt, the tactile, behind him. He seems obsessed by the idea of a complete state of passivity, choosing to 'let the world fall softly from my hand' ('Motifs'). The affairs of men seem increasingly remote:

> The distant world in an obituary.
> We do not hear the tappings of its dread.   ('The Jungle', Part iv)

It takes an effort to recall that Lewis was a Welsh schoolmaster, trained as a historian — a sensible, intelligent man who exuded competence. It was with his voyage out to India that the formidable contradictions within his work emerged. Conditions aboard ship during the voyage out in November and December, 1942, were overcrowded and oppressive. It was characteristic of the man that he noted in a letter that a soldier had been courtmartialled for saying that the officers were more comfortable aboard ship than other ranks. His job was Entertainments Officer and he was kept busy to the point of distraction organizing lectures, forums, Hyde Park Corner discussions, and Brains Trusts. Passages in Lewis's poem about the voyage, 'A Troopship in the Tropics' (*New Statesman*, 24 April 1943) are among his last exercises in documentary realism:

> Deep in the foetid holds the tiered bunks
> Hold restless men who sweat and toss and sob;
> The gamblers on the hatches, in the corner
> The accordionist and barber do their job.

The second half of the poem goes beyond the immediate experience of the voyage and tries to understand it in other terms. Despite the overwhelming presence of *things* aboard, there are 'tranquil pools of crystal-clear reflexion': amidst the confusion of the crowded decks there are 'simple donors of goodness'. Welsh songs are heard in the circling darkness. Even 'the ruthless Now grows kind'.

'A Troopship in the Tropics' is leading us through the documentary realism of 1930s poetry towards a quite different, more introspective, more passive mode of writing. Even Lewis seems mildly bemused at the new direction of his thoughts, noting how 'Strange desires drift into the mind'. His letters from the voyage out to India are full of detail about conditions on board, and contain fascinating descriptions of the ports of call in Brazil and South Africa. Lewis clearly possessed an acute and prophetic sensitivity to race relations. But later in the voyage a different note appears in his correspondence:

> Oh, time is long! And yet this voyage has been so placid in a way, it's been a complete seclusion of the spirit despite the crowded cabins and decks and messrooms; there's been only the sea, and the sun and the moon, the ship's steady voyaging and the ultimate purposes all far away, never touching us, distant as the horizon. That is why I've been able to write so much poetry; and why, now that I've given up my entertainments job and sought a few days' freedom before the shrinking chaos of unloading our mighty luggage from half a dozen holds and directing the coolies to load it on to the trains, why I am living in a world of pure contemplation, letting daily life revolve on the circumference of the circle, while at the centre my thoughts and emotions form their altering pattern and make their music.

Lewis, who had signed the *Horizon* manifesto on war writers, knew that a consciousness 'chopped into useless fragments' could not produce whole art. The conditions of life during the war were especially hostile to poets. His discovery that writing was at least possible within that 'world of pure contemplation' put him in touch with the roots of his own artistic coherence. He might have written quite different poems had there been no war. But the experience of profound distractedness which it exacerbated, gave Lewis a different perspective, and a new resolve as a poet.

Soon after arriving in India he wrote that he was going 'to rinse my mind of preoccupations, to write no more poems about Europe and to speak as I found' (*New Statesman,* 1 May 1943). Lewis's work from India was received with some resentment. Roy Fuller remembers thinking that it signalled an 'abdication from responsibility'.[46]

Lewis's dilemma now revealed itself through his increasing frustration with army life. In a letter to his wife Gweno he described coming across 'a tiny shrine set in a desolate plain', and how he had remained, expectantly, before the Buddha. 'But it was no good. I only knew that it was closed to me as long as I was a fussy little officer sahib with a hundred unimportant jobs on his mind.' He turned this experience into a fine poem, 'Karanje Village'. It begins with a sweeper telling him that the village possessed a temple with a roof of gold. But when he arrived there was only 'the long-nosed swine and the vultures/Groping the refuse for carrion'. He then proceeds with a long descriptive catalogue of the village, animals and people, in a sarcastic tone. At this moment, having established the basic irony of the richness of the spiritual promise of the shrine and the impoverished, disgusting nature of the village in which it was set, he introduces the 'little Vishnu of stone':

> Silently and eternally simply Being,
> Bidding me come alone
> And never entirely turning me away,
> But warning me still of the flesh
> That catches and limes the singing birds of the soul
> And holds their wings in mesh.

The people of India (whose poverty 'is like acid in the brain', as he wrote in the *New Statesman*, 1 May 1943) were not to be reached in a hurry by such a message: they were like 'Hard stones flung out of Creation's silent matrix'; nor can there be much hope for a generalized love ('we must love one another or die') in such a harsh land. His answer is quietist: 'I am seeking less and less of the world.'

Many poems in *Ha! Ha! Among the Trumpets*, Lewis's posthumous collection of 1945, enforce the same understanding. In 'The Jungle', Lewis's longest and most ambitious poem, he evokes a 'stagnant pool', the 'indolence' of the sun, and the 'black swollen leaf' of a clearing in the jungle — all becoming part of the 'sinister content' of his sleep. He has come to the pool for refreshment, but wonders if that must mean an utter dissolution and abandonment.

> As though all strength of mind and limb must pass
> And all fidelities and doubts dissolve,
> The weighted world a bubble in each head . . .

He described the 'wandering and fortuitous' paths which people take to arrive at the pool, cataloguing the 'humming cultures' of the West:

> But we who dream beside this jungle pool
> Prefer the instinctive rightness of the poised
> Pied kingfisher deep darting for a fish
> To all the banal rectitude of states,
> The dew-bright diamonds on a viper's back

To the slow poison of a meaning lost
And the vituperations of the just.

The third section of 'The Jungle' expands a powerful image of 'the black spot in the focus', by which Lewis meant the blind spot in the eye, into a metaphor bringing general insight into the human condition:

. . . though the state has enemies we know
The greater enmity within ourselves.

As he had done at the end of 'Karanje Village', Lewis begs forgiveness for this 'strange inconstancy of soul'. The final section of the poem emphasizes his feeling of remoteness from the 'distant world':

The act sustains; there is no consequence.
Only aloneness swinging slowly
Down the cold orbit of an older world
Than any they predicted in the schools. . .

Lewis began by experiencing abandonment as a release of untapped creative energies. But he also sensed that it contained threats and other kinds of problems. Writing to his wife in April 1943, he remarked that

. . . although I'm more and more engrossed with the single poetic theme of Life and Death, for there doesn't seem to be any question more directly relevant than this one of what survives of all the beloved, I find myself quite unable to express at once the passion of Love, the coldness of Death (Death is cold) and the fire that beats against resignation, acceptance. Acceptance seems so spiritless, protest so vain. In between the two I live.

Later in the month he experienced a particularly shattering dream in which he was 'enticed, seduced and destroyed' by the 'long octopus arms' and 'hungry hard mouth' of a shapeless poem that will never be written. The dream so rattled him that he wrote, 'I couldn't *live* with the thoughts that encircled this particular poem, and I was afraid of being alone with them after I'd put the lamp out.' The following spring and summer saw Lewis's letters enlivened by a reborn hunger for the integrity of experience for its own sake. He had had a glimpse of annihilation by the very forces of the *daemon* which he had protected and encouraged. He recoiled with an intense desire to survive, to live. 'I turn insatiably to more and more life', he wrote on 26 May. He identified 'life' not so much with the richness of his own experience, though that remained important, but with 'the simple human material', the Welsh soldiers in his outfit, who 'seem to have some secret knowledge that I want'. He became increasingly obsessed by the idea that it was only in battle that the 'secret knowledge' would finally be revealed to him. 'The Assault Convoy', a poem of this time, describes his anxieties at the delay of a battle. Even more significantly, Lewis intimates what is hinted at in letters home: that he was finding it increasingly difficult to write. Whether it was the premonition of a final, suffocating poem, never to be written, or an epiphany only to be experienced in the battle that was continually postponed (Lewis is said to have made repeated requests to be transferred to a frontline unit in Burma), it was poetry itself which lost out:

> The nihilist persistence of the sun,
> The engines throbbing heatedly all night,
> The white refineries of salt and dust
> Forbid the mind to think, the pen to write . . .

Lewis went into action in Burma in 1944 and shot himself (accidentally, a court of inquiry found) after his first inconclusive engagement with the Japanese. In one of his last letters to his wife, he wrote that 'I've put a huge burden on you always, through my poems which have spoken more openly of the danger and the jeopardies than either of us could or would with the living voice. I don't want them to mean forebodings to you or to me. They're universal statements . . .'

Lewis's work shows the *general* crisis of creativity governing, like some dark star, a finely talented poet. The war intensified Lewis's loathing of an oppressive social order which, through racism, class, military hierarchy, or caste, created the alienation of self from self:

> My soul cries out with love
> Of all that walk and swim and fly . . .   ('Odi et Amo')

His experience on board ship, and then in India, gave him the hope that this *angst* might be swept aside by a deliberate act of abandonment. He hoped to free himself from 'the banal rectitude of states', from 'the drag and dullness of my Self ', by quiet and contemplation. He was powerfully caught by the sheer inhospitable otherness of India, but was shattered by the consequences that followed from an act of abandonment. The sun's persistence was 'nihilist', not necessarily more conducive to creativity than the wretched busyness of life aboard a troopship, or on a military base. As though he were a figure out of Conrad, Lewis tried to make a statement about the ultimate configuration of the real world. But an act of abandonment, an 'abdication from responsibility' in Fuller's hurtful phrase, left Lewis only able to say something about the *meaning* that an individual gives to the real:

> The real always fades into the meaning . . .
>   ('The Assault Convoy')

And that was the precise nature of the crisis which runs through the literature of the war. Reality itself was too vast, impersonal, oblivious. All that was left was the rubble of meanings, a series of personal landscapes. In that sense there could be no universal statements, as Lewis hoped, or any 'war poets' either; Alun Lewis's work shows why.

Poems, Roy Fuller's first book was published in 1939. Years later, speaking at Oxford on 'Poetic Memories of the Thirties', he recalled his ambition as a young poet:

> It's hard indeed to recover one's attitude to the spate of poetry in which one was so completely immersed. But certainly at the start of the period one disapproved of the public school and university chumminess that sometimes accompanied the left-wing poetry. And at the end of the period one disapproved even more of the personal romanticism and reckless obscurity represented by one side of Dylan Thomas's verse. One was searching, hopelessly it seems now, for a poetry with impeccable political orientation, yet as rich and free as the great English poetry of the past.[47]

In the late 1920s Fuller bought, and read, Ezra Pound's *Selected Poems,* and T. S. Eliot's *Poems 1909-1925.* A chance meeting with John Davenport introduced him to early Empson in *Cambridge Poetry 1929,* to Auden's *Poems* of 1930, and to Stephen Spender, who had five poems in *Oxford Poetry 1930.* It was a good moment to begin an education in poetry.[48] From Auden, as from a schoolboy hero, Fuller wrote, 'one took a tone of voice, catchphrases, beliefs – the very cut of one's poetic personality'.[49] Fuller's early poems are exercises in the Audenesque, with the tone, scenery, symbolism and use of scientific and technological metaphors bearing witness to the dominant style of the age. He was a fellow-travelling solicitor, sharing the political frustrations of the left, that combination of rage and paralysis before the slump and the rise of fascism. (Fuller was twenty-one when Hitler came to power.) Faith in Uncle Joe, the certain knowledge that war with Hitler must come, the equally strong conviction that the Tories would sell out to fascism, and a desperate faith in the revolutionary potential of the proletariat (sullenly brewing beneath the deceptively calm surface of English society), dominated the apocalyptic cast of mind of Fuller's generation. He was an intellectual, sharing their isolation from the mainstream of the labour movement; as a literary intellectual, a poet, he was a member of a sect within a sect. The most brilliant evocation of the ethos of self-educated petty-bourgeois left intellectuals in the 1930s, after Orwell's *Keep the Aspidistra Flying* (1936), is Julian Symons's memoir, *Notes from Another Country* (1972). Symons, working for the Dickensian Mr Budette's Victoria Lighting and Dynamos, and editing *Twentieth Century Verse,* was close to Fuller and published his early poems and reviews.

That first book in 1939 could hardly be called an ambitious or even an independent-minded volume of poems. Alternatives to the Audenesque were available in the neo-Georgianism of J. C. Squire's *The London Mercury,* in the surrealism sponsored by Herbert Read and David Gascoyne, and in the American moderns: Wallace Stevens, Hart Crane and Marianne Moore, all generously represented in Michael Roberts's *Faber Book of Modern Verse* (1936), and W. C. Williams, who was not, but whose *Collected Poems* had been noticed, obtusely, by Geoffrey Grigson in *New Verse* (April 1934). In any event, Fuller's grasp of the Audenesque was confident enough to suggest that *Poems* was no mean achievement for a first book.

The central poem is 'End of a City', above which Marx, Auden and surrealism hover benignly. The city, inevitably, was a symbol of the condition of England. An initial perspective is granted by a flight of birds. (How often one finds, even in self-proclaimed left writers, the lingering romanticism of the artist as freewheeling bird, above class interests; or else, picked up from Baudelaire, a pathetic symbol of those finer spirits crushed by an uncaring world: hence 'The voice of the weeping and isolated bird' in Fuller's 'Summer 1940'.) We see the monuments, white walls, buildings, the articulations of the city — aqueducts, drains, fountains — but there are no inhabitants. The whole scene is stagnant. Only birds move freely about. There is a 'soft wear of stone by water', melted from 'static glaciers': an image of the surface calm of England during the depression. Though we see no signs of movement in these 'monuments of easy living', the interior contradictions are intensifying:

> But the crack is widening
> Between the sun and moon, the rest and flow,
> The vomitorium and immense sewers.

As the city comes to life 'the naked slaves awake,/Who face another epoch of draining work'. A buddha-like figure, JA, sits within a mouldering, deserted temple.

> This was he who ordered
> For his tremendous dropsy the sanitation,
> But whose emissaries sent timely hence
> Brought no green leaf to soothe his helplessness.

The poem ends in apocalypse: roused by a trumpet, the 'oldest inhabitants' emerge:

> . . . they come
> Like grass between the stones, but grass like hair,
> And growing goatishly along the sewers,
> Over the stage, the temple and on JA.

Despite the poem's conclusion, the dominant feeling is of paralysis; the whole is marked by a chill timelessness. Fuller's vision of England's situation seems undialectical, even ahistorical; and he evades the fundamental problem of consciousness and will. The proletariat are summoned and promptly fulfil their historic role as prime agents of the dialectic almost as though they were part of a natural process. His use of organic metaphors, and of the idea of evolution elsewhere in the early poems, reinforces a fundamentally pessimistic attitude towards the working class — though Fuller's pessimism was lightly masked by long-term confidence in the inevitability of revolution. Like Auden's 'A Communist to Others', the poem's reticence stands for considerably more than Fuller's personal reservations: there are no people in 'End of a City', no messy and contingent life within which the political drama of the age was being played out; nor was there an intellectual class, or any poets, and therefore no problem of the intellectual's relationship to society. The poem avoids the inevitable contradictions between class and ideology on the part of a left-wing lawyer, an intellectual committed to the worker's movement. The lack of dialectical movement in the poem may be attributed to the author's ambiguity over his own role in a situation of revolutionary *praxis,* or even over his place in the dying moments of the corrupt, sterile *ancien régime.* 'End of a City' is burdened down by a dilemma which Fuller sensed, but could not resolve.

His next collection, *The Middle of a War* (1942), contained a small proportion of poems actually written on active service. He had joined the Royal Navy the year before. As in the war poetry of Randall Jarrell, the feeling of an individual swept along by the pressure of events, and of the sheer helplessness of ordinary men (and intellectuals) in such circumstances, govern the book. Such feelings form the social motifs of Fuller's generation.

> Suddenly our relation
> Is terrifyingly simple
> Against our wretched times,
> Like a hand which mimes
> Love in this anguished station
> Against a whole world's pull.   ('The End of a Leave')

As the war went on Fuller's language grew tauter, capable of greater focus; he writes in one passage of the way landscape, even perception itself, suffers distortion by the war:

> Cigar-coloured bracken, the gloom between the trees,
> The straight wet by-pass through the shaven clover,
> Smell of the wet as if already these
>   Were salient or cover.   ('Autumn 1939')

Henry Reed captured this effect with even greater economy:

> . . . there is a row of houses to the left of arc
> And that under some poplars a pair of what appear to be humans
> Appear to be loving.[50]

Fuller's imagination was most closely touched by the enormity of events, 'the grandeur of historical conceptions':

> One confronts the varieties of death and of people
> With a certain sense of their inadequacy;
> And the grandeur of historical conceptions,
> The wheeling empires, appearance of lusty classes,
> The alimentary organizations, the clever
> Extrications from doom, seize the imagination
> As though these forms, as gods, existed cruel,
> Aloof, but eventually for our salvation.　　　('Autumn 1941')

People, quotidian reality, paled before the grand sweep of history for an imagination hungry for the apocalypse:

> . . . on the quay, in our imagination,
> The grass of starvation sprouts between the stones,
> And ruins are implicit in every structure.
> Gently we probe the kind and comic faces
> For strength of heroes and for martyr's bones.
> 　　　　　　　　　　　　　　　　　　('Defending the Harbour')

Thrown into contact with the miscellaneous mass of men in the Royal Navy, Fuller struggled to find a way to incorporate them, and their experience, in his art. In a note in Ian Hamilton's *The Poetry of War* (Alan Ross, 1965) Fuller refers to the salutary effect of 'the proletarianization resulting from service on the "lower deck" '. There is little of the declassed intellectual in Fuller; it seems to have been a more theoretical than real experience for him:

> . . . in the mess, on beds, on benches, fall
> The blue serge limbs in shapes fantastical.
> 　　　　　　　　　　　　　　　　　　('Royal Naval Air Station')

There are abstracted voices, 'obscene realities', in another poem, 'Saturday Night in a Sailor's Home', but the generality of the phrase gives the game away. It simply will not do to say that obscene realities look like obscene realities – at least not in poetry. The aura of petty-bourgeois reservation, pickled forever in Fuller's endless reiteration of 'One thinks' or does, or is, remains undented. In later years he unforgivably refers to 'the herd', 'the poor anonymous swarm', the 'stupidity of slaves'. One gets the same thing in Orwell: a flash of resentment, a moment's lapsed vigilance, before the almighty pressure of the English class system.

But there can hardly be a socialist art without people, without a rock-solid humanism. Inevitably, the type of such an art is Whitman — warm, generous, open, and yet committed to the lot of the ordinary man. Fuller's next book, *A Lost Season* (1944), attempts to make a remarkably uncharacteristic affirmation:

> My living now must bear the laceration
> Of the herd, and always will. What's done
>
> To me is done to many. I can see
> No ghosts, but only the fearful actual
> Lives of my comrades.   ('What is Terrible')

The Whitmanian affirmation appears again in 'A Wry Smile':

> No longer divided — the unhappy echo
> Of a great fault in civilization; inadequate,
> Perhaps, and sad, but strictly conscious no one
> Anywhere can move, nothing occur,
> Outside my perfect knowledge or my fate.

The sentiment is pure Whitman, but it is undermined by the severity of his tone. Fuller's inflection upon 'strictly' opens other levels of meaning, for the aura of the Petty Officer is unmistakable. By temperament Fuller was unsympathetic toward Whitman's prodigality, and how utterly unlike Whitman is his dispassionate comment in 'Sadness, Theory, Glass':

> I feel I should deliver a summing-up
> Of all the passion, boredom, history,
> Of all the suddenly important lives.

In the flesh people were 'incoherent presences' ('Night'), whose 'pathetic personal trash' ('Autumn 1942') cluttered up one's life. He wanted to enact a particular kind of reality and humanity in his verse, but it wasn't something which could be easily picked up, like a fashionable verse style or political line. Fuller's evolving political commitment presupposed a relationship to 'the people' that was constantly being undermined by his temperament, by his class position, by the complex net of personal and ideological factors which gave rise to the tension between Fuller's politics and his class position. We need to isolate, to concentrate upon, a particular 'moment' in his creative life, bringing contradictions and tensions to the surface, in order to understand the relationship a writer establishes between himself and his age. For we need to see that Fuller's dilemma was approaching the intolerable by the time he published *A Lost Season,* and thus to appreciate how ready he was for a general withdrawal from the stage of political commitment. There was a deliberate echo of Auden in the poem 'Winter Camp' when he stated that 'man must be political or die'; but there is a stale confession of failure in the dedicatory epistle to *Epitaphs and Occasions* (1949):

> We would have moved, were held, alas
> In the paralysis of class.

Fuller's subsequent career presents a dismal, familiar spectacle of steadily advancing technical mastery and an impoverishment of energy and spirit. He was inclined now to accept his fate, to acknowledge, as he explained in 'Obituary of R. Fuller', that

> . . . his life had all been spent
> In the small-bourgeois element,
> Sheltered from poverty and hurt,
> From passion, tragedy and dirt.

He polished his metric. Several poems in *Counterparts* (1954) show Fuller dabbling with a Cabala of energies; even when he praises the irrational, he never quite shakes off the tone of the 'waking rational life':

> I would like to renounce the waking rational life,
> The neat completed work, as being quite
> Absurd and cowardly; and leave to posterity
> The words on book-marks, enigmatic notes,
> Thoughts before sleep, the vague unwritten verse
> On people, on the city to which I travel.
>
> ('Rhetoric of a Journey')

In Fuller's Oxford lectures he projects the image of a craftsman, a professional, committed to a poetry enriched by 'the wealth of historical reference, the insights of science, the sophisticated vocabulary and syntax' which, like some glorious ancestral property had been 'accumulated' over the centuries. But in the decade after the war Fuller wrote inconsequential, polished poems about finding a spider in a bathtub, a robin singing in a garden, walking alone through snow, a visit to a derelict church, and poems on reading Soviet novels, and on Gide's death. This was an 'abdication from responsibility' of the kind of which Fuller himself had accused Alun Lewis. By the mid-1950s Fuller's position as a polished occasional poet was fairly secure. Yet he was capable of a kind of crassness which, even then, was unusually forthright:

> I will cease to blame the stupidity of the slaves
> Upon their masters and nurture, and will say,
> Plainly, that they are enemies to culture,
>   Advancement and cleanliness.   ('Translation')

There would be no great uncertainty about *whose* advancement is being meant.

At some point in the early 1950s Fuller began to write fiction. He had tried writing for children after the war, and emerged, as did Julian Symons, as a prolific and interesting novelist, 'trying to delineate in fiction the moral reality of the world I know'.[51] The consequences for his verse did not appear until *Brutus's Orchard* (1957), which contains some of Fuller's finest work. Despite the general impression that his novels are able in the way the novels of C. P. Snow are 'able', writing fiction is clearly something Fuller does with skilful conscientiousness. The novels sustain problems of greater social import than the poems, and may, at some deep level, stand for a reaction against the formalism of his verse.[52] He will never write a bad poem, nor will he attempt risky failures or technical innovations. His refined style is only approached by Philip Larkin among poets writing today. But Fuller may never understand why his achievement may be less than an unadulterated good for English poetry, or why a brilliant formalism in which 'the last trace of conviction/Has long since been extinguished', as he wrote in 'On the Mountain', and which played no small role in shaping the emergent tone of 1950s poetry, can be scarcely less than disastrous for an entire generation of poets and readers who have not been taught to ask for more.

Chapter 2

The 1950s

The 'collapse' of the poetry market after the war, and the reaction against modernism; literary intellectuals in the new prosperity; Larkin, the saddest heart in the supermarket; Donald Davie on the road to Palo Alto; a cento from the new age; Richard Wilbur and some versions of formalism (Donald Hall, Anthony Thwaite); the Movement meets its anti-type in Charles Tomlinson; Charles Tomlinson meets his anti-type in Theodore Roethke: two poets who tell us what it meant to dissent from the reigning orthodoxies; William Carlos Williams takes the measure of American life in *Paterson*; but Charles Olson wasn't impressed; Allen Ginsberg opens a Pandora's Box with an elegy for the bohemia of the 1940s and a prayer for the restless spirit of his mother; three ex-formalists take us into the 1960s: W. D. Snodgrass, Robert Lowell, Sylvia Plath.

Selected Chronology

1950

Kenneth Allott, ed., *Contemporary Verse*
W. H. Auden, *Collected Shorter Poems 1930-44*
Basil Bunting, *Poems: 1950*
John Ciardi, ed., *Mid-Century American Poets*
Robert Lowell, *Poems 1938-1949*
F. O. Matthiessen, ed., *Oxford Book of American Verse*
Arthur Rimbaud, *A Season in Hell*, trans. Norman Cameron
Delmore Schwartz, *Vaudeville for a Princess*
Wallace Stevens, *The Auroras of Autumn*
Richard Wilbur, *Ceremony*
W. B. Yeats, *Collected Poems* 2nd ed.

F. W. Bateson, *English Poetry: A Critical Introduction*
John Berryman, *Stephen Crane*
Richard Crossman, ed., *The God That Failed*
Richard Hoggart, *Auden: An Introductory Essay*
F. R. Leavis, *New Bearings in English Poetry* reissue
Charles Olson, 'Projective Verse' in *Poetry New York*
Ezra Pound, *Letters*, ed. D. D. Paige

1951

W. H. Auden, *Nones*
Keith Douglas, *Collected Poems*, eds. John Waller and G. S. Fraser
Robert Frost, *Complete Poems*
Rolfe Humphries, trans., *The Aeneid of Virgil*
Randall Jarrell, *The Seven-League Crutches*
Philip Larkin, *XX Poems*
Richmond Lattimore, trans., *The Iliad of Homer*
Robert Lowell, *The Mills of the Kavanaughs*
Marianne Moore, *Collected Poems*
Adrienne Rich, *A Change of World*

Michael Roberts, ed., *The Faber Book of Modern Verse,* new ed., with a
    Supplement by Anne Ridler
Theodore Roethke, *Praise to the End!*
Charles Tomlinson, *Relations and Contraries*
John Wain, *Mixed Feelings*
W. C. Williams, *Collected Earlier Poems*
— *Paterson, Book Four*

William Empson, *The Structure of Complex Words*
Hugh Kenner, *The Poetry of Ezra Pound*
Robert Motherwell, ed., *Dada Painters and Poets: An Anthology*
Wallace Stevens, *The Necessary Angel*

1952

Robert Creeley, *Le Fou*
Thom Gunn, ed., *Poetry from Cambridge, 1951-1952*
Geoffrey Hill, *Poems* (The Fantasy Poets, No. 11)
David Jones, *The Anathemata*
Louis MacNeice, *Ten Burnt Offerings*
W. S. Merwin, *A Mask for Janus*
Edwin Muir, *Collected Poems,* ed. J. C. Hall
Frank O'Hara, *A City Winter*
Adrienne Rich, *Poems* (The Fantasy Poets, No. 12)
Dylan Thomas, *Collected Poems 1934-52*

R. P. Blackmur, *Language as Gesture*
Donald Davie, *Purity of Diction in English Verse*

1953

G. S. Fraser and Iain Fletcher, eds., *Springtime*
Thom Gunn, *Poems* (Fantasy Poets, No. 16)
Kenneth Koch, *Poems*
Charles Olson, *In Cold Hell, In Thicket*
—*The Maximus Poems 1-10*
—*Mayan Letters,* ed. Robert Creeley
Ezra Pound, *Translations,* ed. Hugh Kenner
Theodore Roethke, *The Waking: Poems 1933-1953*
Anthony Thwaite, *Poems* (The Fantasy Poets, No. 17)

G. S. Fraser, *The Modern Writer and His World*
Randall Jarrell, *Poetry and the Age*

1954

e. e. cummings, *Poems 1923-1954*

Donald Davie, *Poems* (The Fantasy Poets, No. 19)
Roy Fuller, *Counterparts*
Thom Gunn, *Fighting Terms*
Anthony Hecht, *A Summoning of Stones*
Weldon Kees, *Poems 1947-1954*
Philip Larkin, *Poems* (The Fantasy Poets, No. 21)
C. Day Lewis, *Collected Poems*
Louis MacNeice, *Autumn Sequel*
W. S. Merwin, *The Dancing Bears*
Marianne Moore, trans., *The Fables of La Fontaine*
Wallace Stevens, *Collected Poems*
W. C. Williams, *The Desert Music*
The Letters of W. B. Yeats, ed. Allan Wade

Malcolm Cowley, *The Literary Situation*
Elder Olson, *The Poetry of Dylan Thomas*
Ezra Pound, *Literary Essays,* ed. T. S. Eliot
W. C. Williams, 'On Measure — Statement for Cid Corman', in *Origin*

1955

A. R. Ammons, *Ommateum*
W. H. Auden, *The Shield of Achilles*
Elizabeth Bishop, *Poems*
Gregory Corso, *The Vestal Lady on Brattle*
Donald Davie, *Brides of Reason*
William Empson, *Collected Poems*
D. J. Enright, ed., *Poets of the 1950's*
Lawrence Ferlinghetti, *Pictures of the Gone World*
Donald Hall, *Exiles and Marriages*
Philip Larkin, *The Less Deceived*
Federico Garcia Lorca, *Poet in New York,* trans. Ben Belitt
Ezra Pound, *Section: Rock-Drill*
Adrienne Rich, *The Diamond Cutters*
Louis Simpson, *Good News of Death*
Stephen Spender, *Collected Poems 1928-1953*
Charles Tomlinson, *The Necklace*
Richard Wilbur, trans., *The Misanthrope*
W. C. Williams, *Journey to Love*

R. P. Blackmur, *The Lion and the Honeycomb*
Donald Davie, *Articulate Energy*
John Wain, ed., *Interpretations*

1956

W. H. Auden, ed., *The Faber Book of Modern American Poetry*

John Berryman, *Homage to Mistress Bradstreet*
Robert Conquest, ed., *New Lines*
George P. Elliott, ed., *Fifteen Modern American Poets*
G. S. Fraser, ed., *Poetry Now*
Allen Ginsberg, *Howl*
W. S. Merwin, *Green with Beasts*
Marianne Moore, *Like a Bulwark*
Charles Olson, *The Maximus Poems 11-22*
Richard Wilbur, *Things of This World*
Louis Zukofsky, *Some Time*

Robert Duncan, 'Notes on Poetics, Regarding Olson's *Maximus*', in *Black Mountain Review*

1957

Norman Cameron, *Collected Poems*
Donald Davie, *A Winter Talent*
Roy Fuller, *Brutus's Orchard*
Thom Gunn, *The Sense of Movement*
Donald Hall, Robert Pack and Louis Simpson, eds., *The New Poets of England and America*
Ted Hughes, *The Hawk in the Rain*
Denise Levertov, *Here and Now*
Louis MacNeice, *Visitations*
Frank O'Hara, *Meditations in an Emergency*
Theodore Roethke, *Words for the Wind*
Howard Sergeant and Dannie Abse, eds., *Mavericks*
Stevie Smith, *Not Waving But Drowning*
Jack Spicer, *After Lorca*
Anthony Thwaite, *Home Truths*
Richard Wilbur, *Poems 1943-56*
James Wright, *The Green Wall*

Kingsley Amis, *Socialism and the Intellectuals*
John Bayley, *The Romantic Survival*
R. P. Blackmur, *Form and Value in Modern Poetry*
Cleanth Brooks and W. K. Wimsatt, *Literary Criticism: A Short History*
T. S. Eliot, *On Poetry and Poets*
Northrop Frye, *Anatomy of Criticism*
Frank Kermode, *Romantic Image*
Wallace Stevens, *Opus Posthumous*

1958

Gregory Corso, *Bomb*
— *Gasoline*

Lawrence Ferlinghetti, *Tentative Description of a Dinner Given to Promote the Impeachment of President Eisenhower*
Thom Gunn, *Fighting Terms*, rev. American ed.
Stanley Kunitz, *Selected Poems 1928-1958*
Denise Levertov, *Overland to the Islands*
Jacques Prévert, *Selections from Paroles*, trans. Lawrence Ferlinghetti
Charles Tomlinson, *Seeing is Believing*
W. C. Williams, *Paterson, Book Five*

A. Alvarez, *The Shaping Spirit*
Robert Penn Warren, *Selected Essays*

1959

Donald Davie, *The Forests of Lithuania*
Geoffrey Hill, *For the Unfallen*
Kenneth Koch, *Ko; or, A Season on Earth*
Robert Lowell, *Life Studies*
Marianne Moore, *O To Be a Dragon*
Ezra Pound, *Thrones*
Jerome Rothenburg, trans., *New Young German Poets*
Delmore Schwartz, *Summer Knowledge: New and Selected Poems 1938-1958*
Louis Simpson, *A Dream of Governors*
W. D. Snodgrass, *Heart's Needle*
Gary Snyder, *Riprap*
James Wright, *Saint Judas*
Louis Zukofsky, *A 1-12*

David Jones, *Epoch and Artist*
Charles Olson, 'Letter to Elaine Feinstein'
Yvor Winters, *On Modern Poets*

The 1950s

Eliot's reputation was at its glorious zenith in the late 1940s. He alone remained of the 'men of 1914', the generation of the great modernists: Lawrence, Joyce and Yeats were dead; Pound, an accused traitor, was in an insane asylum. Eliot was an 'international hero', as Delmore Schwartz put it: 'the width and the height and the depth of modern life are exhibited [in his poetry] . . .; the agony and the horror of modern life are represented as inevitable to any human being who does not wish to deceive himself with systematic lies'.[1] It was the old critical intimidation again, mastered early on by Eliot himself, by which only the deceived or dishonest could fail to recognize that 'agony' and 'horror' which accompanied the tragic view of modern life as seen through the eyes of the nervously conservative *zeitgeist* of the 1940s. Eliot's *Notes Toward the Definition of Culture* (1948) experienced a remarkable success. The first English edition ran to 6,000 copies; Harcourt Brace's print order in New York was for 7,500. The plays (19,950 copies of *The Cocktail Party* were printed in 1950), essays, poems, and the *Four Quartets,* were equally successful. Eliot received the Order of Merit in the New Year's Honours List in 1948, and the Nobel Prize for Literature later in the year.

Little of this rubbed of on, or, it seems, greatly interested the younger poets in England. The editor of *Poetry Quarterly* wrote that, *'All* publishers agree that the sales of bound volumes of verse are now so low that it is more than probable that in the coming years the new and unpublished poet is going to find it extremely difficult to get a hearing.'[2] Even poets of some standing were experiencing long delays in publication, or having manuscripts rejected outright. After sitting on a manuscript by Richard Eberhart for a year, Ian Parsons of Chatto and Windus replied with some discouragement in July 1949 that 'the sales of books of verse are so small as to be almost non-existent. Even the most established poets have taken a knock and, for any but the favoured few, a sale of two or three hundred copies is the very best that can be hoped for.'[3] The collapse of the 'market' after the war caught everyone by surprise. The redesigned twenty-seventh number of *Penguin New Writing,* published in 1946, had an initial print order of 100,000. A year later that figure had declined to 80,000. By 1949 it was down to 40,000. Allen Lane wound up the series in 1950 after forty numbers. Lehmann's great empire was gone. 'As we toiled away at the huge piles of MSS at our desks in Egerton Crescent', he wrote, '. . . it seemed very difficult to believe that the change was taking place, that the temperature which had altered so much during the war years was dropping fast.'[4]

What was taking place in England had less to do with literature than with the pattern of life which emerged, especially in the 1950s, with postwar prosperity. The forms which the war had imposed upon cultural life had for six years seemed virtually permanent. The very idea of 'life' was redolent of peace, the future; during the war (as Alun Lewis discovered) one learnt to live day by day. Writing of Oxford during the early years of the war, Philip Larkin pointed out that 'perhaps the most difficult thing to convey was the almost complete suspension of concern for the future'.[5] Demobilization signalled the release of ordinary concerns for careers, jobs and pleasures. The mood now was for security, efficiency, and for a capitalism — judiciously balanced by nationalization and state intervention in the economy — which, with the Marshall Plan, would see to the aspirations of the people. There could hardly be an imaginative response, an image of British socialism, to the various acts of nationalization, beginning with the Bank of England, which had precious little meaning for ordinary people. In an essay on Paul Nizan, Jean-Paul Sartre writes 'that shoes and boots were set out in all French chimneys and Santa Claus filled them with American canned goods'. The replacement of the 'Master' by a white-collar élite of managers confirmed James Burnham's *The Managerial Revolution* (1941); and made little difference to the man on the shop floor. The greatest material benefits came through the National Health Service. 'Thanks to the nurses and Nye Bevan/The N.H.S. is quite like heaven.'[6] That wasn't the way to greet the new age, either; but again, expectations were drowned in the oncoming tide of disillusionment, and the slowness of the economic recovery after the war. Those who hoped to usher in a new age of English culture with socialism saw the aspirations of the common people expressed in terms of increased consumption. The popular art form of postwar prosperity was the cinema; people seemed to read less, certainly fewer 'serious' books.

The predominant note in poetry is one of sadness and nostalgia, a positively hangdog tone of regret at a dimly perceived alteration in the social base of art itself. The war years conclusively ended that last flowering of private patronage which emerged in close alliance with the modernist generation: Harriet Shaw Weaver and the *Egoist,* Robert McAlmon and *Contact,* Harold Loeb and *Broom,* Harry Crosby's Black Sun Press, Harold Monro's Poetry Bookshop, Sylvia Beach's Shakespeare

& Co., John Rodker's Ovid Press, Nancy Cunard's Hours Press. From now on it was left to the great foundations and universities to pick up the tab for high culture. (One notable exception was Marguerite Caetani, an American heiress, who edited *Botteghe Oscure* from her ancestral palazzo in Rome.) The new audience for art seemed more like a consumer than a patron or colleague. In this situation, literature was merely one among numerous expressions of cultural activity in competition for our time, attention and money. Literature had been bureaucratized, lost its 'aura'.[7] Society seemed to be a massive supermarket, a highly complex system which pretended to be solely designed to fulfil the needs of the consumers. And the supermarket becomes a symbol of our prosperity: nowhere are our values more vividly on display. But the postwar consciousness of consumerism specialized in a cautious ambivalence, typified by Randall Jarrell's witty essay 'A Sad Heart at the Super-market', in which he offered a plangent diagnosis of the future of culture in a consumer society. The same note is echoed by Allen Ginsberg, 'shopping for images', in 'A Supermarket in California', and by Lawrence Ferlinghetti in 'The pennycandystore beyond the El'. Ed Dorn's 'On the Debt My Mother Owed to Sears Roebuck', and Jarrell's 'Sears Roebuck' work an obvious vein of nostalgia. Howard Nemerov's 'Grace to be Said at the Supermarket', and Michael Hamburger's 'Notes on a Supermarket', are doleful satires; Theodore Roethke catches the right note: 'Frigidaires snoring the sleep of plenty' in 'Last Words'. Everywhere the need to *choose* works through society with a diffuse but insistent voice:

> . . . every nook and cranny of flesh
> Is spoken to by packages and wiles.
> 'Buy me, buy me', they whisper and cajole . . .
> (Karl Shapiro, 'Drug Store')

> I name an age of choice and discontent
> Whose emblem is 'the difficult to choose'
> (Donald Hall, 'The World, The Times')

> born March 26 1930 I am led 100 mph o'er the
> vast market of choice
> what to choose? what to choose?
> (Gregory Corso, 'In the Fleeting Hand of Time')

> . . . goods, deeds, credits, debts.
> Have it your own way, life:
> I'm just here to die, but I
> would rather live it out as a fool
> and have a short life in contempt
> and idle graces, but, instead,

the office telephone goes off
and voices out of its dark night
command me, 'Choose, Choose...'

(Alan Dugan, 'Not to Choose')

Hence John Lehmann's comment about *Penguin New Writing*: 'What we had underestimated was the ease with which the great outer circle of those who had become readers, and often eager readers, when there were few competitors for the occupation of leisure hours, would slip away.' Prosperity brought a kind of social change which literary mandarins deplored; more means worse. Lehmann attacked a familiar bogey in 'low level commercial exploitation' which was queering the pitch for his literary magazine. People closest to the event characteristically understood less than they saw, but the changes were glaringly *there*. The small 'boom' upon which *Penguin New Writing* had bobbed about did not survive the decade. Left to their own devices, the 'great outer circle' sank back in the movies, into the cultural gloom.

One of the most persistent explanations for the postwar cultural 'decline' laid the blame for everything on modernism. Philip Larkin has suggested that the creative tension between artist and audience has slackened, and finally perished, since the turn of the century. At the root of the problem, he explained, was the modernist predilection for 'irresponsible exploitations of technique in contradiction of human life as we know it'.[8] In 1952, Davie wrote that 'one cannot avoid the fact that the poet's churches are empty, and the strong suspicion that dislocation of syntax has much to do with it'.[9] Three distinguished products of Cambridge English — Thom Gunn, Donald Davie, and Charles Tomlinson confidently stated that the epitome of restless modernism, Ezra Pound, could now be completely written off.[10] Modernist and symbolist versions of literary history were acidly rewritten by Davie in *Articulate Energy* (1955), 'anxious to show the inadequacy of the symbolist and post-symbolist tradition'; by Frank Kermode, who held up Milton as an example to young poets in *Romantic Image* (1957); and by Graham Hough, who endorsed 'the ever present lyricism' and the 'very varied, meditative yet musical rhythm' of Thomas Hardy in *Image and Experience* (1960). There was renewed academic enthusiasm in England for all things Victorian. The romantic poets (and critics, thanks to John Wain), and the Victorians in general were being read with greater sympathy and attention than at any time in the preceding half century.[11] What was at first a tentative revision of modernist hagiography quickly turned into a mini-purge. According to Davie (always quick with the tactical exaggeration), 'the development from imagism in poetry to fascism in politics is clear and unbroken'.[12] Philip Hobsbaum, a product of Downing College, argued that 'The Waste Land' 'has helped to corrupt the poetic techniques of nearly half a century'.[13] Reviewing *Oxford Poetry 1948,* John Wain made a shrewd assessment of the mood of young Oxford poets at the apogee of Eliot's fame:

> No less than three [poems] are on classical Greek themes, treated in a romantic vein; one is on Salammbo; one on T. E. Lawrence; others about the more emotional aspects of Sacred History; and while only one poet has taken the countryside as his ostensible theme, Nature — as understood by poets from Wordsworth to Rimbaud — supplies about two-thirds of the imagery of the book. And if the Thirties poets are no longer potent, there are signs of an even more far-reaching emancipation; not one of these thirty-five poets seems anxious to write like Mr Eliot. I had long suspected that the echo of his voice was growing fainter, and this proves it.
> And so the lesson of this book is that English poetry has now thoroughly learnt the lessons of modernism . . .[14]

Despite an undergraduate vogue for *Lions and Shadows,* and a reverence for Orwell (more political than literary, certainly, and not widely felt by Orwell's contemporaries), there was a vacuum created by the eclipse of the 1930s generation which helped to define the mood of the 1950s. William Empson was being strongly urged as the heir to the Eliot 'line' by Wain,[15] but he had ceased to write poems; Auden's departure, and the evident impoverishment of the poetry of MacNeice, Spender and Day Lewis by the late 1940s, made a difference; as did the fall of the entrepreneurs (Grigson retreated from the poetry scene, Lehmann lost his empire, Michael Roberts died in 1948); the generation is littered with deaths, broken careers, silence. It was not yet time for sympathy, though. The poets of the 1930s, wrote Alan Ross, now seem

> . . . mere fakers
> Of unruffled and pedantic songs, who oblivious
> And outgrowing history, grow silent to us —
> Their world and their words subsiding like flat champagne.

Davie was much more ambivalent, writing of 'These poems about "abandoned workings," ' which

> . . . show
> Worlds more remote than Ithaca or Rome.
>
> The Anschluss, Guernica — all the names
> At which those poets thrilled or were afraid
> For me mean schools and schoolmasters and games . . .[16]

The world of the 1930s poets seems so far away, so accessible to 'time's derision'; yet they were brave men, possessing undoubted courage. Maybe, Davie asks, despite the preferred 'neutral tone', it would be better to praise them than to have their qualities wholly obscured. Significantly, that praise is only forthcoming in Davie's poem as a parodistic version of the era.

What seemed like a lesson learned to Wain in 1948 looked more like a legacy squandered to Charles Tomlinson, writing in 1961:

> The effect of those generations who have succeeded to the heritage of Eliot, Pound, and Yeats has been largely to squander the awareness these three gave us of our place in world literature, and to retreat into a self-congratulatory parochialism.[17]

The saddest heart in the postwar supermarket was, and is, Philip Larkin. When editing the recent *Oxford Book of Twentieth-Century Verse,* Larkin took a long look at 'the vast market of choice' in the stacks of the Bodleian Library and then turned the whole enterprise over to his *alter ego,* that epitome of 'self-congratulatory parochialism', Larkinism. Donald Hall cast the *Oxford Book* into the depths with a memorable, unfair tirade broadcast on the B.B.C. in 1974, blaming Larkinism on *le vice anglais,* gentility. But Hall was surely wide of the mark. Larkinism is the 'moment' of a particular generation, when a new relation to society, to literature, was crystallized. It appears in Larkin's *Oxford Book* as though quick-frozen and preserved in a state of suspended animation for twenty years. The sleeper has awoken, taken one look around, and said 'no'.

It is Larkin's 'tragic view of life', not his temperament, which is at issue. He is not particularly religious (unlike Eliot and Auden), but shares their pessimistic view of the world. Failure, death, loneliness, and emptiness haunt his verse. The one positive note, when Larkin identifies what is valuable and permanent in life, seems to be closely connected with ceremonies and rituals. Otherwise, the alternatives are either materialistic and vulgar or idealistic and without warrant. Yet reading Larkin is anything but dispiriting. One often nods with assent: here, surely, is the way things are:

> ... waking at the fumes
> And furnace glares of Sheffield, where I changed
> And ate an awful pie, and walked along
> The platform to its end ...   ('Dockery and Son')

Things impose themselves upon us remorselessly:

> Look at the pictures and the cutlery.
> The music in the piano stool. That vase.   ('Home is so Sad')

> cheap suits, red kitchen-ware, sharp shoes, iced lollies,
> Electric mixers, toasters, washers, driers —   ('Here')

The catalogues are never random or pleasureful. Far from it. *Red kitchen-ware, after all!*

> . . then the perms,
> The nylon gloves and jewellry-substitutes,
> The lemons, mauves, and olive-ochres . . .
>
> ('The Whitsun Weddings')

> Lemon sapphire, moss-green, rose
> Bri-Nylon Baby-Dolls and Shorties
> Flounce in clusters. ('The Large Cool Store')

It is the candy-floss society. The very term 'candy-floss society', rooted in the sustained, casual prosperity of English life in the 1950s and early 1960s, seems dated. Even in *High Windows* in 1974 he showed little sense that things had changed much. The feel of *The Whitsun Weddings* was described by A. Alvarez as that of 'post-war provincial England in all its dreariness, with the boredom of shortages no longer justified, the cheap, plastic surface of things nobody wants and everybody buys'.[18] Larkin seems very little interested in the changes which have taken place between 1954 and 1974, and Alvarez's description looks increasingly like the permanent landscape of Larkin's work. The 1950s, that Tory *ancien régime* when the 'affluent worker' emerged, bloated with prosperity, doesn't feel very much like the real world in which *High Windows* was being bought and read with such enthusiasm. It would be cruelly unfair to link Larkin with the cynical and pervasive cashing in on nostalgia for the 1940s and 1950s which is so common today; but Larkin reads increasingly as though he *is* dated, and that he scarcely cares one way or the other. The point is not that he fails to be 'up-to-date', of course, but that his critical perspective, his eye for satire and irony, comes full-blown from the fretful and agonized materialism of the 1950s, when technological change, and new patterns of consumption, were 'problems', and unemployment, redundancies, inflation and terrorism were not.

> The crowd
> Is young in the M1 cafe;
> Their kids are screaming for more —
> More houses, more parking allowed,
> More caravan sites, more pay. ('Going, Going')

What does Larkin think they *should* want? In the same poem he invokes a shadowy 'England gone', a world of

> . . . shadows, the meadows, the lanes,
> The guildhalls, the carved choirs.

and which in turn reminds us of the earlier passage in *The Whitsun Weddings,* when Larkin writes of 'unfenced existence':

75

> Here leaves unnoticed thicken,
> Hidden weeds flower, neglected waters quicken,
> Luminously-peopled air ascends;
> And past the poppies bluish neutral distance
> Ends the land suddenly beyond a beach
> Of shapes and shingle. Here is unfenced existence:
> Facing the sun, untalkative, out of reach.　　('Here')

The final qualification, that it is out of reach, is at once reassuring (there may actually be places where there can be no more houses, parking or caravan sites), but also devastating in that the consoling and curative resources of nature are 'out of reach' of those whose need is great. There has rarely been an English poet who found nature so profoundly 'untalkative'.[19] Permanent values for Larkin emerge from the lives and values and customs of people; but not from *all* of their values, for at the heart of Larkin's tragic view of man's fate is the belief that the dream of personal fulfilment and hopes for an enhanced existence, are the products of self-deception. Things never quite turn out the way they might. Behind the 'spectacled grins' and the five percent profit in 'Going, Going', there are the polluted estuaries. The 'sparkling armada of promises' in 'Next, Please' never quite manages to reach the dock. The 'warm spring rain of loving care' in 'Faith Healing', his acidulous portrait of a Billy Graham revival meeting in London, lasts for 'some twenty seconds'. Love in particular is a bottomless bran-tub of promise:

> The glare of that much-mentioned brilliance, love,
> 　　Broke out, to show
> Its bright incipience sailing above,
> Still promising to solve, and satisfy,
> And set unchangeably in order.　　('Love Songs in Age')

But in the end, loved or loveless, there is the same bleak message:

> Life is first boredom, then fear.
> Whether or not we use it, it goes.　　('Dockery and Son')

Yeats, improbably, is the strongest influence on Larkin's first collection, *The North Ship* (1945). What seems rather more important is that from the outset there is the sense of regret and loss, of the actuality of love, but also of its inaccessibility. Despite the presence of Yeats, the presiding spirit of *The North Ship* is none other than J. Alfred Prufrock. Poem XX is the most vividly Prufrockian of Larkin's early poems, beginning as it does with a powerful passage:

> I see a girl dragged by the wrists
> Across a dazzling field of snow,
> And there is nothing in me that resists.
> Once it would not be so;

What seems at first threatening, especially when the speaker's passivity is so quickly brought out, is given a different meaning in the next stanza. He sees that 'she laughs and struggles and pretends to fight', and is intensely disturbed.

> I have heard the mermaids singing, each to each.
> I do not think that they will sing to me.
> I have seen them riding seaward on the waves
> Combing the white hair of the waves blown back
> When the wind blows the water white and black.

Some Yeatsian imagery, and the sight of two workmen, release an unhappy feeling of limitation in the speaker, combining hopelessness and exhaustion. 'Each dull day and each despairing act' remind him of the world of physical sensation and sensuality from which he is excluded.

> And I have known the arms already, known them all —
> Arms that are braceleted and white and bare
> (But in the lamplight, downed with light brown hair!)

The workmen, clearing snowdrifts with shovels and spade, come to stand for the speaker's emotional deprivation, but he transforms the symbol, fighting to resist the pointed arguments of reality

> . . . a tedious argument
> Of insidious intent . . .

into a mythological fantasy. There are no 'human voices' to wake us, only the dream of a 'snow-white unicorn' and its golden horn. Poem XX in *The North Ship* concludes with what is an untypical Larkin note. The evasion of the real world is successful.

Larkin has scarcely 'developed'. The voice he found in *The Less Deceived* remains adequate for what he has to say. There have been two influences: Yeats, who was absorbed and then discarded after *The North Ship*, and Hardy, who remained. An earthy streak, all 'sods' and 'fucks', reminding us that Larkin belongs to Lucky Jim's generation, has emerged, but the procession of poems is an orderly one. Having found his voice, he has remained faithful to it — and to its limitations. Larkin is anything but a restless poet, seeking a revolution of the sensibility, new kinds of technical excellence. Between *The North Ship* and *The Less Deceived* a substantial change took place; it represents the most interesting period of his career as a poet, and yet the least well known. It may be that as in the case of Roy Fuller, his desire to write novels played an important role. Both of Larkin's novels appeared immediately after the war: *Jill* was published by the Fortune Press in 1946, followed a year later by *A Girl in Winter*. They are over-written yet moving stories which reveal that Larkin had a great deal to say. Not so much a desire to express himself (the cautious deflections of the Larkin *persona* suggests the opposite), but to organize and make sense of experience which was in itself inchoate. In his longer poems there is often a prosey feel about them, a simplicity and straightforward 'story' which owes a great deal to his desire to be a novelist. But novels require circumstantial evidence and believable plots, whereas Larkin's instinct was to distill a complex moment of experience into an image, a momentary revelation of insight, for which poetry was more suitable. Poems like 'The Whitsun Weddings', 'Show Saturday', 'Dockery and Son' and 'Church Going' have the construction of short stories. In 'Show Saturday' Larkin uses his undoubted skill at construction for his major effects; the rapid panorama of movement, gestures, noises, machines, demonstrations and competitions builds up steadily upon an increasingly insistent rhythm until the end of the fifth stanza when the show ground begins to empty. The profuse life of the day is withdrawn: 'Back now, all of them, to their local lives'. But the idea of the show, its inner social meaning, remains, 'hidden there like strength', ready to emerge next year with renewed life. Despite Larkin's contempt for the 'myth-kitty'[20] behind so much modern writing, 'Show Saturday' portrays the revivification of fertility rituals in an England that remains familiarly available to common sense. In the show Larkin finds an expression of the habitual, even ritual behaviour upon which is based the values of a civilization. We might say that civilization *is* a country show for Larkin.

There will always be a generation gap, let us say, between the poets who begin poems, 'Rising at dawn to pee . . .' (Roy Fuller, 'In Memory of My Cat Domino: 1951-66') or 'Groping back to bed after a piss' (Larkin, 'Sad Steps'), and those who find this intrinsically risible. More seriously, Larkin's work confronts us with a dominant feeling of loathing towards the 'prosperity' of English life, and a bitter awareness of what it has cost — physically, environmentally, spiritually. The literary social democrats have a defence to put forward. The 'innocence' recalled in Larkin's 'MCMXIV' exists only in the nostalgic perspective of the present. Many children in Edwardian England would have known hunger and real deprivation. It is obvious that the common people were certainly much worse off then than now. At this point Larkin might point to 'Deceptions', a poem about a young girl in Victorian London who has been drugged and 'ruined' while unconscious. Yes, he knows that things were much worse then. But there is no debate, no political alternative. Larkin's sense of the meaning and value of ritual, the place of the ceremonial in ordinary life, scarcely answers the arguments made by social democracy. Larkin is of a generation of writers in England (Wain, Amis, Braine, Davie, Osborne) who are indeed sad hearts at the supermarket. But Larkin's memories of 'a serious house on serious earth', his belief in custom ('Show Saturday') and habit ('To the Sea'), leaves him in precisely the same position as his right-wing friends, with their Black Papers, the defence of private medicine and public schools, and the proudly proclaimed 'right' to be unequal: they cannot persuade us that the 'sparkling armada of promises' had, as Larkin certainly feels, *always* been false — no matter how far life in England (the 'first slum of Europe', Larkin fears) is from their realization.

Donald Davie regarded his own first book of criticism, *Purity of Diction in English Verse* (1952) as a manifesto for the poetry of the Movement, the chief achievement of which was to 'hoist into prominence, and keep there, the poems of Philip Larkin'.[21] In a postscript to the 1966 reissue of *Purity of Diction,* Davie says it was a manifesto 'under a thin disguise', and still is. The claim was only partially correct, and has become increasingly less so as Davie himself moves away from Larkin's 'heroic insularity', away from Kingsley Amis's view that

> ... nobody wants any more poems on the grander themes for a few years, but at the same time nobody wants any more poems about philosophers or paintings or novelists or art galleries or mythology or foreign cities or other poems.[22]

This is Amis, naturally, providing the definitive statement of the insular and philistine side of the Movement. Davie has his quarrels with his old colleagues. The blistering tone of his review of Larkin's *Oxford Book of Twentieth Century Verse* in *The Listener* of 29 March 1973 is another sign of the distance he has travelled in the past twenty years.

There has been a consistency of sorts underlying Davie's work, a persistent adherence to a body of ideas which he has described as 'rational conservatism'. But Davie's carefully gauged propriety of tone, and the undeniable streak of priggish self-righteousness, is on occasion overthrown by less temperate formulations. His dealings with Ezra Pound over the years remain central, not merely because Pound embodied in modernism a literary tradition which Davie opposed; but also because Pound was too brilliant a technician, too genuine a scholar, too thoroughly committed to 'literary civilization' as Davie puts it in the Modern Masters volume in 1975, to be the object of unequivocal feelings. Davie's *Ezra Pound: Poet as Sculptor* is a case in point. It appeared in 1964, well over a decade after Hugh Kenner's pioneering study, *The Poetry of Ezra Pound.* Kenner was (and is) Pound's subtlest apologist, making a case for the poet when Ezra Pound the man was an accused traitor, locked away, seemingly for life, in an insane asylum in Washington. It was an impassioned piece of advocacy, like all of Kenner's books. Davie had no such project in mind, although it is hard to see what precisely he intended as he discussed Pound's development in a leisurely fashion. It is only when Davie suddenly breaks off into a series of increasingly wild claims, hasty generalizations and over-heated denunciations, that Davie's purpose comes clear. The object of his attack is *The Cantos,* and Pound's use of mythology, history and morality. He undermines Pound's claim to use history, calling it ruinously 'wasteful and repeatedly arbitrary'; the technique of composition by juxtaposition, the ideogrammic method which Pound learned from Fenollosa, does not 'deceive' the reader: Pound has simply been improvising; the whole plan of *The Cantos* 'is absurdly, even insanely presumptuous'; and finally, 'Pound has made it impossible for anyone any longer to exalt the poet into a seer.'[23]

Here the deeper motive, or at least a version of it, appears. Davie's attitude towards the seer-poet, and the correct antidote, appears in his very earliest work. Reviewing an anthology of Pacific coast poetry edited by Yvor Winters in the November 1950 issue of *Poetry London,* he writes:

> For the young English poet resentful of the tyranny of the 'image' in the restricted sense of 'metaphor' (whether inflated into symbols, worried into conceits, or compressed into 'striking' epithets), this American anthology points in a direction which may provide a wholesome alternative, i.e. it points to a renewed poetry of statement, openly didactic but saved by a sedulously noble diction, from prosiness.

The programme of Davie's thought seems to have emerged fully formed. The key links in the argument are (to simplify): symbolist or post-symbolist poems work by the manipulation of images; meaning flows into and out from the interstices between images; this meaning depends upon a dislocation of syntax, which is the 'essential secret' of the symbolist technique; but there is 'a connection between the laws of syntax and the laws of society, between bodies of usage in speech and in social life, between tearing a word from its context and choosing a leader out of the ruck'; therefore, to dislocate syntax, to write in the post-symbolist fashion like Pound and the modernists, 'is to throw away a tradition central to human thought and conduct'. 'One could almost say', he goes on, 'that to dislocate syntax in poetry is to threaten the rule of law in civilized community.' The competition cannot be very great for a sillier analogy than the one Davie proposes between the 'laws' of syntax, and the 'laws' of society. And this was the 'manifesto' of the Movement! 'I like to think that if the group of us had ever cohered enough to subscribe to a common manifesto, it might have been *Purity of Diction in English Verse.*'[24] Very little is added in *Articulate Energy* (1955), beyond the statement of Davie's explicit motive to undo the harm done by the symbolist and modernist traditions in poetry and criticism, his adherence to 'rational conservatism', and the assertion that 'where there is authentic syntax in poetry . . . the poet retains hope of the conscious mind's activity'.

The landscape of Davie's poetry suggests a subtler mind — no less bleak or conservative than Larkin's — but less sympathetic, less humane. For all Davie's belief in 'images of celebration', he is the last poet in the world capable of writing a 'Show Saturday'. This assessment of Davie's austerity seems cruelly unfair, especially after a reading of 'Pietà' from *Essex Poems,* the most unflawed creation in the three hundred pages of his *Collected Poems.* But Davie is also the author of:

> May the humanitarian
> Blackmail be paid no longer;
> Instead may you work a little.
>
> ('New Year Wishes for the English')

And of this, in 'England':

> . . . the girls from the nearest college
> of Further Education
> spread their excited thighs . . .

This inevitably reminds us of Yeats's 'staggering girl, her thighs caressed By the dark webs . . .' a rather severe comparison for Davie. He is also prone to an unattractive self-pitying whine:

> My native tongue was leased
> Fawningly, long ago
> To the too long appeased
> Long pitied vulgar.
>
> ('Brantôme')

His career seems to fall into two distinct phases, divided by the half-decade following his visit to California in 1957-8. After graduating from Cambridge, he lectured at Trinity College, Dublin, and then at Cambridge, where he was fellow of Trinity College, from 1950 to 1957. This was the period of his Fantasy Poets pamphlet in 1954, and of the first two books of verse (*Brides of Reason* in 1955, *A Winter Talent* in 1957), and the first two critical studies. 'He aims at the restricted gloom of Cowper', noted G. S. Fraser, 'the moral weight of Johnson, and affable flow (though less often, this) of Goldsmith.'[25] Davie jocularly referred to himself as 'a pasticheur of late-Augustan styles' in 'Homage to William Cowper'. The style of his poems in the 1950s is dry, precise, carefully plain. They are written as though the entire corpus of literature since the late eighteenth century has been an unfortunate mistake. The occasional contemporary reference, such as the ponderous 'At Dachau Yeats and Rilke died' from 'Hawkshead and Dachau in a Christmas Glass', and more recently, the slight references to Jan Palach and Salvador Allende in 'Oxfordshire' in *The Shires,* constitute a kind of shorthand which did not greatly interest Davie. Or at least, did not seem important enough to use more than infrequently, though he rather savours the sweeping cultural generalization *à la* George Steiner ('The British imagination, it may be, has never to this day recovered from the shock of Passchendaele').[26] In 'Among Artisans' Houses' first published in Donald Hall's periodical, *New Poems,* at the end of 1953, an observation is given a weight of meaning, a *gravitas,* which seems uncomfortably programmatic. The details seem to exist for the moral, or at least the conclusion, inevitably tacked on with a restrained but decisive rhyme. Davie reveals undoubted powers of social observation (as, for example, in 'Belfast on a Saturday Afternoon'), but there is a nervous inability to leave well-enough alone. A poetry of 'statement' had actually to *say* something, after all. What he has to say is not consistent or clear; the most notable failure being 'Hawkshead and Dachau'. There is an argument with romanticism throughout Davie's early work, and an ambivalent relationship to the poets of the 1930s; but the 'civil sense' embodied in terrace houses in Plymouth in 'Among Artisans' Houses';[27] the 'neutral tone', so quickly made a notorious slogan, from 'Remembering the 'Thirties'; the 'types of ideal virtue' in 'Dream Forest'; and the defence of his temperament in 'A Winter Talent', do not constitute more than fragments of a system of values. 'The Wind at Penistone' seems to speak, if obliquely, for a larger dilemma: the landscape of Yorkshire is one of bleak reserve, the clenched fist, with which — in human terms — Davie feels uneasy ('close-fisted people/Are mostly vulgar'). In poetry, that 'stern-game' played with life, he can find no sustenance either:

> . . . coming home
> The poet falls to special pleading, chilled
> To find in Art no fellow but the wind.

The poet is a divided man, alienated, distracted, a 'Water Walker' as Richard Wilbur describes the dilemma in *The Beautiful Changes* (1947).

The adaptation of Mickiewicz's *Pan Tadeusz,* which appeared from the Marvell Press in 1959 as *The Forests of Lithuania,* suggests two important developments in Davie's art.[28] He here reveals a greatly heightened sense of the profusion of nature, the choking, alien presence of the great forests of Eastern Europe, and in another passage, a conversation between Dombrowski and Maciek, Davie shows for the first time the swing and energy of colloquial speech.[29] Mickiewicz, in the prose translation of G. R. Noyes in Everyman's Library, was a crucial figure in the process of change which carried Davie beyond the pat civilities of *Brides of Reason* and *A Winter Talent.*

Davie's period of transition is roughly coterminous with his return to Cambridge, this time as a fellow of Caius College, between 1959 and 1964. The sequence for Francis Parkman in 1961, 'With the Grain', and 'For Doreen, A Voice from the Garden', form the crucial link with *Events and Wisdoms*. He does not praise polish, refinement, or purity, so much as show a new awareness of the 'natural'. There is a new sensitivity to nature and landscape in 'Low Lands'. In one sense, this was clearly against the grain of his temperament. He makes the point in 'Barnsley Cricket Club':

> Hard to instruct myself, and then my son,
> That things which would be natural are done
> After a style less consummate . . .

It was about this time that Davie published 'Poetry & Landscape in Present England' in *Granta*. Davie's essay, now reprinted in *Thomas Hardy and British Poetry,* brings to the surface the political, social and ecological context of his new awareness of landscape:

> Britain as a whole is the most industrialized landscape in the world; . . . here the nonhuman has been exploited and violated by the human more consistently and over a longer period than anywhere else.[30]

It was English poetry, Davie goes on, which first expressed 'ideas of elemental sanctity and natural piety'; but now 'in a landscape where virtually all the sanctuaries have been violated, all the pieties blasphemed', it is poetry which figures among the chief victims. 'Our poetry suffers from the loss, or the drastic impoverishment, of the traditional images of celebration.' *Events and Wisdoms* is dominated by a sense of the corruption of the quality of life by the supermarket mentality. 'Chemicals ripen the citrus', he notes in 'In California'; 'Beef in cellophane'. Only in 'Agave in the West' does he arrange a direct confrontation between the natural and the civilized. Ironically, the result is not as anticipated:

> Leaving the wilderness, she counts the loss
> Of a world of signs — in algae, moss,
> Guano, lichen, all the blooms of stone;
> In cross-grained baulks and boles, in timber grown
> Noble in groves or into monstrous shapes;
> In rock-formations, cloud-formations, landscapes.
> I like the sidewalks of an American city:
>
> Sunstruck solitude of parking lots;
> Taut vivid women, hair close-shaved from the armpit;
> Glass walls run up, run out on the canyon's lip.
> Barber my verses, pitiless vivid city.

The second distinct phase of Davie's career came when he left

Cambridge in 1965 to take up a chair at Essex, a new university designed on progressive lines. The remarkable conjunction of poets at Essex created a brief renaissance. Ed Dorn was visiting professor between 1965 and 1968. The poet Tom Clark was there from 1965-7, co-editing with Andrew Crozier the most un-English poetry magazine of the decade, *The Wivenhoe Park Review,* becoming *The Park* when Crozier moved to Keele University in 1968. (Robert Lowell came to Essex after Davie's departure.) His Davie's stint at Essex, coinciding with the fierce politicization of universities in Britain generally, and Essex in particular, between 1966 and 1968, was clearly a devastating experience for him, ending with his decision to leave England altogether for a chair at Stanford. The effect of his time at Essex still reverberates in Davie's poetry. Writing of the county in *The Shires* (1975), he lamely notes:

> Constable's country merits
> Better than I can give it
> Who have unfinished business
> There, with my own failures.

His professional 'failures', either as an administrator or teacher, do not surface in the poems. The general ambience within the university does:

> Diatribe and
> Denunciation, where
> I spend my days . . .

At times, the specific crisis at Essex University, torn by sit-ins, seems merely an instance in Davie's thinking of a general malaise affecting the culture of England, too susceptible to grotesque alien influences:

> Like you I look with astonished fear and revulsion
>   at the gross and bearded, articulate and good-humoured
>   Franco-American torso, pinned across
>   the plane of human action, twitching and roaring.
>   ('To Certain English Poets')

In a fond echo of MacNeice's 'Bagpipe Music', Davie records the final collapse of the millennium-long tradition of English poetry:

> The Gutenberg era, the era of rhyme, is over.
> It's an end to the word-smith, now, an end to the Skald,
> and end to the erudite, elated rover
> threading a fiord of words. Four-letter expletives
> are all of that Ocean's plankton that still lives.   ('To Helen Keller')

What survives, along with Davie's prim euphemism, 'four-letter expletives', are the 'self-communers' in the devastating 'Pentecost', who are eloquent in pidgin. The sense of failure and pollution dominates the landscape:

Diesel-fumes cling to wistaria   ('For Doreen')

Landscapes of supertax
Record a deathly failure
As clearly as the lack
of a grand or expansively human
Scale to the buildings of Ilford

The scale of that deprivation
Goes down in no statistics.   ('Thanks to Industrial Essex')

In view of such unimaginable horrors, little remains of the national character:

'A nation of theatre-people,
Purveyors, not creators,
Adaptable cyphers, stylists,
Educators, dandies.'   ('From the New World')

Larkin's 'Homage to a Government', first printed in *The Sunday Times* of 19 January 1969, expressed a not dissimilar state of mind. Davie seems to withdraw in simple despair:

I cannot abide the new
Absurdities day by day,
The new adulterations.   ('Epistle. To Enrique Caracciolo Trejo')

In the same poem he notes the precise form of his discontent: we have been reduced to a language maimed by 'its incapacity to venerate/Life, or the going of it'. It was the loss of those 'images of celebration', the 'sense of elation'[31] which was the burden of the best poetry, which stood for the crippled and diminished sense of life in present-day England. Feeling the absences, the flaws, so acutely, Davie was able to point to some positives, something to be celebrated, such as excellence ('Ezra Pound in Pisa'), the need for the metaphysicality of poetry ('Or, Solitude');

More than ever I need
Places where nothing happened,
Where history is silent,
No Tartar ponies checked, and
Endurance earns repose.   ('Behind the North Wind')

Davie had asked in 'A Letter to Curtis Bradford' about the differing meaning of history in England and America. At home history was to do with 'man with man', in America 'you met with spirits'. The decision to emigrate might just as well have been taken when, travelling through Southern France, he wrote:

Goodbye to all the centuries. There is
No home in them, much as the dip and turn
Of an honest alley charmingly deceive us.

('Rodez')

There is no 'goodbye' to the past, whether it provides a 'home' or not. America has often been a refuge for European intellectuals, exiled from intolerable conditions; but it has never offered, since the closing of the frontier, for immigrants or natives, a pastoral serenity and silence; or, since then, freedom from 'new adulterations'. It may very well be a charming place, free from 'the too long appeased/Long pitied vulgar', but even Palo Alto isn't Arcadia.

A cento from the new age. Davie's 'How dare we now be anything but numb?', from 'Rejoinder to a Critic', may have put it too boldly, but the movement against modernism, against 'the edge-of-the-crowd poetry of the 'thirties, whether wise-cracking or weeping in its evasions', was now complete.[32] Richard Howard: 'We wanted to find as many constraints as possible.' Anthony Thwaite: 'An acceptance of quiet apprenticeship has replaced the firebrand and the manifesto.' Howard's models at Columbia in the late 1940s were Elizabethan or metaphysical; Wain was reading Empson at Oxford; John Hollander, Howard's contemporary at Columbia, found in Wallace Stevens 'a fruitful kind of restraint'. On the occasion of Stevens's death in 1955, William Carlos Williams wrote:

> He was a formalist as much as Rimbaud or Baudelaire or Remy de Gourmont were so. The poems of Walt Whitman meant nothing to him, the entire 'free verse' movement left him cold — which marks in the beginning (because he never went astray) the modern return to accepted verse forms of the present day . . .

Richard Wilbur, an assistant professor of English at Harvard, on restraint:

> If art is a window, then the poem is something intermediate in character, limited, synecdochic, a partial vision of a part of the world. It is the means of a dynamic relation between the eye within and the world without. If art is conceived to be a door, then that dynamic relation is destroyed. The artist no longer perceives a wall between him and the world; the world becomes an extension of himself, and is deprived of its reality. The poet's words cease to be a means of liaison with the world; they take the place of the world. This is bad aesthetics — and incidentally bad morals.
>   The use of strict poetic forms, traditional or invented, is like the use of framing the composition in painting: both serve to limit the work of art, and to declare its artificiality: they say 'This is not the world, but a pattern imposed upon the world or found in it', 'this is a partial and provisional attempt to establish relations between things'.

Donald Hall, completing a B. Litt. at Oxford between 1951-3, was a crucial conduit into England of Harvard formalism: 'I have come to think that all human action is formal; all personality is an aesthetic structure, a making something exist by statement: like saying a word. Symmetry becomes the root of morality, conduct, and judgment, and reality is a terrifying chaos outside form glimpsed only occasionally, and never, of course, understood without a translation into form.'

Older critics were not readily persuaded by this. Contemporary English poetry, write Marius Bewley, who was not an elder but sounded like one, 'has entered into one of those periods of extreme aridity and discouragement'. T. S. Eliot confessed to John Lehmann 'a sense of disappointment that so much less has come of it than one expected, so little that gives one any great hope for the future'. Only Lowell and Wilbur escaped the great man's censure and were published by Faber and Faber. Herbert Read (and just about everyone else) identified a 'failure of nerve':

> . . . eyes are dazzled and once again a veil of rhetoric is drawn over the vision of the poet . . . it is the hour of the twittering machines. We listen to them as we drink our martinis or smoke a cigarette, and for an hour or two we feel content. Then the night comes and there is no voice to fill the silence . . .

Hot on the heels of the 'New Elizabethans' and the Festival of Britain, a gloomy insularity prevailed:

> . . . English culture, in the last few years — in reaction, maybe, to shifts of world power — has become much more self-protectively insular. The bright young men no longer read Kierkegaard, Kafka, Sartre, and what have you, but rediscover Bagehot, George Gissing, 'Mark Rutherford', or Arnold Bennett.

Which sounded strikingly like the 'age of respectability' in America where:

> . . . the greatest demand probably will be for tamer and less controversial talents, and . . . we are not likely in the immediate future to see any splurge of raucous, experimental writing or of aggressive and programmatic criticism.

Two judgments:

> It is more important for a poet to have a sense of humour than a social conscience. (Adrian Mitchell, 1954)

> . . . I feel a certain sympathy for these young people, though they are so cautious and, so it seems to me, so sad, and so careful not to hope. (Edwin Muir, 1956)

Everywhere the 'reality' out there was inhospitable. The new prosperity meant mindless consumption, not a better life; the reassertion of the sanctity of profit became a proposition, an image, to be sold by professional persuaders; everywhere there was insecurity, loneliness, bureaucratization, conformity, the cold war, and McCarthyism. Only in the universities was this pressure noticeably eased, if you didn't mind signing a loyalty oath, that is. Artists, poets, free-floating literary intellectuals, gradually found themselves signed on to be writers in residence or visiting professors, participants at Breadloaf Writer's Conference, guests at Yaddo writer's colony, taken on Guggenheim junkets in Italy or England, commissioned by the Bollingen Foundation or awarded the Pulitzer, nominated for the National Book Award or that of the National Institute of Arts and Letters. Universities served the muse by publishing new poetry (particularly Yale and Wesleyan), and by underwriting literary journals and quarterlies, each with a hatful of prizes and fellowships. Inevitably there was much discussion of the new situation of the poet, no longer a denizen of bohemia, but a crisp, scholarly fellow, wearing a bow tie, teaching Metaphysical Poets on Monday-Wednesday-Friday at ten. The universities were little islands of culture, *gemütlich* and calm, good places to hold conferences and symposia, to edit proceedings, to write text books and book reviews, to be critics of literature, and even, sometimes, to write poems.

The problem was one of mediation between that alien 'reality' and the inner consciousness. The economic mediation could be left to the great corporations and universities. In poetry, we call it an age of formalism, uniform to both England and America. By formalism we mean the interposition of *technical* imperatives between the poet and 'reality'. The Audenesque had served such a function, and embodied a recognizable fund of techniques and a characteristic diction; it was a stylization of reality (inevitably), but also a way of accommodating reality, of admitting the possibility of the poet as poet intervening in the world around him. The hope was utopian, but courageous. With its eclipse, the hope and courage seemed equally out of place. It was scarcely possible now to write poems overtly committed to 'the harder reality of social change', as one communist critic put it.[33] There was a new and overriding interest in technique; the poem-as-manifesto, or the poem-about-poetry became annoyingly commonplace. The obsession with technique paradoxically sat side by side with a deep-seated hostility towards the modernists, for whom the importance of technique had been an untiring theme. This, certainly, was Pound's contribution. 'Technique,' he wrote, 'is machinery for the transmission of power. You do not judge an engine by the polish on the outside of the boiler nor by the shriek of its whistle. One might be supposed to consider the precision of its driving machinery.'[34] 'Precision' is Pound's term; in the 1950s it would have been 'form', often enough form for its own sake, with little concern for the 'transmission of power'. The term meant something less combative to the young formalists. It was widely acknowledged that the younger American poets were showing great skill in strict verse forms and intricate metrical patterns. 'But the complication of form which they pursue', complained Bewley,

> ... frequently seems to be achieved with facility rather than sustained with conviction or a poise that is not brittle. There is a disquieting tendency to refer to these poets as 'great technicians'. I say it is disquieting because a highly ordered form in poetry ought to relate ... to patterns of feeling and living ...[35]

The identification of a disjunction between the elaborate forms of the formalists, and the thinness of feeling in their poems, is crucial, forming as it does the basis for the whole attack on formalism. As a mode of poetry it was felt to be inherently arid, that the end result of cherishing 'complication of form' was complication for its own sake. The phrase 'academic verse', for interesting cultural reasons, has come to stand for poetry which was polished but not sustained by any great power of feeling. Alvarez, despite his long string of academic awards and research fellowships in the 1950s, describes this kind of poetry as 'academic-administrative verse, polite, knowledgeable, efficient, polished, and, in its quiet way, even intelligent' (*The New Poetry*, 1962).

Formalism emerged as the 'cause', one might say, of the generation of poets born in the 1920s. They were perhaps too young to have made a strong commitment to the Popular Front, but not too young to understand what Orwell was saying about the Spanish Civil War, what Koestler said in *Darkness at Noon* about the trials of the Old Bolsheviks, and certainly not too young to see the meaning of the Molotov-Ribbentrop pact and the dismemberment of Poland. They came into maturity in a radically different literary and political climate. Donald Davie, who was born in 1922, has written in an interesting autobiographical essay on T. S. Eliot of going up to Cambridge when the Left Bookshop was still in Rose Crescent 'to remind me that this was the university from which John Cornford and Julian Bell had gone to die in Spain ...'

> ... for men and women who had gone up to university only eighteen months before me had had time to invest something in the ideology of the Popular Front, and to this day that investment (as I know, for I am speaking of my closest friends) makes them wryly suspicious and resentful of Eliot as a thinker about society and as a force in politics. I had no such difficulties; but for me, growing up

89

just when I did, Eliot's pessimistic conservatism seemed tough-minded and straight-talking . . .[36]

The break between generations was sharp and irrevocable. It is illuminating in this regard to consider three 'first' books of poetry published between 1947 and 1957: Richard Wilbur's *The Beautiful Changes* (1947), Donald Hall's *Exiles and Marriages* (1955), and Anthony Thwaite's *Home Truths* (1957). All three books were published when their authors were in their mid-twenties. Four different books (for example, 'first' books published during this period by Robert Duncan, Charles Olson, Gregory Corso and Allen Ginsberg) would tell a quite different story, but one is looking here for a particular tradition and its exemplars. There was no sudden break after 1957. Geoffrey Hill's *For the Unfallen* was published in 1959, Sylvia Plath's *The Colossus* in 1960, and X. J. Kennedy's *Nude Descending a Staircase* in 1961. There is a residual unfairness in isolating the earliest work of poets who, like Hall and Thwaite, have gone on to write very different kinds of poetry in their maturity; the purpose rather is to understand something of the mechanics behind the way a body of assumptions and practices became nearly universal.

Allen Ginsberg's *Howl* was published in 1956, the year when Richard Wilbur's *Things Of This World* scooped the Pulitzer and the National Book Award. Praise for Wilbur was immoderate:

> There is a sense of mastery but of struggle, of order claimed from chaotic forces never allowed to assume disproportion, yet valued as formative . . . One returns to the idea of balance, or orderliness, or excellence, of a good centrality, nothing excessive, nothing divisive, which is to say that Wilbur has achieved a natural and full harmony in his poetry.[37]

Eberhart is making an act of homage to the virtues of the metropolis, to the values of 'a good centrality'. Wilbur's undoubted virtues are those of a class and a region, the anglophile East, the Ivy League colleges, the protestant culture of America, discovering in formalism a new and potent mode of social control. By 1956 American poetry had been dominated (as far as the younger poets were concerned) by Lowell and Wilbur, Wilbur and Lowell, for a decade. 'One reviewer praised Wilbur's elegance,' Louis Simpson wrote, 'and Lowell's passionate complexity. Another reviewer said that though Lowell was passionate he was also graceful, and though Wilbur was elegant this should not blind us to the intensity of his metaphysics.'[38] Harvard and Columbia were hotbeds of formalism, New Criticism, and literary intrigue. Yet it was Lowell who abandoned left-wing Harvard for Kenyon College and the strict versification of Allen

Tate and John Crowe Ransom; and it was Lowell who cracked the ice on the academic pond with *Life Studies* in 1959. And there is no small irony in Ginsberg, an ex-student of Lionel Trilling's at Columbia, announcing at a poetry reading at his old university in 1958 that 'no one at Columbia knew anything about prosody; the English department was stuck in the nineteenth century, sensible of no meter other than the old iambic pentameter'.[39] When the reaction against formalism set in, the supreme virtues of 'grace', 'elegance', 'precision' and 'discipline' began to look rather empty and pretentious. By 1962 (in America at least) poetry in the formalist mode seemed a little dated. A reviewer in *The Kenyon Review* complained that *The Colossus* was 'self-consciously literary', 'pot-bound' and 'lumpy'. Wilbur was the chief target, though sometimes remaining unnamed, in the early numbers of Robert Bly's *The Fifties* in 1958 and 1959. Wilbur's reputation has scarcely survived the 1950s, suggesting a shift in taste less sudden than the collapse of committed poetry between 1939 and 1941, but seemingly a good deal more permanent.

Wilbur, then, presents us with a body of values, a stance, a caste of mind, which finds little sympathy with the general readership of poetry, and which forces his defenders on to an apologetic note. 'I know I shouldn't say this,' they usually begin, 'but I've secretly loved Wilbur, the old dispensation of rhymes and regular verse forms, despite the heroic achievements of the new.' Wilbur insisted upon the limits of poetry:

> Poets are often intelligent men, and they are entitled to their thoughts, but intellectual pioneering, and the construction of new thought-systems, is not their special function.[40]

And upon the unfashionable idea that knowledge matters:

> ... there seems to me no disadvantage to poetry's being intellectually sharp, and to its having some knowledge behind it. Good poetry always has had that; there have never been any good ignorant poets.[41]

The dominant mode of formalism was established with *The Beautiful Changes.* It is obviously an impersonal poetry, steeped in the propriety of Eliot and the New Criticism. 'My first poems,' Wilbur has written,

> ... were written in answer to the inner and outer disorders of the Second World War, and they helped me, as poems should, take a hold of raw events and convert them provisionally, into experience.[42]

The tone is cool and ironic, displayed by an array of technical accomplishments — so polished are Wilbur's poems that he might easily be mistaken for one of the refiners and polishers who come along in the wake of the great innovators. But this is not the case: formalism was, if not invented, at least perfected by Wilbur.

The argument which runs throughout the whole of the collection is for the sufficiency of 'things of this world'. He connects this with his dissatisfaction with the poetics of Edgar Allan Poe, which 'tends toward brushing aside and annihilating everything in the natural world, everything that stands between Poe and the realm of pure spirit', and with his own argument with the whole vatic or bardic tradition. He writes in 'Praise to Summer':

> Does sense so stale that it must needs derange
> The world to know it? To a praiseful eye
> Should it not be enough of fresh and strange
> That trees grow green, and moles can course in clay,
> And sparrows sweep the ceiling of our day?

In theory, Wilbur finds himself in the camp of Whitman, Pound and Williams, on the side of the 'world of concrete particulars'. 'Things *are*,' he writes in 1953. 'The cow is there. No poetry can have any strength unless it continually bashes itself against the reality of things.' He resists the hasty imputation of meanings on to natural objects:

> It's hard to tell the purpose of a bird;
> for relevance it does not seem to try.
> No line can trace no flute exemplify
> its travelling; it darts without the word.
> Who wills devoutly to absorb, contain,
> birds give him pain.   ('In a Bird Sanctuary')

It would be reasonable to assume, on the basis of this argument in Wilbur's work, that his poems are gritty with objects, places, animals, people, things. But he seems unable to let a 'praiseful eye' go about its business unmolested. Poem after poem betrays a struggle to link 'meanings' and symbolic functions to his wonderfully acute eye. He has said that he valued the 'resistance of the world, its independence of the mind', but his poems reflect a continual assertion of the imagination against the 'things of this world'. The things which Wilbur sees come through with great freshness and intensity:

> Cut open raw, it looses a cool clean stench,
> Mineral acid seeping from pores of prest meal . . .   ('Potato')

>   . . . his hands thick tines
> Touch the gold whorls of her Corinthian hair.   ('Place Pigalle')

> You know those windless summer evenings, swollen to stasis
> by too-substantial melodies, rich as a

running-down record, ground round
to full quiet. Even the leaves
have thick tongues.   ('Cigales')

The problematic status of Wilbur's role as observer is explicitly raised in 'Water Walker'. This poem works through a delicate skein of metaphors which express the urge to embrace the world and to renounce it, the desire to be a part of a community and to be alienated from it. 'Water Walker' is an uncharacteristic personal statement on the question of commitment. The opening images of the infidel, and the Caddis fly, stand between two worlds, not within the communion of faith, nor wholly outside it; not of the water, nor, completely, of the air. They stand suspended between two worlds, '. . . knowing/Both, with his breath, to be real'. Wilbur stands in a similar relationship to his parental home, with its

> . . . odors of halls and the fade of familiar voices,
> Stair creaks, piano tunes falling oñ rugs,
> Wall paper palimpsests . . .

He then introduces another water walker, Saul, who might have been content to remain obscurely at home but who chose to carry 'Jew visions to the Greeks'. Saul gains by the process that made him 'grow/stranger to both'. Wilbur wants to 'observe', to 'watch and wait/And praise'. But to do justice to things is to acknowledge that the condition of being a water walker is permanent — that one remains a prisoner of the 'cherished, tyrannical' dilemma.

'Water Walker' is a parable, an 'animal-morality poem' as Randall Jarrell remarks in an acute comment in *Poetry and the Age*. It is difficult to do more than acknowledge Wilbur's desire to observe and praise, to remain completely committed to the here and now, the things of this world, before deciding that he, too, has axes to grind. In fact, Wilbur does not approach the real directly, but accepts its necessary deflection through formalism: 'The relation between an artist and reality is always an oblique one, and indeed there is no good art which is not oblique.' In an essay in the *Quarterly Review of Literature* in 1953 Wilbur took issue with William Carlos Williams's contention that it was desirable to concentrate upon 'structural reforms and inventions'. 'Instead of talking about the need of a perpetual revolution of the entire sensibility', Wilbur explained,

> . . . in the incessant task of achieving relations to the always changing face of reality. To this latter purpose I have seen sonnets, villanelles, inversions and all that Dr Williams reprehends do great services in the last few years, and when this is so, one cannot say that the poets have surrendered to traditional forms.
> They have taken them over, rather.[43]

Wilbur's work continually raises the question of whether the 'traditional forms' can be taken over and made adequate for 'the incessant task of achieving relations to the always changing face of reality'. He said yes, and so did the majority of poets in the 1950s. He saw the permanent need for a poetry of the real, but also that the real was only to be reached through form. 'In each art,' he writes in the same essay, 'the difficulty of the form is a substitution for the difficulty of direct apprehension of the object.' Wilbur was deeply caught up in the 'difficulty of the form' − to the apparent exclusion of the 'direct apprehension of the object'. It is his preoccupation with form which explains why his work is so disregarded by contemporary taste.

After a brilliant undergraduate career at Harvard, where he edited the *Advocate* and won prizes for his poetry and Latin translation, Donald Hall won a Henry Fellowship and went to Christ Church, Oxford, in 1951. While at Harvard he had been the friend and disciple of Richard Wilbur. Anthony Thwaite recalls the great fervour of Hall's evangelism for Wilbur at this time. The American contingent at Oxford had a strong literary flavour. Adrienne Rich was there on a Guggenheim Fellowship after taking her B.A. at Radcliffe in 1951. Her first book, *A Change of World*, had been selected by Auden for the Yale series of Younger Poets in the same year. George Steiner, then under the guise of the poet F. George Steiner, was at Balliol College, contributing poems to *Oxford Poetry 1952* and *New Poems.* Hall, Rich and Steiner were all graduate students, mature, successful, worldly and self-confident, whose collective influence on Oxford poetry has been little understood. The atmosphere at Oxford was clearly transitional. The immediate postwar students, in whom John Wain noticed such strong neo-romantic inclinations, had already gone down. In 1952 Michael Shanks, then President of the Oxford University Poetry Society, established contacts with the painter and printer Oscar Mellor. Together they designed a series of small pamphlets by younger poets with close connections with Oxford. Shanks was succeeded as editor of the series by Donald Hall, who was in turn followed by George MacBeth and Anthony Thwaite. With the sixteenth pamphlet the series was extended to a group of slightly older poets from Oxford (Larkin, Wain, Amis, Holloway), and a contingent from Cambridge (Gunn, Davie) was brought in. There was an American flavour to the earlier numbers (Hall, Steiner, Rich, and later Theodore Roethke's pupil from the University of Washington, Richard Selig). The plan was that Mellor would do the printing on his hand press at Eynsham. The editor would be appointed by O.U.P.S. The 'Fantasy Poets' venture was soon extended to take in the annual volumes of poetry from Oxford. The 1952 volume, edited by Derwent May and James Price, was published by Basil Blackwell (contributors included A. Alvarez, Hall, Geoffrey Hill and Steiner). Mellor published the 1953 volume, edited by Hall and Hill. Many contributors appear in both volumes. New boys included Edward Lucie-Smith, George MacBeth, Adrian Mitchell and Anthony Thwaite. A further venture by the Fantasy Press was a small poetry magazine, edited by Donald Hall (and for a sixth and final number by Jonathan Price and Geoffrey Hill), entitled *New Poems*.

The Fantasy Press was a remarkable venture, for which Mellor deserves great credit. The pamphlets and other publications were typographically conservative (compared for example with Geoffrey Grigson's *New Verse*), but this was in keeping with the contents. The poems of Hall would look rather odd in sans-serif. The 'Fantasy Poets' series, *New Poems,* and the annual *Oxford Poetry* collections were augmented by Elizabeth Jenning's *Poems* and Lucien Stryk's *Taproot* in 1953, Thom Gunn's *Fighting Terms* in 1954, Tomlinson's *The Necklace* and Davie's *Brides of Reason* in 1955, the first proper 'books' of poems to be published by Mellor. The contributors were interchangeable in the three main ventures: a generation of poets were able, with remarkably little fuss, to see their work in print. The Fantasy Press was only retrospectively useful for Larkin (whose first book was published by the Fortune Press in 1945), Wain or Amis, whose first books were published on a very limited scale by the School of Art of the University of Reading (*Mixed Feelings* in 1951, *A Frame of Mind* in 1953). It was very much the show of the 'younger' formalists* — Hall, Hill and Thwaite — who, indeed, had other irons in the fire at Oxford. *Mandrake,* the magazine founded by John Wain, survived until 1952. *The Isis* was edited by Thwaite in 1954. *Trio,* a lively poetry magazine, was edited in turn by George MacBeth, Anthony Thwaite, Quentin Stevenson and others from 1952 to 1955. The selection of poets for the Fantasy Poets series reflects 'Oxford taste', little difference being noticeable between poems appearing in *Oxford Left* and *Oxford Tory*. And it was Oxford taste behind Conquest's anthology, *New Lines,* 1956. Between 1952 and 1954 the Fantasy Poets included six of its nine contributors. Given the small size of Mellor's pamphlets, they seem an earlier, and more interesting weather vane, than either *New Lines* or G. S. Fraser's *Poetry Now*.

* The first twenty-six poets in the Fantasy pamphlets were Elizabeth Jennings, Pearce Young, James Price, Donald Hall, Simon Broadbent, Peter Dale Scott, Paul West, F. George Steiner, Lotte Zurndorfer, Martin Seymour-Smith, Geoffrey Hill, Adrienne Cecile Rich, Michael Shanks, Michell Raper, A. Alvarez, Thom Gunn, Anthony Thwaite, Arthur Boyars, Donald Davie, Jonathan Price, Philip Larkin, Kingsley Amis, Richard Selig, Adrian Mitchell, J. E. M. Lucie-Smith, John Holloway. (All published between 1952 and 1954.)

The great cham at Oxford during his remarkable two years at Christ Church between 1951 and 1953 was Donald Hall. He was responsible for *New Poems,* the best-edited of all the Oxford poetry magazines. It was clearly transatlantic: Robert Bly was the 'New York Representative', and poems appeared by Bly, Steiner, Rich, Selig and Hall himself. Jennings was a regular contributor, as were Geoffrey Hill and Thom Gunn. Davie's 'Among Artisans' Houses' appeared in it. There were poems entitled 'Epithalamium' (Broadbent) and 'Epithalamion' (Hall); 'Elegy' (Rich), 'Final Elegy' and 'Requiem' (Thwaite), and 'In Memory of Jane Fraser' (Hill). To go by the titles alone, you might think *New Poems* was edited by apprentice funeral directors, and published courtly, gracious verse. Not one poem in the run of six numbers is directly concerned with contemporary life. The greatest interest of these poets (with some exceptions) is style, rather than what they can say through poetry.

One striking feature of these poems reminds us of Davie's 'Remembering the 'Thirties': 'England expected every man that day/To show his motives were ambivalent.' In Thwaite's uncollected 'Final Elegy' in the Winter 1952 issue there is a portrait of the poet as a man divided. Half of him 'lay underground', among 'the verbal worms' of the unconscious. The 'sky bound half' of the rational man was 'too fluent, sensitive and young'. Thom Gunn's 'Wind in the Street' (in the Spring 1953 issue), heavily revised for *Fighting Terms,* is a dramatic monologue of a man in a state of terrible indecision:

> I may return, meanwhile I'll look elsewhere:
> My want may modify to what I have seen.
> So I smile wearily, though even as I smile
> A purposeful gust of wind tugs at my hair;
> But I turn, I wave, I am not sure what I mean.
> I may return, meanwhile I'll look elsewhere.

The feeling of uncertainty, divided aims, and indecision had an unintentionally comic flavour in Lucie-Smith's 'October Thames':

> . . . I am never poor, nor ever fear
> The failing of the autumn, or the stream,
> Am caught forever in the amber word
> Whose hardened resin holds me quick in stone
> And keeps me here.

What relief, amid all the sombreness of *New Poems,* to learn that Lucie-Smith does not fear the 'failing of the autumn'!

The most elaborate statement of the mood of ambivalence is in Hall's Newdigate Prize poem 'Exile', published in *Oxford Poetry 1953,* and in Hall's *Exiles and Marriages* (1955). A sympathetic critic of Hall's poetry acknowledges the 'formal skills, dexterity, irony, and intelligence' of

Exiles and Marriages; on the other hand, the volume exhibits 'a gift for knowledgeable polished versifying' which seems 'dated and very slight'. [44] The tidily executed four-line stanzas of alternate rhyming lines, the deadening finality of the rhymes ('I drop a sixpence in the luckless box/To bribe the devil and avoid the pox'), the use of elaborate, finicky stanzas (such as the triplets of 'Syllables of a Small Fig Tree'), and his pleasure in moderately obscure traditional verse forms, gives the unfortunate impression that Hall spent most of his time in those days with his nose buried in the *Princeton Encyclopedia of Poetry and Poetics,* or the contemporary equivalent. At one point Hall satirizes an effete aestheticism:

> *Finesse* be first, whose elegance deplores
> All things save beauty, and the swinging doors;
> Whose cleverness in writing verse is just
> Exceeded by his lack of taste and lust;
> Who lives off lady lovers of his verse
> And thanks them by departing with their purse;
> Who writes his verse in order to amaze,
> To win the Pulitzer, or *Time*'s sweet praise . . .

MacNeice and Plomer seem to warm to subjects like this rather more quickly. Hall goes through the motions of satire, but it is a manner – like so much of his early poetry – that betrays no urgency or even conviction. The positive absence of forcefulness is the main consequence of the studied constraint and formality of *Exiles and Marriages.* Yet Hall certainly has a subject: loss and self-isolation, remembered emotional wholeness and present-day reserve and ambivalence. For all its calculation, 'Exile' is no mean feat, translating as it does the specific emotion of his very fine 'An Elegy for Wesley Wells' into a more general statement affirming the powers of memory and imagination before an impoverished reality. The real for Hall is either a hollow mockery of the past, or else a sea, a storm, a 'terrifying chaos' which is incomprehensible without the mediation of form:

> It is by choice and form
> We build defenses from the storm,
> Imposed upon vacuities of space.   ('Epithalamion')

'Reality,' he wrote in 1953, 'is a terrifying chaos outside form glimpsed only occasionally, and never, of course, understood without a translation into form.'

There are only two poems on public themes in Hall's first collection. One outraged poem, 'Rhyme of Appointed Death', is about a hanging. The other, 'The World, The Times', reads like an oblique parody of an editorial. It certainly reveals nothing so crude as partisanship or propaganda. The poem is about the need to choose – the classic existential dilemma – in a world in which freedom of choice is circumscribed by necessity, and by mortality. 'We live by choice, and choose with every act/That form or chaos move from mind to fact.' That there are no 'simple' answers was in itself an answer, a choice, which helped to define the conservative acquiesence in 'complexity', and which eventually reflected a process of accommodation between the intelligentsia and society. Irving Howe's essay 'This Age of Conformity' (*Partisan Review*, January-February 1954) voiced a significant dissent, revealing for the assumptions he makes about the role of intellectuals in society, and for the numerous wounds, self-inflicted and otherwise, caused by McCarthyism.

In a symposium in *Trio* in June 1953, Alistair Elliot, literary editor of the *Isis* and a contributor to *Oxford Poetry 1953*, made the following observation:

> I don't think that poetry should try to remedy social situations, in this respect, the 30s poets are a waste of time. One's ideas on morality, politics and so on, should not be allowed to intrude into poetry . . .

Thus we see the transformation of the gospel of Wilbur's formal skills into a dogma, a manner to be picked up, a style – the formalism of the 1950s. The narrowing assumptions and slick dismissals, the welcomed self-limitations and cautious tone, were all closely connected with what the younger poets understood by the gospel of formalism according to Donald Hall. It didn't stick, not even for the keenest disciples. 'When I was an undergraduate at Oxford', remarked A. Alvarez,

> . . . an American – who shall be nameless – arrived in Oxford and went around saying 'poetry is the most important thing in the world and one must be professional about it'. Well now, in the face of the kind of 'frou-frou' that passed as a literary life in Oxford at that time this was marvellous. It seemed to me that I wanted to stand on the chairs and cheer. It seemed to me something very good, and almost rather brave to say. Well, I've seen the chap more or less ever since – less more recently. When I went to America about five years later, I found him ravaging around on the literary scene, with a wife and two kids, and an ice-box as big as Verlaine's garret, still saying that poetry is the most important thing in the world. It seemed ludicrous. He had simply never grown up.[45]

Anthony Thwaite's Fantasy Poets pamphlet appeared in 1953. The cool formality of his style was studied and technically correct. The poems hint, however, at a romantic and emotional temperament:

> . . . you provoke, though severance, desire
> Which is the burden of my narrow love.   ('Requiem')

> Lie with me now and hear transmuted sound
> Wail in our wilderness of solitude   ('Bodies and Music')

Form smartly reins in any dangerous tendencies. These poems, four or five chunky stanzas long, intricately rhymed, speak of their nature more vividly through their form than through Thwaite's ostensible subjects. When he published his first book, *Home Truths,* with the Marvell Press (the list of subscribers before publication is a wonderful period document) four years later, only one poem, 'Music by Water', survived from the Fantasy pamphlet. The style seems more evolved, the formalism stricter. Behind *Home Truths* was the witty, argumentative, paradoxical style of the minor Metaphysicals (though not the outrageousness of Donne), and the easy regularity of the Augustans. As in Davie, what was wanted was a poetry of statement, of direct utterance. Thwaite seems to have a great deal to *say* in his first book, unlike most of his Oxford contemporaries. He insists upon the 'point' or the 'moral' with the fervour of English nonconformity. The poems are always under control, with tight stanzaic forms, a steady iambic pentameter, and a way with rhymes which seems notably defter than Donald Hall's early verse. (Rhymes in formalist poetry serve to intimidate the reader, to extort acquiescence; the word-magic allows no time to wander off, break concentration, to let the armoured consciousness relax. It is a profoundly puritanical poetry.)

Thwaite's early poems are in one way or another about love, and the transient states of ambivalence and exile which complicate one's capacity to love. Characteristically the poems transform what may have been highly local and specific emotional or psychological states, or situations, into something imaged, realized, objectified. The subject-matter is part of the programme. Writing in *Encounter* in May 1954, thinking generally of his generation, Thwaite described a poetry which

> . . . does not try to illuminate 'Society' with brash and sanguine slogans; rather, it concerns itself with the individual confronted by human problems (such as love, authority, and power). The resultant poems are quieter, less immediate, less 'obvious' because they are reaching for a kind of truth which is more subtle and delicate.

There is very little feel for society in *Home Truths,* or for authority or power, for that matter; society has simply ceased to exist. Or at least it only exists in negative and passive observations, such as his description in 'The Poet at Lake Nojiri' of

> . . . the lake
> Choked with atomic rain.

More typical, perhaps, in early Thwaite is a sense of conflict between the perfections of art and the 'harsher ache' of the real world in 'The Dream' and in the lucid 'Japan: Aesthetic Point'. Poems about poetry were very much in vogue, and in 'To a Northern Poet' Thwaite turns the art-reality tension into a division between kinds of poets: one is all 'formal gardens', valleys, temperate weather; the other type must learn to discard 'formal reason' for the 'working reason of the heart' by learning 'a stricter craft, a leaner power'. Thwaite treats the theme of exile in 'Three Kinds' and 'From Home'. Both poems are exercises in definition (literally: unfolding the meanings of exile); but he was working too close to Hall's long poem, 'Exile', to do much with the topic. The title poem, 'Home Truths', is one of the most overtly personal in the book, or so it would appear. The experience of being evacuated to America during the war (1940-4) and of compulsory military service mostly spent in Libya (1949-51), may stand somewhere behind this poem, as it does behind the whole of his next collection, *The Owl in the Tree* (1963). Domesticity, whether cosy and suburban, or in the general sense of the ordinariness of life for most people in England, dominates Thwaite's treatment of the major experiences of birth and death. Home stands for certainty and security:

> . . . a place
> Where nothing furious can fall
> And tear me from a sheltering wall
> And show a leering, vagrant face.
>
> Homeward I go, secure in this:
> Nothing can alter this at least,
> This house, this home, these certainties
> Which shut out, with calm thoroughness,
> The beggar, thief, and homeless beast.   ('Home Truths')

In the last poem in *The Owl in the Tree,* 'Manhood End', Thwaite describes a visit to the chapel of St Wilfred. Looking up to the roof, he notices a sixteenth-century carving of a husband and wife 'kneeling together, meant/For piety and remembrance'.

> But on their right
> I grasped with sudden shock a scene less pure —
> A naked woman, arms bound back and tight,
> And breasts thrust forward to be gnawed by great
> Pincers two men held out.

The full meaning of this emblem is unclear, but its shocking juxtaposition with the praying husband and wife speaks clearly enough:

> How we are shifted, smashed, how stones display
> The names and passions that we cannot mend.

Home, then, is a great deal more than a fanciful conceit. In a world where people are thus treated, and of which (looking back to Auden) we may be sorely tempted to 'say Alas' but feel we 'cannot help or pardon', Thwaite has come to one of his great themes: not 'I'm all right, Jack', but 'You've got it easy, haven't you?' 'Manhood End' seems to me a more interesting poem than 'Home Truths'. It represents a considerable movement on Thwaite's part towards the recognition of the usefulness of the personal, contingent nature of experience. 'Manhood End' is an act of remembering something sunk deeply within our own past. 'Home Truths' can mention a banal half-truth: 'Home Sweet Home', and then qualify but not dismiss it entirely. In his later treatment of the theme in 'Manhood End' the poem does not simply state what it is about, it enacts its meaning, makes it part of an ongoing experience and not merely an attempt to persuade.

Many of Thwaite's more recent poems emerge out of 'Manhood End'. It is the place where his long-standing passion for archaeology finally becomes usable. This, too, is a great development from *Home Truths.* Describing a visit to a Noh theatre, his main concern seems to be the clear indication that it forms no part of *his* heritage. After concluding that he felt 'ignorant and bored', he leaves. But no observation rather leaps off the page:

> All grace and knowledge are inherited
> From what our fathers did and what they said.   ('At the *Noh*')

In context, this is part of a self-examination before a sense of tradition radically different from any he has known. His conservative understanding of tradition in his mature work is deeper than Larkin's, less parochial, possessed of an historical sense, for which the plausible explanation is that Thwaite (unlike Larkin) has lived for extended periods outside England. He was lecturing in Japan between 1955 and 1957, and in Libya for a much more important stay from 1965 to 1967. The interest in archaeology has broadened considerably into a sense of the past only approached by Geoffrey Hill among his contemporaries.

Thwaite has moved steadily away from the formalism of the early 1950s, without in any way abandoning the idea that poems should be well made. (Pound to René Taupin, May 1928: 'Und uberhaupt ich stamm aus Browning. Pourquoi nier son père?') He rather mournfully relishes the idea that writing poetry well, as he does, makes him a back number, a voice in the wilderness. Anyone who talks about rhyme and strict versification, who preaches 'Erudition. Admonition. Discipline', is going to sound a little peculiar in the present literary climate. But if that is what has made possible *New Confessions,* and the power of inventive and sustained growth which that volume represents, we are going to have to think twice about what makes good poets, and then think twice again.

We turn now to the forms of dissent in the 1950s, beginning with Charles Tomlinson. One of course assumes the benevolent impact of his entrepreneurial-cum-critical activities — the Zukofsky issue of *Agenda*, and the Black Mountain issue of *The Review* (both in 1964); the sympathetic essays on Bunting (*Agenda*, Autumn 1966), Williams (*Encounter*, November 1967), and George Oppen (*Grosseteste Review*, 1973); the superbly edited collections of criticism on Marianne Moore (1969) and Williams (1972). Tomlinson is the fiercest home-grown critic of the Movement and all its progeny, a scourge of provinciality, a living recrimination to his contemporaries. Like most prophets, he can be tiresomely self-important, sometimes identifying the malaise of the age with the fate of his own message. One way or another, Tomlinson is in a class of his own. The combativeness of his approach to contemporary culture comes right out of Pound, from the programmatic certainties of Eliot and the New Critics. At times he sounds like the kind of intellectual who flowered on the Continent between the wars, the men who were attacked so eloquently by Julien Benda in *La trahison des clercs* (1927), the anti-democratic intellectuals who saw in aristocratic life the only sustaining values for an artist in an age of bourgeois materialism. Tomlinson writes of tradition, tradition as the modernists understood it, and not the patchwork of Hardy-Housman-Thomas-Graves. Yet there is little in Tomlinson, in his public pronouncements, to link him with T. S. Eliot's notorious proclamation in the preface to *For Lancelot Andrewes* (1928): 'The general point of view [of these essays] may be described as classicist in literature, royalist in politics, and anglo-catholic in religion.' A document like Tomlinson's *The Poem as Initiation* would have seemed fair game for Eliot, nosing around for even newer heresies as he had in *After Strange Gods* (1934). Despite this, the tone of Tomlinson's discontent with the degradation of bourgeois England, with the 'characteristic defilement of our time' (the demolition of an architectural heritage and the 'sacrifice of fine relationship'),[46] places him firmly with the right-wing anti-democratic intelligentsia, the reactionaries discussed in John Harrison's volume of that title: Yeats, Wyndham Lewis, Pound, Eliot, Lawrence. He might complain that such views are met on all sides by a yawning willingness to accommodate, by the maddening English habit of compromise. He doesn't want to compromise, does not believe that humanism, utilitarianism, or democracy, provide the best (or only) standards of value. Unlike the poets of his generation, from Larkin to Davie and Thwaite, who accept some version or other of conservatism, Tomlinson is more restless and radical.

Tomlinson's early work remains unpublished. 'My real enthusiasm when I left Cambridge in '48 was Walt Whitman', he told Ian Hamilton in

1964. 'I think my . . . unpublished Blake-Whitman "prophetic books",
written and illustrated in '49 had the grain of something new but they
were technically wretched. I needed cramping technically. I needed a real
obstacle.'[47] The fruit of that discipline emerged in *Relations and
Contraries,* Tomlinson's first book, published by The Hand and Flower
Press in 1951. The title was aptly selected, for it indicates the two areas of
general concern: problems of perception and meaning, and social
criticism, of which there are several biting examples. The book is alive to
symbolism and romanticism (these concerns situate Tomlinson in the
neo-romanticism of the 1930s and 1940s); there are poems dedicated to
Blake ('Peace Between Us, William Blake' and 'Variations on a Theme by
Blake') and to Yeats ('Monuments: *Variations on a theme of Yeats*'). By
'cramping' he mostly means rhyming stanzas, such as he employs in
'Liebestod' for an elaborate metaphysical conceit:

> As beams refracted from the stone
> Create the seen dimensions
> And yet in no wise they declare
> It's inner dark to outer air,
>
> Each mind mirrors each with light,
> Each other's reflex and delight,
> Though outer word is inward fiction,
> Light's truth dark's contradiction.

Tomlinson demonstrates a rather stagy Swiftian disgust,

> Love is an empty shell and sex a vent
> Through which the gods pile refuse on our earth,
> A snuff of star-fire laid in excrement.   ('Disgust')

and a highly-developed dislike of the vulgar:

> Mauve-blue mascara round the eyelid skin
> Becomes a fetish when desires no longer warm.   ('Underground')
>
> Randy queens on celluloid, sleek tarts;
> Ice-cream and nickel-odeon gems.
>
> — The poor man's pantheon . . .   ('Democracy')

When Tomlinson writes of 'the pimping usury of advertisement' in 'The
Dead', there is Pound's sanction behind the poem, the Pound of *Lustra,*
'Hugh Selwyn Mauberley' and Canto XIV. Yeats is there as well:

> Daily was holy bread;
> Each parish owned its poor
> And to this door

All came and all were fed.
Here fraternity,
No flatterer of the crowd,
In order flowed
From root up to the summit of degree.   ('Monuments')

He really means it. Writing about Yeats in an essay published in 1965, Tomlinson specifically endorses Yeats's courageous 'triumphant contempt', and his poems on the great houses of the Ascendancy:

> What, indeed, properly speaking, is Yeats's 'aristocracy' but a circle of friends, centred it may be on an hereditary figure like Lady Gregory, but essentially free of the petty tyrannies of feudal dependence? One of his aristocratic ladies wrote plays and another wrote poems. The circle of friends was a circle of artists or of promoters of the arts.

The aristocracy are O.K., then, in their manifestation as patrons of the arts. That leaves a lot of aristocrats, one might assume, to account for, but it is enough for Tomlinson that we have the 'tradition': Jonson, Carew, Herrick, Marvell, Pope. Even Pound, after a lifetime's effort to extend the meaning of tradition, was rebuked by Tomlinson in 1954: 'Whatever else we may derive from these essays [Pound's *Literary Essays,* edited by Eliot] — and Pound's comments are often of the greatest interest — the lack of centrality and the lack of any complete conception of tradition cannot but point us to the absence of the discipline of an organic literary-critical approach.'[48] Such a discipline was to be found in Cambridge English, or so Tomlinson at that time believed.

He published two further volumes in the 1950s: *The Necklace,* brought out by Oscar Mellor's Fantasy Press in 1955, and a more substantial collection, *Seeing is Believing,* in New York in 1958. Both volumes show the influence of Wallace Stevens, in Tomlinson's sense of the metaphysicality of perception, and of William Carlos Williams, in his feeling for the moral weight residing in the sheer existence of 'things', the non-human. The relationship between Tomlinson and the two American poets is crucial to his subsequent development, and deserves treatment in greater detail than is possible here. It is hard, I think, to claim the greatest originality for Tomlinson. He has perfected a style, but not invented one, assimilating a spectrum of apparently contradictory tendencies.

In January 1957 he published a review of D. J. Enright's *Poets of the 1950s* in *Poetry.* His verdict on the poets collected together by Enright, who were quickly to become the Movement, is stunningly harsh. They represent a new *Kulturbolschewismus,* a hostility to tradition, which Tomlinson deplores: ' . . . Amis and Larkin display an inadequate sense of civilized values . . .', Conquest does not 'wait for the revelation' but 'for the chance to secrete his reflections on to the landscape'. 'Poetry can surely be moderate, elegant, humane,' he writes,

> . . . as the poets of the fifties variously demand. It must also be *le pain spirituel, amor intellectualis Dei,* even if it expresses only delight in the shapes, colors, and textures of the created universe. Such spiritual realities the poets of the fifties seem all too willing to forgo, in their compromise of moderation with the world as they find it.

A somewhat better-known version of Tomlinson's case appeared as 'The Middlebrow Muse' in *Essays in Criticism* in April 1957. Here he blames Larkin's 'intense parochialism', and generally the failure of any of these poets to 'escape beyond the suburban mental ratio which they impose on experience', on a 'debased form of humanism':

> They show a singular want of vital awareness of the continuum outside themselves, of the mystery bodied over against them in the created universe, which they fail to experience with any degree of sharpness or to embody with any instress or sensuous depth.

Tomlinson saw himself as the anti-type of the Movement poets. 'Thus Mr Amis', he notes with prim displeasure, 'according to *The [Daily] Express,* opts for blondes, billiards, bars and progressive jazz-clubs. Mr Larkin abominates Mozart, never goes abroad, is a mild xenophobe. The beer mug (we learn from the *[Times] Educational Supplement)* "is never far from Mr Wain's hand".' Nothing from that lot about *le pain spirituel* or even *amor intellectualis Dei.* Tomlinson was not, then, a sad heart in the supermarket, but an angry one, outraged by poets who (he felt) were deliberately letting down the side. The Tomlinson regimen involved less literary democracy, and a 'redirection away from the constricted world of the merely social that was becoming so deadening for English verse'.[49]

Tomlinson wanted a poetry adequate to a complex perception of the finite nature of man, the complete otherness of nature, and of the proper, indeed moral, burden of perception. He writes in the fine poem 'A Meditation on John Constable' in *Seeing is Believing* of 'the labour of observation', registering Constable's light, the play of cloud, sun and the movement of wind:

> . . . what he saw
> Discovered what he was, and the hand — unswayed
> By the dictation of a single sense —
> Bodied the accurate and total knowledge
> In a calligraphy of present pleasure.

Tomlinson's powers of description are considerable:

> Massed darks

> Blotting it back, scattered and mellowed shafts
>   Break damply out of them, until the source
> Unmasks, floods its retreating bank
>   With raw fire.

The central terms are *illusions, persuade, convince* and *accept*: the illusions of art persuade or convince, but are not complete until we accept them unreservedly:

> . . . their deft restrictions
> Convince, as the index of a possible passion,
>   As the adequate gauge, both of the passion
> And its object.

In the earlier poem from *The Necklace,* 'Observation of Facts', he put the relation on a simpler level:

> Facts have no eyes. One must
> Surprise them, as one surprises a tree
> By regarding its (shall I say?)
> Facets of copiousness.

'A Meditation on John Constable' and 'Observation of Facts' carry the whole of Tomlinson's poetic. The 'deft restrictions', the business of counting syllables or the steady effort to maintain a rhyme scheme, become part of a ritualization of art, a mode of meditation, to delay or disjoint a process or observation of an act (Tomlinson's celebrated 'Swimming Chenango Lake' is an example) 'to make the consciousness pause over the stages of the act. It meditates an event while taking a grip on external reality and attempting to adjust the consciousness to that reality'.[50] The natural world seems a great deal more 'real' for Tomlinson than do the people who, from time to time, enter the landscape. Despite this, *American Scenes* (1966) and *The Way In* (1974) contain some brilliant character sketches. It is that desire 'not to try to reduce objects to our own image, but to respect their otherness and yet find our way into contact with that otherness', as he observed in *The Poem as Initiation,* which so remarkably sets his work apart. It is a very pure, scrupulous poetry, affording a narrow but intense kind of pleasure.

If Tomlinson suggests an antithesis to the Movement, the antithesis to Tomlinson was Theodore Roethke. He was an older man, but early on sensed that the tidy gentility of formalism was a dead end. Roethke's major contribution comes before the full expression of dissent in the middle of the decade, but reminds us that the alternatives to formalism, latent or manifest, were frequently as hostile to each other as they were to formalism.

For most of his working life, Theodore Roethke was a teacher as well as a poet. The combination suited him exceptionally well, and he is remembered as a dedicated and sensitive teacher. His professional career effectively coincided with the canonization of Eliot as 'international hero', the incorporation of the modernist movement into the mainstream of English and American literature, and the arrival of the New Critics. Roethke watched all three developments with growing unease. As early as February 1934 he wrote, 'I'm tired of all this Eliot-Pound worship. Eliot's a good poet, but there are others.'[51] A decade later Roethke chose the sympathetic ear of William Carlos Williams for the complaint that 'the conceptual boys are too much in the saddle: anything observed or simple or sensuous or personal is suspect right now. Anything with images equals Imagism equals Old Hat.' Although Williams's personal relations with a wide variety of critics were amicable, he too expressed deep-seated distaste for the 'whole "enlightened" group, the self-elevated masters of our world of poetry today . . . with whom . . . I grow wearier and wearier, since from them I get not a breath of anything new . . .'[52] This is a theme running through *Paterson*:

> . . . clerks
> got out of hand forgetting for the most part
> to whom they are beholden.
>
> spitted on fixed concepts like
> roasting pigs, sputtering, their drip sizzling
> in the fire   (Book I, part iii)

Roethke's attitude was even more explicit. He complained in a letter in 1948 about 'the dreary text-creepers, the constipated agrarians, and the other enemies of life'; this theme spilled over into his notebooks: 'Moan somewhere else, text-creepers.'[53] In his superb essay 'The Age of Criticism' Randall Jarrell uses the visit of a pig to a bacon-judging contest who was impatiently shooed away ('Go away, pig: What do you know about bacon?') to illustrate the changed relationship between poet and critic. Roethke, Williams and others yearned for justice — Snowball and Napoleon organizing the barnyard revolt.

During the 1930s Roethke was vaguely leftish, a fellow-traveller, a reader of *New Masses* who pronounced himself willing to join the League of American Writers. He boasted in a letter of having placed a poem 'with mildly revolutionary implications' with the *Sewanee Review* (appearing as 'Sign Though No Sign' in the January-March 1938 issue). He steered clear of any closer involvement with Popular Front literary politics, and published not in the *New Masses* but, willy-nilly, in the best English and American journals. Roethke cultivated the right literary editors, craved praise, longed for recognition, in what are among the most painful letters in American literature.

Despite the significant vein of satire and social criticism running through his first book, *Open House* (1941), which proclaimed its roots in the 1930s, there was another, more personal note — or at least the desire for a personal voice:

> I'm naked to the bone
> With nakedness my shield.   ('Open House')

Roethke achieves some of his best effects with images, physical signs of psychological unease:

> You feel disaster climb the vein.
>
> There's canker at the root, your seed
> Denies the blessing of the sun,
> The light essential to your need.   ('Feud')

The substance of the poem is a state of mind, 'chill depths of the spirit', a personal history, a pathology. 'The Premonition' contains a particularly vivid moment when an unexpected disturbance of water causes the reflected image of his father to disappear. The early Roethke is something of a formalist, with tidy stanzas and accomplished rhymes; but the real energy of these poems comes through their images, gestures, signs, spirits, echoes. The faculty of reason becomes part of the problem:

> Sometimes the blood is privileged to guess
> The things the eye or hand cannot possess.   ('The Signals')

'I'll deliver you, dear doves, out of the rational, into the realm of pure song' (*Notebook*, p. 207). In 'Epidermal Macabre' he pronounces himself willing to dispense with 'fake accoutrements of sense'. In this Roethke was with Yeats and Lawrence, 'blood-thinkers', critics of a desolating rationality. Roethke proposed an 'open house' at the most fundamental levels: he implied access to the personal when Eliot's doctrine of impersonality, and the donnish notion that it was heretical to pursue an author's intention, were tantamount to holy writ. Beyond that, Roethke wanted access to the deepest recesses of personality, sensibility and psychic energy — and even beyond that to the primal roots of growth, nurture and biological existence. Kenneth Burke captures the right note in his essay 'The Vegetal Radicalism of Theodore Roethke', published in *The Sewanee Review* of January 1950, and Roethke thanked him for it: 'I can only say that I never expected during my own life, that close and perceptive a reading.' Yet, for all that, *Open House* served merely to hint at Roethke's direction.

Things began to come right for Roethke with a group of short poems which were published immediately after the war. He had tried out the manner as early as 'The Minimal' in *Harper's Bazaar,* November 1942. Then 'Carnations', 'Flower Dump', and 'Child on Top of a Greenhouse' appeared in *The New Republic* in early February 1946, followed within the month by 'Moss-Gathering' and 'Weed Puller'. 'Old Florist' appeared in the same month as *Harper's Magazine.* When Roethke collected the sequence in *The Lost Son and Other Poems,* published by John Lehmann in London in 1948 (of his contemporaries only Richard Eberhart, who had studied at Cambridge and published in *Cambridge Poetry 1929* and *New Signatures* in 1932, had an independent English public and publisher), the effect was stunning. There was nothing at all like these poems in American literature. The central fact of the poems was the greenhouse, a large commercial enterprise founded by Roethke's grandfather in Saginaw, Michigan, which had many acres under glass. Roethke appears to have had some of his most intense childhood experiences there, and he gave it a full burden of symbolic and erotic meaning as 'a kind of man-made Avalon, Eden, or paradise' (letter to Burke, 27 February 1945). The greenhouse was an intensification of nature, where an artificially stimulated growth ran wild. It was, as advertised, 'the largest and most complete floral establishment in Michigan', but it remained a profoundly ambivalent symbol in Roethke's imagination:

> What was the greenhouse? It was a jungle, and it was paradise; it was order and disorder: Was it an escape? No, for it was a reality harsher than reality. (*Notebook*, p. 150)

Roethke recalled its self-sufficient completeness; it was a 'world', a remarkably auspicious place for a young poet to grow up in. The greenhouse was the great stage for his father, Otto, about whom there is a delicate, subdued poem in *The Far Field* (1964). Otto Roethke was a complex figure, with the traditional Prussian love of order and insistence upon discipline. All this, Roethke wrote to Kenneth Burke in 1949, he had sublimated 'into a love for, and a creating of the beautiful (the flowers)'.

The greenhouse poems are literally bursting with life:

> . . . still the delicate slips keep coaxing up water;
> The small cells bulge.   ('Cuttings')

> Nothing would give up life:
> Even the dirt kept breathing a small breath.   ('Root Cellar')

Despite this, the poems are not celebrations. The restlessness of growth, uncontrolled, reaches Roethke:

> I can hear, underground, that sucking and sobbing,
> In my veins, in my bones I feel it, —   ('Cuttings (*later*)')

and it leaves him depressed, even disgusted:

> All pulse with the knocking pipes
> That drip and sweat,
> Sweat and drip,
> Swelling the roots with steam and stench,
> Shooting up lime and dung and ground bones, —
>   ('Forcing House')

He is intensely there, in the landscape or groping among the roots and plant life. Nothing could be further from Tomlinson, abusing Conquest for 'secreting' his reflections on the landscape. Roethke's response is to a nature whose richness, confusion and power seems overwhelmingly real:

> . . . dank as a ditch,
> Bulbs broke out of boxes hunting for chinks in the dark,
> Shoots dangled and drooped,
> Lolling obscenely from mildewed crates . . .   ('Root Cellar')

In 'Weed Puller' Roethke carefully balances the sense of 'perverse life' running rampant with unabated sexual suggestiveness, and the aggression demanded of himself, 'hacking', 'digging', 'yanking', 'tugging'. The 'fetor' of weeds, tangled roots and soft rubble, are what he struggles against. The contact with nature which was imposed on Roethke from an early age was anything but sensitive or appreciative. In a greenhouse there was precious little time to 'fart around' with sunsets, like Wordsworth. He must learn to impose his will, act decisively and violently, become a repressed authoritarian — become his father, in effect. It left Roethke with 'the sense of being defiled'.[54]

The first half-dozen lines of 'Moss-Gathering' describe precisely the physical process of taking a piece of moss in both hands and lifting a sizable chunk clear. The poem breaks in half at this point, going on to describe Roethke's reaction to what he has done — a sense of loss, meanness, defilement, and even desecration. There is something rather awkward in this, not so much false as something that seems rather too obviously planned. The wonderfully acute description with which the poem begins is made to seem merely the pretext or occasion which enables Roethke to say something whose ultimate source has nothing to do with gathering moss. The conjunction of description and emotion here seems rather crude and mechanical, and suggests the limitation of the greenhouse poems as a whole. The greenhouse was too artificial, too carefully planned, effectively to release Roethke's immense powers of intuition. He needed a landscape less structured, less immediately burdened with textbook symbolic meanings.

Roethke's breakthrough came in an untitled series of longish poems in free verse which he published between 1947 and 1952. Their full significance has been obscured by the circumstances of their publication. Some appeared in *The Lost Son* in 1948 and the rest in *Praise to the End!* in 1951. One poem was added, and the sequence was presented as an integral whole, in *The Waking* (1953), and this arrangement was retained for *Words for the Wind* (1957). But with the posthumous *Collected Poems* of 1966, edited by Roethke's wife Beatrice, the sequence was broken up, with a brief note to that effect. The transition between *The Lost Son* and *The Far Field* is now a great deal harder to follow. By disrupting the sequence, Roethke's most extraordinary achievement is left in a disconcerting critical limbo. The poems I am referring to are 'The Lost Son', 'The Long Alley', 'A Field of Light', 'The Shape of Fire', 'Praise to the End', 'Unfold! Unfold!', 'I Cry, Love! Love!', 'O, Thou Opening, O'. In this sequence Roethke was writing with a freedom, an openness, an intuitive gaiety, which is one of the great achievements of contemporary American verse. They are utterly unique, pure Roethke. W. D. Snodgrass, who describes these poems as 'the wildest and most experimental poetry of the period', cautiously remarks that 'even now, many years since these poems appeared, I do not feel that I really understand them, or feel certain how ultimately successful they are'.[55]

'The Lost Son', alone among the poems in the sequence, can be said to possess a structure, and Burke's reading of it seems definitive. One can only see the sequence as constituting a massive, implicit rejection of structure as such, a rebuke to the fetishism of structure in the age of triumphant formalism. He was later to go back on this, but here, at least, he found a style which collected energy to itself, and grew quickly and surely into a flow of perceptions and intuitions taking us into his own consciousness. It is not the confessional, self-parodying, mannered style of middle Lowell and late Plath. Some aspects of Roethke's view of things are familiar, such as his attitude towards reason:

> Reason? That dreary shed, that hutch for grubby schoolboys!
> The hedgewren's song says something else.
> I care for a cat's cry and the hugs, live as water.
> I've traced these words in sand with a vestigial tail;
> Now the gills are beginning to cry.
> Such a sweet noise: I can't sleep for it.
> Bless me and the maze I'm in!
> Hello, thingy spirit.   ('I Cry, Love! Love!')

The song of the hedgewren, cry of a cat, noise of gills, open our way to the cacophonous presence of nature, and of Roethke's rapt attention. He recalls at one point that 'I've been asleep in a bower of dead skin' ('Praise to the End!'), but he has opened himself completely to the natural world.

> Listen, love,
> The fat lark sang in the field;
> I touched the ground, the ground warmed by the killdeer,
> The salt laughed and the stones;
> The ferns had their ways, and the pulsing lizards.
> And the new plants, still awkward in their soil,
> The lovely diminutives.
> I could watch! I could watch!
> I saw the separateness of all things! ('The Long Alley')

Sylvia Plath, in an autobiographical sketch written for the B.B.C., half-consciously echoed Roethke: 'As from a star I saw, coldly and soberly, the *separateness* of everything. I felt the wall of my skin: I am I. That stone is a stone. My beautiful fusion with the things of this world was over.'[56] Roethke did not share Plath's louring sense of alienation. The discovery of the separateness of things was for him an act of homage so elemental, so decisive, as to impart sheer delight. This passage continues:

> My heart lifted up with the great grasses;
> The weeds believed me, the nesting birds.
> There were clouds making a rout of shapes crossing a windbreak of
>   cedars,
> And a bee shaking drops from a rain-soaked honeysuckle.
> The worms were delighted as wrens.
> And I walked through the light air;
> I moved with the morning.

As early as 'The Light Comes Brighter' in *Open House,* Roethke had shown fine powers of descriptive writing, which were enhanced by the massive effort of sheer observation in the greenhouse poems from *The Lost Son.* There is a slight loss here of specific description, but an enormously effective sense of ensemble — the cumulative effect of a multitude of observations, some quite general ('the ferns', 'the weeds', 'the worms') as well as the kind of close detail at which Roethke excels: the ground warmed by the killdeer, the rain dropping from the honeysuckle. The only poetry at all like this in American literature is Whitman's; Roethke's achievement is more emphatic, more brilliant, though without Whitman's sweeping perspective. Roethke's presence is so complete and unreserved that he might almost be aiming deliberately at harnessing a faculty of observation every bit as precise as Tomlinson's to a totally different poetic. Roethke's poetry of this period constitutes a kind of risk that even Whitman, content to compile his objects or observe his landscapes from a greater distance, did not often take. They are locutions, words spoken — not *in* nature, not dramatic monologues, but emotions recollected in 'perpetual agitation'. The address is almost always to the reader and not — how easy the absurdity — to the plants and animals themselves.

> I believe! I believe! —
> In the sparrow, happy on the gravel;
> In the winter-wasp, pulsing its wings in the sunlight;
> I have been somewhere else; I remember the sea-faced uncles.
>
> ('Praise to the End!')

When he (infrequently) does speak softly to the animals, it is out of an excess of love. Their separateness entitles them to a civil address:

> Arch of air, my heart's original knock,
> I'm awake all over:
> I've crawled from the mire, alert as a saint or a dog;
> I know the back-stream's joy, and the stone's eternal pulseless
> longing.
> Felicity I cannot hoard.
> My friend, the rat in the wall, brings me the clearest messages;
> I bask in the bower of change;
> The plants wave me in, and the summer apples;
> My palm-sweat flashes gold;
> Many astounds before, I lost my identity to a pebble;
> The minnows love me, and the humped and spitting creatures.
>
> ('Praise to the End!')

These poems do not possess a form, or structure; there is no plot, no narrative or dramatic situation. They simply move from image to image, with nothing more than the fecundity of Roethke's sensibility, and the fineness of his eye, to give them shape. Inevitably, they are remarkably alike. What makes them unique is a discovered voice, and a way of using that new-found freedom of movement with a system of rapidly shifting metrical stresses. The last poem in the sequence, 'O, Thou Opening, O', which appeared in *Poetry* in October 1952, carries the dominant mood of exaltation:

> I'm twinkling like a twig!
> The lark's my heart!
> I'm wild with news!
> My fancy's white!
> I am my faces,
> Love.

A return to traditional versification, Roethke's old *bête noir,* was first signalled by 'Elegy for Jane' in *The Kenyon Review* in 1950. This is either

113

a deeply-felt poem of the purest sentiment, or sickly, gauche and sentimental; it is a poem of considerable emotional opacity. It suggests one thing, certainly, that the intuitive, joyous freedom of his verse at this period was at loggerheads with the studied formality of the elegiac tone. 'Four for Sir John Davies', a homage to Davies's philosophic nature poem, *Orchestra, or, a Poem on Dancing* (1596), is a further attempt on Roethke's part to find a measure at once slower, more formal and a great deal more solemn, and to move away from the warmth of 'My Papa's Waltz' and the impulsiveness of

> Alone, I kissed the skin of stone;
> Marrow-soft, danced in the sand.   ('A Field of Light')

Roethke's account of the composition of the poem, written some eleven years later, tells us that it came at the end of 'a longish dry period' which signalled a crisis in his career. He had been reading the sixteenth-century poets Ralegh and Davies, and studying the five-beat line, when the first part of 'Four for Sir John Davies', 'The Dance', and the presence of Yeats, suddenly confirmed the availability of 'the poets dead', and in a way helped to bolster Roethke's sense of his own identity, deeply shaken by his inability to write. The experience of psychic visitation galvanized Roethke, and led to much of his late work where the influence of Yeats, and of course the Eliot of *The Four Quartets,* is persistently present. That his last book, the posthumous *The Far Field,* was a great success (over 35,000 copies of the American edition were printed between 1964 and 1967) was no more than due homage; the poetry, however, is more diffuse and tired than in his earlier books. The psychic visitation and reanimation which he experienced may have been real to him but have nothing to do with the judgments which we make about his verse. Roethke's literary collapse was as sudden as MacNeice's, though from a pinnacle of considerably greater originality. It may never be possible to explain with any certainty its causes. (Roethke's comments don't actually explain what happened to his poetry.)[57] We are left with a return to formalism, the dark lorelei of Plath's poem, come to 'sing/Of a world more full and clear/Than can be'.[58]

Roethke's ambition was too close (but not *that* close) to traditional lyric poetry to raise the question of form in contemporary poetry. Two major poems of the postwar period, William Carlos Williams's *Paterson* and Charles Olson's *The Maximus Poems,* both of which come in the expansive wake of Ezra Pound's *Cantos,* suggest how remarkable a phenomenon is the Poundian long poem. When modernism was felt, at last, to be finished, the re-emergence of a primary type of modernist ambition may need some explaining. One might say that there is a 'moment' for the Poundian long poem: the primary condition is a period of cultural contraction, when either through external constraints such as war or censorship, or through the appearance of a new and confident orthodoxy, certain kinds of energies, certain subjects, are driven underground, repressed, or denied access to the customary modes of publication. There is a sense of persecution and neglect, of dislocation, anomie, and a bitter feeling that the energies of society have been misdirected. Sometimes social change is blamed, or capitalism, or urbanization, or industrialization, or even tendencies in thought; the 'dissociation of sensibility' which Eliot located in the seventeenth century is one classic formulation. Part of the desire of the suppressed victims is to revive, or reconstruct, older modes of thought or patterns of life (Olson's *polis*) which have been abandoned or discredited by the advance of rationalism, or utilitarianism, or pragmatism. They want to identify in the past the roots of the present malaise, and in this their quarrel is with history: they want to rewrite our consciousness of the past in order to remake our consciousness in the present. Poetry like this seems to be written when the avowed values of society, as expressed in its dominant culture, seem intolerably at variance with the way a particular group tend to see themselves, and their place in society. Often enough, the real argument is with the advanced capitalism of the West, against which mysticism or primitivism will be juxtaposed. But by declaring anathema the customary tools of analysis, the poems without exception surrender the capacity to speak at a level roughly corresponding to 'the enemy'. The terms of Olson, in particular his 'pejorocracy' (the rule of the worst), act as a ju-ju, a mystical charm, or else as a sheer term of abuse; the poem has, when we put it down, no place in the real world where distinctions like that are a little harder to make.

In the 1930s William Carlos Williams, winner of the Dial Award in 1926 and the Guarantor's Prize in 1931, was a neglected and isolated figure. He wrote to Pound on 15 March 1933:

> What shall you say about me? That I have a volume of verse which I have been in the process of making for the past ten years, that it is the best collection of verse in America today and that I can't find a publisher — while, at the same time, every Sunday literary supplement has pages of book titles representing the poetry of my contemporaries . . . No doubt it means that my conception is not that of my contemporaries, either in the academies or out.[59]

Things had begun to look up for Pound ('After a decade's delay Faber apparently is trying to get my stuff into print . . .', he wrote to John Drummond from Rapallo in May 1933), after a long period of neglect; Williams was confirming the same old story about America that Pound had known for years. Williams was forced to give his new material to little presses, one-man operations, with little chance of financial reward. He sent a collection of stories to Angel Flores for the Dragon Press in 1932. A group of young disciples, Louis Zukofsky, Charles Reznikoff and George Oppen, published *A Novelette and Other Prose* in the same year as TO Publishers, with a new name, The Objectivist Press, they issued Williams's *Collected Poems* in 1934. The Alcestis Press published two collections of Williams's verse in 1935 and 1936 (in editions of 165 copies each). For two decades Williams had seen in the rootless cosmopolitanism of *The Waste Land* an unmitigated disaster for American letters; he was scarcely more sympathetic to the kind of poetry which was being publically fêted in America (MacLeish, Robert Hillyer, Audrey Wurdmann, Robert Coffin and Frost won the Pulitzer prize for poetry between 1933 and 1937). Williams was without a regular publisher until the advent of James Laughlin's New Directions in 1937.

He remained outside the mainstream of American literary life in the 1930s, and played no role in Popular Front literary politics. After considering a special issue of *Contact* devoted to communist writing, Williams wrote to Nathanael West that, 'All we'll get by a Communist issue is a reputation for radicalism and not for good writing – which is our real aim' (14 July 1932). He wrote to Kay Boyle later in 1932 that

> ... poetry is related to poetry, not to social statutes. It will, nevertheless, make its form of what it finds. And so does seem to be a social eye. It is nothing of the sort. It remains itself. It remains related only to poetry.

Williams was completely resistant to the Marxist idea of committed or propagandist poetry. His clearest statement on the politics of American culture comes in a letter to the editors of the *Partisan Review* in April 1936. He describes Marxism as something fundamentally alien to the American tradition. The 'deep-seated ideals' behind American democracy are, no matter how often abused, identified with a certain good humour and pragmatic self-confidence. 'My opinion is that our revolutionary literature is merely tolerated by most Americans, that it is definitely in conflict with our deep-seated ideals.' The conclusions which Williams arrived at during the 1930s were, in a sense, alternatives 'in the American grain' to the revolutionary and proletarian literature of the *New Masses*. Williams looked back, without much enthusiasm, to an older American tradition, that of Walt Whitman: 'Whitman was never able fully to realize the significance of his structural innovations. As a result he fell back to the overstuffed catalogues of his later poems and a sort of looseness that was not freedom but lack of measure. Selection, structural selection was lacking.'[60] When he surveyed modern American poetry, he thought highly of the work of Cummings, Wallace Stevens, and Marianne Moore, but only Pound, among his contemporaries, really mattered: 'Pound is one of the few moderns worth reading . . . I don't think that he has solved anything for us. His line is a classic adaptation, no more' (letter to Kay Boyle, 1932). He concludes, in the same letter, with a verdict which he never seriously questioned: 'there is no workable poetic form extant among us today'.

Williams's feeling for the survival of 'deep-seated ideals' recalls an earlier America, the gaiety of Pound's imagined *risorgimento* of 1912 in *Patria Mia* and the bustling energies of Greenwich Village before America entered the war. Williams was, temperamentally, a large-minded man, a liberal in the American parlance. He was more attuned to the implications of modern science than any of his literary contemporaries, and seems to have absorbed its promise. 'We live in a new world, pregnant with tremendous possibility for enlightenment', he wrote to one correspondent. By the late 1930s, and in particular in an essay entitled 'Against the Weather', which appeared in Dorothy Norman's *Twice a Year* in 1939, some of the essential Williams ideas appear: the crucial importance of structure; a hint at the concept of measure; and the rejection of symbolism. But it was not until he had begun writing *Paterson* that Williams, who was then in his mid-sixties, expressed in 'The Poem as a Field of Action' (a lecture given at the University of Washington in 1948) the importance of an art fully adequate to the modern world. Social and economic changes were affecting every aspect of life. Only in the structure of poetry have these changes been ignored. Traditional metrics began with the idea of the fixed foot: 'I am sure the attack must be concentrated on the *rigidity of the poetic foot*' (*Essays*, p. 289).

> Thus from being fixed, our prosodic values should rightly be seen as only relatively true. Einstein had the speed of light as a constant — his only constant — What have we?

Williams saw the basis for an adequate response to the contemporary world to be rooted in a technical revolution in poetry:

> Set the overall proposal of an enlarged technical means — in order to liberate the possibilities of depicting reality in a modern world that has seen more if not felt more than in the past — in order to be *able* to feel more . . .

The concept of 'measure' is one of the most elusive categories in modern poetics. Williams intended by it a way of escaping from the fixities of traditional poetic forms, such as the sonnet, 'a form which does not admit of the slightest structural change in its composition', and as a way of escaping from the idea that the five-foot, five-accent, ten-syllable line was 'natural' to English speech, and prosody. Measure in turn suggested verse composition in 'open formation' and the 'variable foot'. The example of Whitman warned against 'a sort of looseness that was not freedom but lack of measure', and Williams insisted upon the close identification of measure with discipline and selection; but always a new discipline, adequate to the new reality. He spelled this out in 'On Measure — Statement for Cid Corman' in 1954:

> The very grounds for our beliefs have altered. We do not live that way any more; nothing in our lives, at bottom, is ordered according to that measure; our social concepts, our schools, our very religious ideas, certainly our understanding of mathematics are greatly altered.
> *(Essays,* p. 337)

Although Williams decisively rejected the Marxist interpretation of the relation of literature to society, he sees that there *is* a connection, and that measure is the crucial test of the adequacy of the response. Writing to Kay Boyle in 1932, Williams suggested that poetic form in the next ten years 'will take its shape from the character of its age'; and this was the burden of his *In the American Grain* (1925), a brilliant collection of prose imitations, in which he looks closely at the forms of prose, and hence at the forms of individual's response, to the experience of America. Measure, then, is not in Williams's definition merely a new system of metrics, or a 'technique' in the narrow sense. It was above all an index of the way contemporary writers understood modern society. Despite his insistence upon the local meaning of culture (he often quoted John Dewey on discovering the universal in the local), it is worth insisting that measure did not correspond to a provincialism or an imitation of a dialect. Einstein and Heisenberg had as much to say about the condition of modern life for Williams as did Major C. H. Douglas and Leo Frobenius for Pound. Williams might have been uncomfortable at the term, but he was an intellectual, an advanced thinker, and a man of scientific training. Pound, who was none of these things, makes a great to-do about science, and treated Williams condescendingly as a small-town New Jersey doctor. It says a lot about Pound; but even more about Williams that he should have come to Pound's aid when he was accused of treason.

The evolution of Williams's thought has been considered at some length, at the expense of a more extended treatment of the poem *Paterson.* It was his doctrine, rather than his practice, that seems to have exerted the stronger influence. When he talks about a poetry adequate to modern life, this means something quite literal and practical in *Paterson*:

> Things, things unmentionable,
> the sink with the waste farina in it and
> lumps of rancid meat, milk-bottle tops: have

> here a tranquility and loveliness
> Have here (in his thoughts)
> a complement tranquil and chaste[61]

A feeling for the domestic geography of the poor, their houses, trees and streets, informs Williams's most notorious statement:

> — Say it, no ideas but in things —

The passage continues:

> nothing but the blank faces of the houses
> and cylindrical trees
> bent, forked by preconception and accident —   (*Paterson*, p. 15)

By this Williams means something rather less barbarous than his hostile critics have assumed. When Eliot uses the phrase 'objective correlative' in the 1919 essay on *Hamlet*, he refers to 'a set of objects, a situation, a chain of events which shall be the formula of that particular emotion'. Williams narrows the meaning of Eliot's formulation because he is not thinking about dramatic or theatrical mimesis, but he does not reject it: he is worried, it seems, about the possible consequences of turning the observed and actual into a symbol, into an idea, instead of allowing its existence to express its own meaning. This is what Williams contributes to a poetry of the real. He has not abdicated the function of poet to the compiler of random catalogues. The measure which enables him to speak of 'things unmentionable' also frees him to make a contradictory but intensely sympathetic judgment upon the scene. He (the poet) detects beauty in the random squalor of the ordinary lives of people. *Paterson* is a massive celebration of that process of detection and sympathy:

> It is summer! stinking summer
>
> Escape from it — but not by running
> away. Not by 'composition'. Embrace the
> foulness
>   — the being taut, balanced
> eternities   (*Paterson*, p. 126)

The poem is, naturally, a great deal more than this. Like Pound, Williams uses historical documents, personal letters, personal reminiscences, as well as a large quantity of mythical and anecdotal material, to support a complex structure of meaning. The city, Paterson, is also a man; the history of a community is the lives of its citizens. It is ultimately about the survival of the *local* as a meaningful reality in American life — something which the great personal mobility of the people, and the increasing uniformity of the society (the same goods in the shops, the same

119

programmes on television, the same kind of education, the same political context), has made less likely as the century goes on.

The form of the poem suggests two things: that Williams has not, any more than had Pound, found a way to control and organize his material; and that the attempt to organize this kind of material was a contradiction in terms. Williams quotes a passage directly to this point from J. A. Symonds's *Studies of the Greek Poets*:

> ... by their acceptance of this halting meter, the Greeks displayed their acute aesthetic sense of propriety, recognizing the harmony which subsists between crabbed verses and distorted subjects with which they dealt — the vices and perversions of humanity — as well as their argument with the snarling spirit of the satirist. Deformed verse was suited to deformed morality. *(Paterson, p. 53)*

But 'deformed verse' wasn't much like 'literature', as seen from the academies; so much the worse for 'literature' says Williams:

> Doctor, do you believe in
> 'the people', the Democracy? Do
> you still believe — in this
> swill-hole of corrupt cities?
> Do you, Doctor? Now?
>
> Give up
> the poem. Give up the shilly-
> shally of art.
>
> What can you, what
> can YOU hope to conclude —
> on a heap of dirty linen? *(Paterson, p. 132)*

I think that in the end Williams felt that literature didn't come to conclusions. That the fact, the thing, and its correct perception, were sufficient unto themselves. He had no instinct for the ways in which things were established in relations, social or political. Such relations as do exist in *Paterson* have little power of analysis behind them. He simply couldn't imagine an America in which 'things', and men, were no longer discrete and independent.

Despite being named as heir presumptive, along with Allen Ginsberg, when extracts from 'Projective Verse' appeared in Williams's *Autobiography* in 1951, Charles Olson was harshly critical of *Paterson*. 'By making his substance historical of one city (the Joyce deal)', Olson wrote to Robert Creeley in March 1951 (*Mayan Letters*, 1953, No. 5),

> Bill completely licks himself, lets time roll him under as Ez does not, and thus ... contributes nothing, in fact, delays, deters, and

hampers, by not having busted through the very problem which Ez has so brilliantly faced & beat.

Olson is more specific later in the same letter. Williams was writing about a 'blueberry America' that had disappeared by 1917. (The significance of the date is unclear: it was the year when *Prufrock* was published, and when the U.S. entered the war; it was also the year when the Russian revolution began, but this can hardly be on Olson's mind). 'Bill, with all respects, don't know fr nothing abt what a city *is*'. Williams found much in 'Projective Verse' which gave him cause to hope. He wrote to Creeley: 'I share your excitement . . . It's the sort of thing we are after and must have . . .'[62] Williams introduces the essay in his *Autobiography* as 'an advance of estimable proportions', a phrase which communicates some small reservation; but it constituted an astonishing recognition for a poet whose output at that time was very small, and whose work was almost entirely unknown. (Olson's brilliant study of Melville, *Call Me Ishmael,* was published in 1947, when Melville studies were still at the stage of primitive accumulation. Since that time, the only reaction to his verse had come from Creeley, writing in the *Montevallo Review* in 1951.) The status today of 'Projective Verse' is uncertain. There always has been an element which regarded Olson as an out-and-out charlatan. From a rather unexpected source, Donald Davie, the essay was described as 'the most ambitious and intelligent attempt by a poet of today to take his bearings, and plot his future course, by his sense of what Pound's achievement amounts to — Pound's and also Williams's' (*Ezra Pound: Poet and Sculptor,* 1964). Marjorie Perloff, in a paper in *English Literary History* (Summer 1973), has looked quite closely at the claims for originality made for Olson's ideas. She argues that 'his main deviation from the Pound-Williams aesthetic is that he muddles their concepts'. ' "Projective Verse," ' she writes, is 'essentially a scissors-and-paste job, a clever but confused collage made up of bits and pieces of Pound, Fenollosa, Gaudier-Brzeska, Williams, and Creeley.' There are other charges to be made against Olson: that he could be pompous, obscure, contradictory, pretentious and a bully. Martin Duberman considers such criticisms in his fine study *Black Mountain: An Exploration into Community* (1972), which contains a notably sympathetic account of Olson's role at the experimental college, but asks, 'What do they come to, other than fallibility?' I think Olson's critics are complaining about his *refusal* to consider his own fallibility; a little humility diverts a lot of criticism.

The major propositions contained in 'Projective Verse' have by now passed from the familiar to the banal:

> . . . the poem itself must, at all points, be a high energy-construct and at all points, an energy-discharge . . .

Form is never more than an extension of content.

One perception must immediately and directly lead to a further perception.

These ideas give 'permission', in Robert Duncan's sense, for a lot of contemporary poetry. There is nothing in Olson which corresponds to Williams's insistence that discipline and selection are integral parts of measure. Olson opens the door for an endless poetry, in which ideas of construction and ensemble have no place. It says a great deal about how thoroughly the values of formalism were discredited that 'Projective Verse' should have played the role which it historically has. One of the chief consequences of Olsonian openness has been the creation of a literature that is hermetic and 'easy': as Simpson put it in *The Nation* (24 April 1967): 'This school has a system of breathing and using the typewriter that will enable anyone to write poetry naturally, without thinking.' There is no place in Olson's essay for the question of audience; it betrays more clearly than anything else in his work the distorting effects of isolation and neglect. That Olson should erect Pound's contempt for the philistinism of Edwardian England into an aesthetic principle shows that Olson had advanced no further than Pound in his thinking about the relationship of a writer to the society in which he lived. Olson's prose style, so hopelessly self-indulgent and rebarbative, says as much, if not more.

Variously in pamphlets, letters, essays, and in his lectures and readings, Olson presents himself as a man who draws sustenance not from other poets or from literature, but from 'thinkers' like Alfred North Whitehead, whose *Process and Reality* is one of the most heavily annotated volumes in Olson's library, [63] and from others — historians, linguists, geologists, morphologists, who helped take Olson back to the earliest stages of civilization to locate a permanent· basis for the 'real'; the alternatives could leave one trapped in the contingent and thus unable to reach the real. Creeley emphasized this aspect of Olson's thought in a conversation with Charles Tomlinson printed in *The Review* (January 1964): 'Olson has always been irritated by the fact that Pound's back wall is . . . fifth century B.C. He goes right there and stops. Olson wants to push it back at least to the Hittites and the Sumerians, wants to think of organizations of intelligence as pre-Socratic.' In this Olson might be compared to David Jones. The first part of Jones's *The Anathemata* (the whole poem was written between 1936-45 and 1947-52, and was published in 1952), entitled 'Rite and Fore-Time', is an attempted re-imagination of the distant past:

> And see how they run, the juxtaposed forms, brighting
> the

vaults at Lascaux; how the linear is wedded to volume, how they do,
                                                            within, in
an unbloody manganese on the grave lime-face, what is done,
     without,
                          far on the windy tundra
at the kill
that the kindred may have life.
                    O God!
O the Academies![64]

There is nothing so subtle as this little lesson in art history in the whole of
Olson. It is tempting to push the comparison a little further, and to look at
Jones's poetic. He begins from the late-Victorian dilemma of a
desacralized universe. The whole of the symbolic life of man is being
progressively eliminated from modern life; the artist of modern life is the
alienated artist. The role of the poet in such dark days is his traditional
one of rememberer. With 'the entire past . . . at the artist's disposal', he is
in a unique position to trace the deposits of a now forgotten unalienated
past:

> What I have suggested is that man-the-artist, finds himself,
> willy-nilly, un-integrated with the present civilizational phase. I
> regard this as a regrettable matter of fact. I also say that there have
> been civilizational phases when this was less marked and that there
> have been true culture-phases when this was not marked at all, when
> man-the-artist was as integral to the pattern as is man-the-mechanic
> or managerial man to our pattern today.[65]

The title of his great poem is made of many layers of meaning:

> So I mean by my title as much as it can be made to mean or can
> evoke or suggest, however obliquely: the blessed things that have
> taken on what is cursed and the profane things that somehow are
> redeemed: the delights and also the 'ornaments', both in the
> primary sense of gear and paraphernalia and in the sense of what
> simply adorns; the donated and votive things, the things dedicated
> after whatever fashion, the things in some sense made separate,
> being 'laid up from other things'; things, or some aspect of them,
> that partake of the extra-utile and of the gratuitous; things that are
> the signs of something other, together with those signs that not only
> have the nature of a sign, but are themselves, under some mode,
> what they signify. Things set up, lifted up, or in whatever manner
> made over to the gods.[66]

The phrase 'utile' is used by Jones to signify the world-view of science. It
has no place for the 'extra-utile', thinking by analogy, signs or sacrament;
but this is precisely the way Jones characterizes the writer's relation to the
past. He must recall past images, and find a language, find words, which

are as valid today as *signa* as they were in the past. It makes the problem of language in Jones's poem nearly impossible. It is an exceedingly difficult poem. (I do not mean to refer to G. S. Fraser's experience. After discussing at great length four lines from Sir John Denham, he concludes that 'for a conscientious critic, *all* poetry is difficult'; or the views of A. Alvarez ['The *Phoenix and the Turtle* is a difficult poem'] and Christopher Gillie ['I once thought that Pope's Elegy was an easy poem'] expressed in the same volume.)[67] Jones poses problems for his readers, however, not out of any contempt, nor because the implications of his poetic leads him to the ridiculous, but because his chosen material is of such massive intractability. One might read *The Anathemata* for years without feeling dispirited (or without much confidence that it will be mastered this time, or even the next):

> the age is obscure —
> and is the age dark?
> The makers of anathemata can, at a pinch, beat out
> utile spares for the mobile columns or amulets for the raiding
> captains and the captains themselves bring certain specifications
> and new god-fears.
> The adaptations, the fusions
> the transmogrifications
> but always
> the inward continuities
> of the site
> of the place.[68]

Olson's interest in history begins from a profound alienation from modern society. One might expect that Jones would 'regret' this fact, but never that Olson would. But the history that interested Olson was not that which Williams dealt with, his 'blueberry America'. 'The substances of history now useful', he wrote to Creeley (*Mayan Letters* No. 5), 'lie outside, under, right here, anywhere but in the direct continuum of society as we have had it.' The contemporary world of Olson, and for so many poets in the 1950s, seemed to be emptied of meaning. According to Martin Duberman, this view played an important role at Black Mountain:

> Not only was the artist at Black Mountain elevated 'as a holy person', but the rest of the world was put down as 'utterly corrupt', unclean. That cluster of attitudes made the community all at once cruel to and protective of its own — and monkishly indifferent to the world outside. Olson had once been a minor bureaucrat in the Roosevelt administration, but by the mid-fifties, with the country blanketed by McCarthyite fear, he put down political involvement as wasted effort.[69]

Olson looked at the past and saw the triumph of humanism. Like T. E. Hulme, he felt we were at the end, the dead end, not only of humanism, but of representational form itself, only good enough now for a 'poor crawling actuarial "real" — good enough to keep banks and insurance companies, plus mediocre governments, etc. But not Poetry's *Truth* ...'[70] He envisages, as did Hulme, the replacement of classical-representational art by the primitive-abstract. The basis for the new art is explained in the essay 'Human Universe':

> If man chooses to treat external reality any differently than as part of his own process, in other words as anything other than relevant to his own inner life, then he will. . . use it otherwise. He will use it just exactly as he has used it now for too long, for arbitrary and wilful purposes which in their effects not only change the face of nature but actually arrest and divert her force until man turns it even against herself. . .[71]

Olson, then, is arguing against the dualism of Western culture, seeing in that split between body and mind the roots of the graver separation between man and a harmonious relationship with the natural world. He describes his programme in 'Projective Verse' as 'Objectism': '. . . that peculiar presumption by which Western man has interposed himself between what he is as a creature of nature . . . and those other creations which we may, with no derogation, call objects'.[72] What courteous politeness to the objects! Olson felt that a kind of permanent revolution of the sensibility was needed to grasp the fact (as he wrote in 'Projective Verse') that 'external reality is more than merely the substance which man takes in'.

The Maximus Poems, of which a third and posthumous volume has recently been published in New York, contains many familiar ingredients of the Poundian long poem. It is, quite simply, a Poundian long poem. His subject in Books I-III, the most overtly traditional part of the poem, is the history and present life of the Massachusetts fishing port of Gloucester. Subsequent volumes show Olson's mystical and visionary inclinations. The elaborately worked-out programme which includes *A Special View of History*, does not make *The Maximus Poems* any more plausible, or more readable; but the inadvertent traces of humanism, the revelations of the man occupying the ordinary reality, might just possibly endure:

> Or the plumbing,
> that it doesn't work, this I like, have even used paper clips
> as well as string to hold the ball up And flush it
> with my hand
>   But that the car doesn't, that no moving thing moves
> without that song I'd void my ears of, the musickracket
> of all ownership . . .

                                    Holes
in my shoes, that's all right, my fly
gaping, me out
at the elbows, the blessing
                            that difficulties are once more

'In the midst of plenty, walk
as close to
bare
        In the face of sweetness,
piss
            In the time of goodness,
go side, go
smashing, beat them, go as
(as near as you can

tear

In the land of plenty, have
nothing to do with it
                        take the way of
the lowest,
including
your legs, go
contrary, go

sing[73]

Those things against which Black Mountain turned its face — the
ordinary life of materialistic America, the whole business of bills, debts,
public opinion, morality and the police — were in the end to be the
instrument of its final closure. Duberman suggests that the decline was
inevitable, once the functions of community began to collapse under
financial and psychological pressures and people at the college
increasingly had to fend for themselves. The Vortex dissipated, and even
the appointment of Charles Olson as rector could only temporarily delay
the inevitable. It was another Brook Farm, a visionary community,
meeting the all-too-common fate of utopian schemes in America. By the
time Robert Creeley arrived at Black Mountain in 1954 there were only
six staff and nine students at the college. Creeley's *Black Mountain
Review* (1954-57) came too late to do much for the institution; as far as
students and staff were concerned, the great days were over; but Creeley's
review played a large role as the myth of the college spread across
America. Olson was the last to go, remaining, to wind up the affairs of the
college and sell its property, for some six months after the last students
had departed. The final issue of the *Black Mountain Review* in the autumn

of 1957 had a prophetic flavour. Work by Kerouac, Snyder, Whalen, McClure, Burroughs and Selby appears, as well as Allen Ginsberg's 'America'. There is a judicious and negative review of *Howl* by Michael Rumaker, and Williams's preface to the then unpublished collection of Ginsberg's early poems, *Empty Mirror*. The initiative had now passed to the 'Beat Generation', of which Ginsberg was the star turn.

As with all forms of dissent in America in the 1950s, the widely-held assumption was, as Olson put it, that political involvement was wasted effort. The pieties of the New Deal survived in the rhetoric of Adlai Stevenson, but it was fairly obvious that no political progress was possible when both the Republicans and Democrats spoke the same language of individual freedom and corporate capitalism. The cold war was at its nadir. The loyalty programmes and oaths, the 'national security' hysteria, and McCarthyism were not sprung on an unwilling, basically liberal citizenry. The spectre of communism, universally acknowledged, produced many varieties of anti-communist political alignments, between the *soi-disant* liberal intellectuals, many of whom had been fellow-travellers, Trotskyists, or Party members in the 1930s, whose anti-Stalinism usurped any more positive political commitments;[74] the victors in the long, successful struggle by right-wingers in the labour unions to eliminate the communist influence; and the strong vein of root-and-branch conservative isolationism, as represented by Senator Robert A. Taft. In this sterile political climate, 'problems' mainly turned upon the necessary price of adjustment to the postwar way of life. Television became a perfect mirror of the new American prosperity, and there was a paperback revolution which made high-brow reading available to a much wider reading public. The popular literature of the 1950s tells us less about the age than do the sociological studies, such as *The Lonely Crowd, The Organization Man, White Collar,* and a little later, *The Feminine Mystique,* which looked at new patterns of attitudes and behaviour in the American middle class.[75] Among intellectuals the general withdrawal of interest in politics, begun in the 1940s, continued. 'So many intelligent academic people,' wrote C. Wright Mills in 1959, 'won't talk seriously about the politics of war and peace, slump and boom, democracy and tyranny. They won't, or they can't, go beneath the official stereo-types.'[76] This was the great age of formalism in poetry, of university novels, and of the New Criticism.

The sources of dissent were almost entirely cultural rather than political. There was a bohemia, anti-bourgeois, anti-conformist, in the old-fashioned Greenwich Village mould. The gay insouciance of the Village in the 1920s was finished; the depression, and the politicization of American culture which followed in its train, saw to that. College boys from Columbia and Harvard still came slumming, wearing their Brooks

Brothers jackets and button-down collar shirts, but the climate was less amusing than in John Reed's day. There had been a cultural and nationalistic movement in Harlem; civil rights was on the agenda; jazz was on the brink of entering whitey's world; and with jazz came the social habits of the jazzmen: most notably drugs, and a drug-argot. It was easy to fall in with the unconventional behaviour, long hair, and sexual liberation of the 1950s bohemia, but something like hard work was required to come to terms with some of the ideas then current in the Village: Kierkegaard, Sartre, and existential thought being the most prominent.

The career of Jack Kerouac is illuminating in this regard.[77] A French-Canadian Catholic from Lowell, Massachusetts, Kerouac won a football scholarship to Columbia University in 1940. Misfortune dogged him: a broken leg prevented him from making the Varsity team, and Kerouac, crestfallen, left the university. He got drunk, enlisted in the Coast Guard and the Marines (on the same day), before finally shipping out as a scullion on board a ship bound for Greenland. Kerouac returned to Columbia in 1942, but walked out after being left out of the team for his first game. He then enlisted in the Navy, couldn't take the discipline, spent six months in a psychiatric hospital, and was eventually discharged in June 1943. It was at this time that Kerouac drifted into the New York scene. He had wanted to write a big novel in the fashion of Thomas Wolfe, but the people he met (Lucien Carr, William Burroughs, Allen Ginsberg) tried to persuade him that Wolfe was passé. They were all, to some extent, involved in drugs and criminal behaviour; what was more disturbing, for Kerouac, was the overt homosexuality.

In an interview in 1972, Ginsberg explained:

> I came out of the closet at Columbia in 1946. The first person I told about it was Kerouac because I was in love with him. He was staying in my room up in the bed, and I was sleeping on a pallet on the floor. I said, 'Jack, you know, I love you, and I want to sleep with you, and I really like men.' And he said, 'Ooooooh, no . . .'[78]

(This is worth quoting because 'Howl' was as much a sexual coming out as a literary one; Ginsberg had been writing poems in the early 1950s which were struggling towards sexual explicitness.) This experience was not uncommon. Lucien Carr murdered a persistent fairy named Dave Kammerer, an event which Burroughs and Kerouac attempted to turn into a novel written in the style of Dashiell Hammett. Ginsberg was in and out of trouble at Columbia. He was caught scrawling 'Fuck the Jews' on a dormitory window in 1945, and suspended from the university. Later, in 1949, a thief and drug-addict named Herbert Huncke used Ginsberg's apartment as a warehouse for stolen property. Though only accidentally involved, he was sent to Columbia University Hospital for psychiatric observation. As he himself describes it in *Junkie* in 1953, Burroughs was picking up a few pennies selling drugs to support his own habit, and was working the subways as a semi-professional thief. In March 1952 Burroughs accidentally killed his wife while playing William Tell with a gun. She had a glass balanced on her head, and he missed. Neal Cassady ('secret hero of these poems, cocksman and Adonis of Denver', as Ginsberg described him in 'Howl') enters the picture in 1947, Ginsberg and Cassady soon becoming lovers.[79] Cassady was a bum and a drifter from Kansas City with a record behind him of car theft and reform school; he was a compulsive talker, an automobile freak, a source of pure energy. Long letters (one goes to 13,000 words), written in Cassady's wild, free style, opened the way for the 'spontaneous bop prosody' of Kerouac's later fiction.[80] The first version of *On the Road* was begun in 1948. *Go,* John Clellon Holmes's *roman à clef,* came out in 1952. *The New York Times* said that 'this is the Beat Generation'. It was onwards and upwards from there.

Ginsberg's evolution was no less tortured. He grew up in Paterson, New Jersey, the son of the poet Louis Ginsberg and Naomi Ginsberg, a Russian Jewish immigrant. 'Kaddish', written in red ink in 1958, published in *Big Table* in 1959, is a heart-breaking description of his childhood and his mother's madness. We understand Naomi Ginsberg's experience as an immigrant, a Jewess, and a communist, through the body of literature written by immigrants, and their children, of which Henry Roth's *Call It Sleep* (1934) is the chief ornament. In Roth's novel it is the husband who becomes paranoid; the disintegration of the family is described through the consciousness of the young son David Schearl. The family crisis is strikingly close to Ginsberg's in 'Kaddish', though a great deal less outspoken. The dilemma facing every immigrant was that they were expected to (and often wanted to) abandon one identity in favour of another. To stop being a greenhorn and become a proper American was considerably more difficult than picking up the language or the customs of the new society. The problem was simpler for men, whose primary relations outside the home might very well have involved substantial contacts with native Americans, or with immigrants who were more assimilated than they themselves. The woman at home, on the other hand, was placed in a situation in which she was traditionally expected to be the custodian of the old values and rituals; yet at the same time she would watch (and sometimes encourage) her husband and children to make the changes that would utterly undermine her position in the family. The immigrant woman proved an exceptionally important figure in the literature of the Jewish newcomers. The courageous and moral Dora comes close to stealing the novel away from the main character in Abraham Cahan's *The Rise of David Levinsky* (1917). An even more interesting example is Charles Reznikoff's *Family Chronicle* (1969), in which the story of the author's mother, Sarah, constitutes one of the most extraordinary portraits of a working woman in American literature.

Naomi Ginsberg's political commitment is less well represented in the literature, although there was a tradition of social democracy and labour organization in the Pale of Settlement in Tsarist Russia and the Jewish presence in certain American unions, and in left-wing politics, was substantial. Naomi Ginsberg was a member of the Party, and her son Allen was brought up in that atmosphere. In the 1930s she began to suffer from acute paranoia. The experience of her madness in 'Kaddish' begins when Allen was twelve. He accompanied her, alone, to a rest home in New Jersey. 'Allen', she said,

> you don't understand it — it's — ever since
> those 3 big — sticks up my back — they did something
> to me in Hospital, they poisoned me, they want to
> see me dead . . . [81]

Riding home on a bus, he wonders if it wouldn't be better if she were dead. The memories of his childhood stand immediately behind his ambition as he prepares for entry to Columbia:

> — Prayed on ferry to help mankind if ad-
> mitted — vowed, the day I journeyed to Entrance Exam —
> by being honest revolutionary lawyer — would
> train for that — inspired by Sacco Vanzetti, Norman
> Thomas, Debs, Altgeld, Sandburg . . .   (*Kaddish*, p. 16)

A call that night at 2 a.m. wakes him with the news that his mother has gone berserk in the rest home. The next day his father takes Naomi to a state mental hospital.

> Naomi, Naomi — sweating, bulge-eyed, fat, the
> dress unbuttoned at one side — hair over brow, her
> stocking hanging evilly on her legs — screaming for
> a blood transfusion — one righteous hand upraised —
> a shoe in it — barefoot in the Pharmacy —   (*Kaddish*, p. 18)

It comes almost as a relief from these moments when Ginsberg recalls the vanished culture of Jewish socialism in New York.[82] The whole experience of left politics for him remains irretrievably caught up in the memory of her paranoia:.

> 'I am a great woman — am truly a beautiful soul —
> and because of that they (Hitler, Grandma, Hearst,
> the Capitalists, Franco, Daily News, the '20s, Musso-
> lini, the living dead) want to shut me up — Buba's the
> head of a spider network —'   (*Kaddish*, p. 26)

The present and the past have become utterly mixed up with each other. All the memories exist on the same plane, with the same potent threat directed at herself, and even her son Allen in time is unrecognizable; he has become a stranger, an enemy. Ginsberg turns the paranoia of his mother into a litany in the fourth part of the poem, invoking Russia and the Communist Party, strikes, Trotsky, Spain, starving India, and then her own personal tragedy of sickness, horror and loneliness. There are passages which evoke great pity and terror; not least in the calmness which follows her first return from hospital:

> One night, sudden attack — her noise in the bath-
> room — like croaking up her soul — convulsions and red
> vomit coming out of her mouth — diarrhea water exploding
> from her behind — on all fours in front of the toilet —
> urine running between her legs — left retching on the
> tile floor smeared with her black feces — unfainted —
>   at forty, varicosed, nude, fat, doomed, hiding
> outside the apartment door near the elevator calling
> Police, yelling for her girl-friend Rose to help —   (*Kaddish*, p. 22)

There were moments of calm recognition:

> 'Don't be afraid of me because I'm just coming
> back home from the mental hospital — I'm your mother —
>   (*Kaddish*, p. 21)

When he sees her, years later, in a madhouse in Long Island, his feeling of shock is palpable, sudden:

> Too thin, shrunk on her bones — age come to Naomi —
> now broken into white hair — loose dress on her
> skeleton — face sunk, old! withered — cheek of crone —
>   One hand stiff — heaviness of forties & menopause
> reduced by one heart stroke, lame now — wrinkles — a
> scar on her head, the lobotomy — ruin, the hand dipping
> downwards to death —   (*Kaddish*, p. 29)

Ginsberg received news of his mother's death by telegram:

> Returning from San Francisco one night, Orlovsky
> in my room — Whalen in his peaceful chair — a telegram
> from Gene. Naomi dead —
>   Outside I bent my head to the ground under the
> bushes near the garage — knew she was better —
> at last —   (*Kaddish*, p. 31)

The incantatory rhythms of the poem come, as the title indicates, from the Jewish prayer for the dead. Like so much of Ginsberg, it gives the feeling of having been written in an anguished, hurried prose, picking up something of Whitman's loose energies along the way, but cast in a form that is more heightened and self-revelatory.

'Howl', written in 1955-6, is Ginsberg's rhapsodic elegy for the bohemia of the 1940s. Here he voices a generalized protest, an angry denunciation of the 'lack-love', 'Moloch'. By the time the poem was published the political climate had sharpened, protest was becoming more specific. In his own work the despair of 'Howl' began to give way to 'America' and 'A Supermarket in California', poems in which Ginsberg celebrates and condemns with increasing specificity the bustling vulgarity and menace of America in the 1950s. Gregory Corso's broadsheet, *Bomb*, came out in 1958, as did Lawrence Ferlinghetti's *Tentative Description of a Dinner Given to Promote the Impeachment of President Eisenhower*, published by the Golden Mountain Press, the purchase of which made me feel nervously subversive and conspiratorial at the age of sixteen. There was nothing at all like 'Howl' in America in 1956, with Ginsberg's talk of God, drugs, booze, sex ('alcohol and cock and endless balls', 'a vision of ultimate cunt and come'), mysticism, homosexuality, suicide, dreams and travels. It is hard to recall today the sanction which came from this poem for almost every kind of independent or rebellious behaviour among the young. For every person who bought and read the poem there must have been twenty who knew about it, who absorbed Ginsberg's messianic libertarianism as from the atmosphere. There were a lot of kids, wandering around the Village in black turtle-neck sweaters, thinking of 'angel-headed hipsters', who would go home, contemptuous and alienated, to Scarsdale or Mamaroneck. The style of youthful dissent in the 1950s took Ginsberg, and Kerouac, with deadly seriousness. What mattered was that 'Howl' came immediately out of personal experience; there is no tedious distinction to be made here between the 'speaker' and the poet, Ginsberg, or between the 'actual' and 'imputed' author. Yet, with the wisdom of further reflection, it seems a little more 'literary' (in that it records an experience selected and arranged) than it once did. Not 'literary' in the sense that it was something Ginsberg got out of Rimbaud, but that the poem seems carefully *made,* that its electric energies have been controlled. There is, of course, the question of the line. When he recorded the poem for Fantasy Records in 1959, Ginsberg explained that

Ideally each line of *Howl* is a single breath unit. My breath is long — that's the Measure, one physical-mental inspiration of thought contained in the elastic of a breath. It probably bugs Williams now, but its a natural consequence, my own heightened conversation, not cooler average-daily-talk short breath. I get to mouth more madly this way.

So these poems are a series of experiments with the formal organization of the long line.

(*Evergreen Review*, November-December 1959)

He goes on to link this specifically with the example of Whitman, but Whitman possessed by the urgency and power of Blake.

Ginsberg's response to the formalism of his contemporaries at Columbia was Blakean and visionary. The long Whitmanic line, Hebraic prayer, and Williams's measure were Ginsberg's response to the intricate stanza and rhyme-scheme. His unabashedly personal presence in the poem (at the end of 'Howl' he describes his purpose to 'stand before you speechless and intelligent and shaking with shame, rejected yet confessing out the soul to conform to the rhythm of thought in his naked and endless head') provides an alternative to the careful deflections of the impersonal Eliotian poet. He is also a political poet, whose politics are visionary and despairing, and whose mysticism was intensely political, celebrating those casualties of Truman's and Eisenhower's America

> who reappeared on the West Coast investigating the F.B.I.
>   in beards and shorts with big pacifist eyes sexy in
>   their dark skin passing out incomprehensible leaflets,
> who burned cigarette holes in their arms protesting the
>   narcotic tobacco haze of Capitalism,
> who distributed Supercommunist pamphlets in Union Square
>   weeping and undressing while the sirens of Los
>   Alamos wailed them down . . . [83]

Ginsberg is a millennial prophet, a celebrator, a radical spirit, whose 'dreadful little volume', as John Hollander wrote of *Howl*, exhibits an 'utter lack of decorum of any kind'. Hollander, writing in the *Partisan Review*, Spring 1957, takes us to the point where the 1950s gets a good first look at the 1960s, and can't imagine why *anyone* would want to write like that.[84]

The 'moment' of formalism was one of cultural contraction. An increasingly isolated and defensive intelligentsia, which saw the abandonment of its traditional adversary function as a tempting though dangerous opportunity to effect a rapprochement with America in the postwar period, managed to praise a dominant style in poetry which turned its back upon the new 'reality' of the cold war. After the death of Stalin in 1953, the possibility of co-existence helped to moderate some of the cruder cold war attitudes. But by that time formalism had an impetus and logic of its own. When the political and cultural climate began to ease in the mid-1950s, the films of social protest and social conscience (Brando in *The Wild Ones*, and *On the Waterfront*, 1954; Chayefsky's *Marty*,

1955, and *The Bachelor Party*, 1956), and the plays of Arthur Miller (*The Crucible*, 1953; *A View from the Bridge*, 1955), tried to speak clearly and immediately to the condition of American life. In England the C.N.D. campaign, following hard on the Suez catastrophe of 1957, opened up political and cultural questions not yet possible in America. Documentaries by Lindsay Anderson, plays by John Osborne (*Look Back in Anger*, 1956), and Arnold Wesker, novels by John Braine (*Room at the Top*, 1957), and journals like *Universities and Left Review*, and then the *New Left Review*, help to define an atmosphere of discontent and social criticism unlike anything since the 1930s. It became marginally harder to carry on writing sestinas and madrigals. There was a contradiction between formalism and the age, which led to a questioning throughout the late 1950s of whether the traditional forms of poetry were any longer adequate for the real world in which the poets lived. This was the period of the fierce, programmatic anthologies by Hall, Pack and Simpson, and by Donald M. Allen, which waged a very symbolic war for the future direction of American poetry (and for English poetry, too, as Alvarez chimed in with *The New Poetry* in 1962). Formalists scoffed, but paid attention. Consider Louis Simpson:

> As for form — if some of the younger poets seem concerned with technique, it would be hard to discover a good poet who has not been.
>
> (1957)

> In America we have no traditions. Writing pseudo-Elizabethan or seventeenth or eighteenth-century English verse in America is not a tradition; it is merely an amusement. In America tradition is another name for laziness.
>
> (1963)

> Repulsions held in common — that's what we find when we look at the work of American poets today. They don't want to write the so-called 'well-made' poem that lends itself to the little knives and formaldehyde of a graduate school.
>
> (1967) [85]

In America the revolt against formalism had, in fact, deep historical roots. Had not Pound and Van Wyck Brooks managed a revolt against an even more hapless genteel tradition? Greenwich Village had been for decades an answer to Main Street. Early on, Pound had made a pact with Whitman, thus affirming a continuity (largely imaginary) between the disaffiliated bohemias of the twentieth century and the eclipse after the Civil War of the hegemony of Boston over American culture. This, in brief, was Santayana's argument in 'Genteel American Poetry' in 1915. He describes a Brahmin poetry which 'modulates in obvious ways the honorable conventions of the society in which it arose. It was simple, sweet, humane, Protestant literature, grandmotherly in that sedate spectacled wonder with which it gazed at this terrible world and said how beautiful and interesting it all was.' Against this 'boundless field of convention, prosperity and mediocrity', Santayana writes, there emerged the figure of Walt Whitman with 'the magnificent intention of being wholly direct, utterly sincere, and bothering about nothing that was not an experience of the soul and the sense'. It was a Pyrrhic victory in Santayana's eyes, in that 'the poetic mind of America suffered a certain dispersion' and the 'average human genteel person' was left without 'any poetry to give him pleasure or to do him honor'.[86]

Santayana could not have known how far along his own age was in a similar cultural revolution: many of the crucial manifestations of modernism were in 1915 scattered across a dozen capitals of Europe; nor would he have known how carefully Pound, for example, was orchestrating and nursing along his own little show with the 'men of 1914', Joyce, Eliot, and Wyndham Lewis. Half a century later the struggle against formalism was virtually over once again, the losers dismissed, like dilettante Mensheviks, to the ash heaps of history. There was no single guiding figure like Pound to manage the propaganda, nor was there a coherent source of inspiration to be derived from Whitman, Pound, Williams, Hart Crane, Wallace Stevens and Marianne Moore. They all provided sanctions of one sort or another, but though the forms of dissent were varied, the enemy was everywhere the same: rhymes, the iambic pentameter, strict stanzaic forms, and the poetry which set itself tasks and elegantly carried the day. You didn't have to be a Santayana to point out the risks: in their desire for a *truer* poetry, for a poetry adequate to the real world around them, these poets sometimes left the ordinary world altogether, or flooded it with myths, drowned it with history, probed through the everyday like a corkscrew, burrowed beneath it like moles, tore it apart like savage beasts, or just sat there, insensible, and celebrated the inhuman. Inevitably the humbug-ratio was pretty high. Bad poems were still bad, though now ambitiously bad or experimentally bad, or self-indulgent, incomprehensible, dull.

The ex-formalists seem, on the whole, rather more interesting than those who had not gone through the discipline. Three such poets who take us from the strict formalism to the 'wholly direct, utterly sincere' 1960s, are Snodgrass, Lowell and Plath. They remain rudely yoked to the term 'confessional poetry', a massively unhelpful concept. Confession is more than metaphorically linked with the idea of absolution, of sin and redemption, and a theology which Lowell explicitly left behind, much ridiculed, in 'Beyond the Alps', and which has no bearing at all on Snodgrass and Plath. M. L. Rosenthal's review of Robert Lowell's *Life Studies* introduces the term.[87] The 'series of personal confidences' which Rosenthal took the book to represent, and the 'incalculable damage' done to Lowell's spirit in allowing himself 'this kind of ghoulish operation' on his father, reminds us of a somewhat politer world, a more genteel time, when poetry was poetry, and talk of one's father as a fool and a failure was not kosher. That the harm might come from talking about it in public, and not from the actual experience of growing up in the ghastly atmosphere of 91 Revere Street, reveals a rather Victorian decorum lying side by side with Rosenthal's evident admiration for the poetry. The term 'confessional poetry' identifies the more sensational elements in the content of the poetry, but not the process of infusion by which the 'I' of the poem and the 'I' of the poet come together in a speech which is utterly natural, and yet heightened, alive, crackling with energy. The very casualness of the tone seems to reject artifice; the poems present themselves as things made, a poem, but also a *thing*, an addition to the sum of the world, with no existence independent of that world. There are no phantasms, myths, or idealized orders; simply, the poem itself, without uplift or symbolic reality, an object, a real object: an art of the real.

In saying that 'in Nature, man alone has the choice to withdraw from the reality in which he lives, and so has the power to die, either metaphorically or literally',[88] W. D. Snodgrass takes sides against anything which might turn the face of art from the sheer actuality of experience. 'The better poems being produced right now tend to be common-sensical, stylistically almost ordinary — such a voice as you might hear in this world, not a voice meant to lift you out of this world.'[89]

Snodgrass's early work was heavily influenced by Lowell: 'You know those big, gorgeous poems that he wrote right after World War II. They just knocked all of us flat . . . Randall Jarrell once said to me, "Snodgrass, do you know you're writing the very best second-rate Lowell in the whole country." '[90] By the time he published *Heart's Needle* in 1959, Lowell's presence had deliquesced into something narrower, but within that smaller scope there is an intensification. Snodgrass, unlike Lowell, does not show much interest in history; the things that matter to him are in the here-and-now. He writes of the return to civilian life at the end of the war in two short, brilliant poems, 'Ten Days Leave' and 'Returned to Frisco, 1946'. The former is a study in dislocation, a portrait of a state of mind now firmly alienated from 'home'. Nothing much seems changed, except in the consciousness of the returned soldier who sees 'the hills, the little houses, the costumes' with fresh eyes, and the clarity of things seen in a dream. 'Returned to Frisco, 1946' describes the emotions felt by a soldier on board a troopship entering San Francisco Bay. There is the same anxiety here, as in 'Ten Days Leave', at the prospect of being 'home once more', for home means the familiar, the known. Soldiers on leave are 'free' to linger over a meal, get drunk, blow their pay, sleep all day. But Snodgrass gives us an overwhelming feeling of manipulation behind this freedom. It primarily comes through the images (the soldiers who had 'scrambled like rabbits' up enemy beaches now 'shouldered like pigs' to catch a glimpse of the shoreline). Overhead there is a seagull screaming for garbage. They are all, soldiers and animals, caught and manipulated in a process of unfreedom.

> Off the port side, through haze, we could discern
> Alcatraz, lavender with flowers. Barred,
> The Golden Gate, fading away astern,
> Stood like the closed gate of your own backyard.

This is a beautifully menacing image. The enjambement of 'Barred/The Golden Gate' links the bridge with the prison, from which no one ever escaped, but now seen in a confused, attractive haze. The Golden Gate becomes the 'closed gate' of a familiar backyard, and of a prison a great deal larger than Alcatraz. In this poem, whose very title has a disturbingly impersonal connotation, the return is to an America of drastically curtailed possibilities.

In his early poems Snodgrass circles around the emotions of a man caught in an environment which is subtly, or overtly, threatening. Physical objects evoke a helpless terror:

> From stainless steel basins of water
> They brought warm cloths, and they washed me,
> From spun aluminum bowls, cold Zephiran sponges, fuming;
> Gripped in the dead yellow glove, a bright straight razor
> Inched on my stomach, down my groin . . .   ('The Operation')

After recovering consciousness, he experiences a heightened visual sensitivity. A series of details, observed with neutral closeness, occupies a mind 'too weak to think of strength', but beginning to fit the pieces of the world together again:

> Opposite, ranked office widows glare; headlamps, below,
> Trace out our highways; their cargoes under dark tarpaulins,
> Trucks climb, thundering, and sirens may
> Wail . . .

Nature, a traditional consolation, is simply unavailable. Snodgrass touches on this in 'A Cardinal', a parody of a romantic nature-and-the-poet poem:

> I tromp off to the woods,
> the little stand of birches
> between golf course and campus

> where birds flirt through the branches
> and the city will be hushed.

This attractive little pastoral vision does not last. The main consequence of his presence is, ironically, to silence nature. 'The weeds sing where I leave.' He has come to listen to nature, but hears a mill whistle, freight cars rattling by, and the sound of trucks and planes. 'Oh, they've all found *their* voices.' The only metre he picks up is from a file of R.O.T.C. cadets marching nearby.

> . . . creating
> for the school and market
> the ground bass of our credo —
>
> faith in free enterprise
> and our unselfish forces
> who chant to advertise
> the ancient pulse of violence.

A cardinal appears suddenly, singing to 'maintain the ancient Law,/and celebrate this ordinal/of the red beak and claw'. Snodgrass mockingly invites the bird to

> sing for the flyboys, birdy,
> in praise of their profession;
> sing for the choirs of pretty
> slogans and catch-phrases
> that rule us by obsession;
> praise what it pays to praise:
>
> praise soap and garbage cans,
> join with the majority
> in praising man-eat-man . . .

But the bird proclaims nothing but itself:

> I want my meals and loving;
> I fight nobody's battles;
> don't pardon me for living.
>
> The world's not done to me;
> it is what I do . . .

Snodgrass's bird sings of a self-interest with which he can oppose the distractions of America. Later in the poem he sums up the message of the cardinal:

> Assertion is their credo:
> style tells their policy.

He senses the characteristic dissociations which the 'silent generation' made, turning away from history:

> Riot in Algeria, Cyprus, in Alabama;
> Aged in wrong, the empires are declining,
> And China gathers, soundlessly, like evidence.
> What shall I say to the young on such a morning? —
> Mind is the one salvation? — also grammar? —
> No; my little ones lean not towards revolt. They
> Are the Whites, the vaguely furiously driven, who resist
> Their souls with such passivity
> As would make Quakers swear.   ('The Campus on the Hill')

But in an interview in 1971, Snodgrass disowned the engagement and social criticism which figures in *Heart's Needle*:

> ... social and political things seem to me of very second rate importance. I'm just not very interested in them. I'm really much more interested in how fathers work than in how presidents work ... simply because that's much more intimately a part of my experience.[91]

Writing about presidents is hardly the only alternative to writing about fatherhood. This is a rather sleazy way to make the basic point that the opening out into a particular kind of experience in his work came at the cost of greatly narrowing the framework: the real has lost its historical and social bearings.

The 'Heart's Needle' sequence is written in an elaborate syllabic versification; the subject is his divorce, and his separation from a dearly loved daughter. As for the syllabics, we can consider Richard Howard's comments upon Snodgrass's poem 'At the Park Dance':

> ... we notice almost simultaneously that the first syllable of each second and fifth line rhymes or assonates with the final syllable of each first and fourth line; and that the stanzas are in fact constructed in paired crescendos of five, six and seven syllables thus bonded by the edge-rhymes, the five- and six-syllable lines ending in an accented syllable, the longer seven-syllable lines ending in an unaccented one, with a single exception (the third line of the third stanza, where the final accented syllable seems to withdraw from the missing seventh syllable).[92]

A detailed rabbinical inspection, now and then, helps reassure us that everything is kosher. Howard goes on in this vein for better than a page (Creeley has called *Alone with America* 'a fine instance of *mandarin* writing — i.e. an "entertainment" of "sensibility" '),[93] proving that he can count syllables and sound accents and rhymes better than just about anyone else in the business. Formalism invites this kind of analysis, and has been buried by it.

The sequence has a specific historical location in the final period of the Korean war:

> We read of cold war soldiers that
> Never gained ground, gave none, but sat
> Tight in their chill trenches. (No. 3)

That static, frozen winter campaign that is getting nowhere is Snodgrass's marriage. In a painful (but also self-indulgent) image, he sees his dilemma as that of the fox who

> . . . backtracks and sees the paw,
> Gnawed off, he cannot feel;
> Conceded to the jaw
> Of toothed blue steel. (No. 5)

The major preoccupation, however, is with Snodgrass's relationship with his daughter. We see her in April, three years old, planting in the garden; an asthma attack, in the complex sixth poem, provides the occasion for a statement of Snodgrass's position:

> Of all living things, only we
> have power to choose that we should die;
> nothing else is free
> in this world to refuse it. Yet I
> who say this, could not raise
> myself from bed how many days
> to the thieving world. Child, I have another life,
> another child. We try to choose our life.

The movement from 'Returned to Frisco, 1946' to 'Heart's Needle' is clearly defined here. The new 'life', and the possibility of choosing it, have eliminated Snodgrass's perception in the earlier poem that he was only 'Free to choose just what they meant we should'.

In an interesting statement which appeared in the *Partisan Review* (Spring 1959), Snodgrass developed the idea of poetic tact:

> Why must ideas and emotions be repressed from conscious statement into details and facts; repressed again from facts into the texture of language, the choice of words, connotations; repressed finally into technical factors like rhyme and echoes of other words . . . Too much consciousness, misapplied, leads directly to mousy poems.
>
> So the poet imitates life, often, by carrying on in his poem a process similar to that of our life. He takes some idea, ordinary enough in itself, and represses it from conscious assertion, so that it can spread into the details, the style, the formal technique.[94]

The process of 'repression' is meant, one hopes, as a metaphor. Nowhere does he place himself so completely within the formalist tradition. It is part of the general critical assumption about his work that Snodgrass pioneered a new subject-matter. But it was only 'new' in poetry, not in life, and hardly seems like one of those epoch-making advances by which a period discovers itself, or a new sensibility emerges. Very few poets exist outside the whole range of traditions and social conventions which governs the public face of our culture. When the contradiction between convention and the lived experience grows too severe, there is a shift, an incorporation, and something startling and new happens, a 'Howl' appears or, on a different scale, a formalist writes 'Heart's Needle'. Pound was said by Eliot to have invented Chinese poetry for our time; Snodgrass may be credited with the invention of the bad divorce.

He believes that 'The Waste Land' was 'about Eliot's insane wife and his frozen sex life'.[95] The images of winter and entrapment in 'Heart's Needle' invite the same kind of interpretation. But there are, as we hardly need to be reminded, some differences: Eliot constructed a form, such as it is — or as Pound left it — to give his 'rhythmical grumbling'[96] other kinds of meanings as well. Eliot may very well have 'repressed from conscious statement' the personal tragedy of his first marriage (so well, in fact, that its personal meaning lay unsurmised for decades); but that is all 'Heart's Needle' is about, despite the trappings of the Korean war. The historical moment of the divorce and separation is only coincidentally that of the war; it almost feels as though it was a small gesture, part of the décor, and quite irrelevant to the 'real' experience of the sequence.

In Snodgrass's second book, *After Experience* (1968), there is a sense of hurt as palpable and remorseless as a nightmare. Images of painful, futile gestures recur. The issue here is survival. 'No virtue can be thought to have priority/Over this endeavour to preserve one's being.' He finds metaphors for this struggle in a moth's 'blind, fanatical drive' which hurls itself against a blank wall; in an amputee on a wheeled platform who fights to get through doors, up stairs; and in a lobster struggling to raise a claw ('With a thick peg in the wrist') in a restaurant window. To locate the existence of some inner, primordial source of energy and will is not, necessarily, to celebrate its presence. It appears as the 'rapacious stiff self-will' of a man dying in hospital, and in an old Indian sitting alone in a teepee, 'Raising his toothless drawn jaw to the light', and singing a song of incomprehensible antiquity:

> . . . for the restless young
> Who wander in and out.

The ironic distance is achieved, but at the cost of a little pastiche Eliot.

After Experience stands as an epitaph upon the wan optimism of *Heart's Needle*:

> Though trees turn bare and girls turn wives,
> We shall afford our costly seasons;
> There is a gentleness survives
> That will outspeak and has its reasons.   ('April Inventory')

Snodgrass is unable to go any further than survival — far enough, one might suppose; but he does not turn his images of desperate defiance into a place where we can live. They seem to exist in a limbo, amidst the emotional wreckage of a life. These images (reminding us of MacNeice) may tell us a great deal about the way we live now, but the more insistent signification is a repressed and paralysed life crisis which has now set in, like lockjaw, like the desperately cold winters of all those poems from the early 1950s.

Since his earliest books in the 1940s, Robert Lowell's career has seemed more important — even more interesting — than the actual poems he was writing at any given moment. The restless growth which that career describes is unlike any since Yeats. When he was an undergraduate at Harvard he wrote poems in imitation of William Carlos Williams's spare, imagist manner; he called on Robert Frost with 'a huge epic on the First Crusade, all written out in clumsy long hand on lined paper'; after going to Kenyon College, and absorbing the influence of John Crowe Ransom and Allen Tate, Lowell began to write poems of enormous difficulty and ambiguity, heavily laden with Roman Catholic religious symbolism. A decade later he tried to write poems 'as open and single-surfaced as a photograph'. There was a return to a more strict formal verse in the 1960s, when Lowell became a public, Roman poet; which was followed by the years spent working with a rhymeless fourteen-line sonnet (from *Notebook 1967-68*, 1969, to *The Dolphin*, 1973), and his decision to move to England. A recent group of poems in *The New Review* (September 1975) shows Lowell writing with a mournful, low-pressure reflectiveness, closer to *Life Studies* in form, yet curiously enervated. His is a protean career, to be cherished and celebrated; there is no one writing poetry today who shows anything like his resilience and capacity for growth.

The rough outline of the career seems inevitably to point towards, or away from, *Life Studies,* which appeared along with Snodgrass's *Heart's Needle* in 1959. Lowell's previous book, *The Mills of the Kavanaughs* (1951), took on a quite different kind of meaning in the light of '91 Revere Street', 'Terminal Days at Beverly Farms', and 'Sailing Home from Rapallo'. *The Mills,* the least highly regarded of any of Lowell's books, was described by him as 'an obscure, rather Elizabethan, dramatic and melodramatic poem'.[97] We see in it not merely the outline of an old family (like Lowell's) in decline, of the past coming to dwarf the present, but also a crisis in the relationship between Anne Kavanaugh and her husband Harry which has strong resemblances to Lowell's parents. 'The Mills of the Kavanaughs' is a masked autobiography not so much of the family as of the relationship between man and wife. Harry left the Navy, as did Lowell's father, in uncertain circumstances after Pearl Harbour. His relationship with his wife has deteriorated through incompatibility and mutual suspicion, which we see most clearly in terms of their sexual failure. Anne recalls their estrangement:

> You went to bed, love, finished — through, through, through.
> Hoping to find you useless, dead asleep,
> I stole to bed beside you, after two
> As usual. Had you drugged yourself to keep
> Your peace? I think so. If our bodies met,
> You'd flinch, and flounder on your face.

Dreaming, she takes a lover. Harry thinks she is speaking in her sleep of a real betrayal, and beats her. The scene ends in recrimination, violence and emotional disaster. Harry survived, just:

> You lived. Your rocker creaked as you declined.
> To the ungarnished ruin of your mind . . .

What goes wrong in 'The Mills of the Kavanaughs' is that we cannot stand back and see them, Harry and Anne, from any other perspective than their own. In a play similarly close to the autobiographical root, Eugene O'Neill was able to achieve this kind of distance in *Long Day's Journey into Night* (1956) by the ironies and cross-purposes introduced by the viewpoint of the children upon the character and behaviour of their parents, and, of course, upon themselves. With both of his parents alive, that is precisely what Lowell was inhibited from doing.

Life Studies was mainly written after his parents died, and their final years figure very largely in the book. 'Sailing from Rapallo' is dated February 1954, when he brought his mother's casket home for burial in Dumbarton. The death within a few years of both parents (to hazard a guess) enabled Lowell to reassume a role in imagination, that of long-suffering son, which he had long since rejected. Resuming the relationship, now utterly severed and a part of 'history', brought with it a freedom to negotiate his way through the flux of his early life, to highlight some things and to remain silent about others. It represents an effort to order his own life. Behind *Life Studies* is a massive effort of recollection. Yet to give the 'truth' about his parents was not his purpose:

I've invented facts and changed things, and the whole balance of the poem was something invented. So there's a lot of artistry, I hope, in the poems ... there was always that standard of truth which you wouldn't ordinarily have in poetry — the reader was to believe he was getting the *real* Robert Lowell.[98]

The emphasis falls on the right place — on Lowell himself. His parents are entitled to be considered not only through his eyes, but that, as they say, is another story. The title of the book seems to say the same thing. The 'studies' from 'life' demonstrate the proficiency of the artist, are essays, provisional versions, not the formal 'portraits' of the academy.

The second half of the book has the ease of conversation caught in a 'fairly gentle style',[99] whose roots lay in prose. Lowell knew and thought highly of Ford Madox Ford, and he turned to Ford's French and Russian masters — Flaubert and Chekhov — when he broke away from his earlier, clotted style. An important interpretation of *Life Studies* and the confessional mode by Marjorie Perloff hinges on this fact.[100] In addition, Lowell has pointed out that the writing of his autobiography (published as '91 Revere Street' in the *Partisan Review,* Fall 1956) triggered off the second half of the book. Once again we see the crucial role which prose plays for modern poetry.[101]

The sequence of publication of the individual poems is revealing. The first part, from 'Beyond the Alps' to 'A Mad Negro Soldier Confined at Munich' were published in 1953-4; '91 Revere Street' two years later, and the whole of the 'Life Studies' poems in 1958-9. The structural break corresponds closely to the death of his parents. The difference between the two halves is stylistic as well. 'Beyond the Alps' places us not so much on a train from Rome to Paris in 1950, but in the heightened, allusive symbolic manner of *Lord Weary's Castle* (1947). The poem turns upon the contrast between Rome and Paris, between faith and reason. The date, '1950, the year when Pius XII defined the dogma of Mary's bodily assumption' (glossed by Cambon as an 'anti-positivist, anti-bourgeois, anti-materialist and therefore anachronistic gesture')[102] is defined by a series of gestures seen and imagined: the steward banging on his gong, Mussolini unfurling a flag, the Pope dropping a mirror, the pilgrims bending to kiss 'Saint Peter's brazen scandal', the Swiss guards pushing back the crowds. Of all the gestures, that of the defeated Swiss Everest expedition, throwing in the sponge like a boxer who has met his match, reverberates most persistently through the poem. The failed expedition is an image of the frailty of human endeavour and human will. The train carries him to Paris, the world of reason:

> Much against my will,
> I left the City of God where it belongs.

There, where Augustine's vision of the struggle between faith and unbelief was to have been decided, something quite ironic has occurred. Mussolini (or 'the breast thumping blimp', in the first version of the poem published in the *Kenyon Review,* Summer 1953) makes his attempt to 'unfurl' Caesar's standard. His presence in the poem must have reminded readers in 1953 of Pound's *Pisan Cantos*, published five years earlier:

> The enormous tragedy of the dream in the peasant's
> bent shoulders
> Manes! Manes was tanned and stuffed,
> Thus Ben and la Clara *a Milano*
> by the heels at Milano
> That maggots shd/ eat the dead bullock
> DIGENES διγενές, but the twice crucified
> where in history will you find it?
> yet say this to the Possum: a bang, not a whimper,
> with a bang not with a whimper,
> To build the city of Dioce whose terraces are the colour of stars.
> (Canto LXXIV)

Lowell had been on the Library of Congress committee which awarded the Bollingen Prize to the *Pisan Cantos* in 1949. 'I've talked to Italians who were partisans,' Lowell remarked to Frederick Seidel in his *Paris Review* interview, 'and who said that this is the only poem on Mussolini that's any good. Pound's quite wily often: Mussolini hangs up like an ox — his brutal appearance. I don't know whether you could say the beliefs there are wrong or not.'[103]   Mussolini's attempt to ape the glory of the Caesars led to the triumph of Italian arms against Abyssinia, but ultimately to his degradation and death in Milan. Nothing as dramatic as this awaits for the Pope, whose gestures are seen as vain. He is something out of comic opera.

> The lights of science couldn't hold a candle
> to Mary risen — at one miraculous stroke,
> angel-wing'd, gorgeous as a jungle bird!
> But who believed this? Who could understand?

Science and reason have no place in the Rome of Mussolini and Pius. Nor were poets at ease there. The third stanza makes a quick, puzzling, break to Ovid, banished to the remote Black Sea by Augustus Caesar for the indiscretion of his *Ars Amatoria*. Lowell, who majored in classics at Kenyon College, can help us with this difficult stanza:

> Until recently our literature hasn't been as raw as the Roman, translations had to have stars. And their history has a terrible human frankness that isn't customary with us — corrosive attacks

on the establishment, comments on politics and the decay of morals, all felt terribly strongly, by poets as well as historians.[104]

Lowell writes in 'Beyond the Alps':

> Rome asked for poets. At her beck and call,
> came Lucan, Tacitus and Juvenal,
> the *black republicans* who tore the tits
> and bowels of the Mother Wolf to bits.

And that is precisely what he had done in the first two stanzas of the poem. Lowell is holding up here an example of a role which he has undertaken. The final stanza brings him back to the train, tired and 'blear-eyed'. He has a momentary vision of Apollo, the god of light, come to

> . . . plant his heels
> on terra firma through the morning's thigh . . .

which causes a sudden distortion of perception:

> each backward, wasted Alp, a Parthenon,
> fire-branded socket of the Cyclops' eye.

The conjunction of the Alps and the Parthenon (symbol of classical Greek rationality), turns us back to the failed Swiss expedition on Everest (symbol of an unattainable reason), and to the goddess of intelligence, Minerva:

> prince, pope, philosopher and golden bough,
> pure mind and murder at the scything prow —
> Minerva, the miscarriage of the brain.

Finally Lowell arrives in Paris, Walter Benjamin's 'capital of the nineteenth-century':

> Now Paris, our black classic, breaking up
> like killer kings on an Etruscan cup.

The image teases us with a sense that here, too, the failure is complete: that neither in faith nor in the worship of pure reason is there a world-view adequate to the modern world. The decision to set the poem during a train journey, suspended between Rome and Paris, seems profoundly correct for Lowell's purpose. He is neither a man of one world or another (Wilbur's image was the water-walker), unlike his father, who 'considered himself', as he writes in '91 Revere Street', 'a matter-of-fact man of science and had an unspoiled faith in the superior efficiency of northern nations'.

Quite deliberately, the 'Life Studies' poems do not invite this kind of close attention. 'I hoped in *Life Studies* — it was a limitation — that each poem might seem as open and single-surfaced as a photograph.'[105]   The great 'confession' in '91 Revere Street' turns out to be pretty mild stuff. His parents had their faults; he himself was 'thick-witted, narcissistic, thuggish' and unhappy. What Rosenthal means by referring to an 'incalculable damage' which Lowell has done to himself seems, like so many quick reactions to *Life Studies,* to be agitated and unbalanced. Parents are there to disillusion their children, to express (unconscious) snobbery, prejudice, or outmoded ideas, to betray their weaknesses in the most damaging way possible. Lowell's father was 'deep — not with profundity, but with the dumb depth of one who trusted in statistics and was dubious of personal experience'. His mother dreamed of a 'Siegfried carried lifeless through the shining air by Brunhild to Valhalla'. Alas, a fish out of water, his father failed repeatedly in his business career. The atmosphere at home was one of 'glacial purity and sacrifice'. Mother, he writes,

> . . . did not have the self-assurance for wide human experience; she needed to feel liked, admired, surrounded by the approved and familiar. Her haughtiness and chilliness came from apprehension. She would start talking like a *grande dame* and then stand back rigid and faltering, as if she feared being crushed by her own massively intimidating offensive.

There are close, over-lapping references to the 'Life Studies' poems in '91 Revere Street'. The poems, particularly those about Lowell's grand-parents and distant family, are fonder, more relaxed, than those about his parents. As the poems approach Lowell's present life there is a mounting sense of tension. Despite this, the dramatic structure of *Life Studies* seems a great deal less insistent than the accumulated presence of *things* :

> snapshots of his *Liberty Bell* silver mine,
> his high school at *Stukkert am Neckar,*
> stogie-brown beams, fools'-gold nuggets,
> octagonal red tiles . . .

> We stopped at the *Priscilla* in Nashua
> for brownies and root-beer . . .

> His favourite ball, the number three,
> still hides the coffee stain.

> The corpse
> was wrapped like *panetone* in Italian tinfoil.

Lowell is the master of the quick sketch, the telling detail which reveals a character, and which gives the texture of the book a gritty richness of accumulated people, places and things. It puts it too melodramatically, but *Life Studies* reeks of humanity. The 'fly-weight pacifist' Abramowitz is savagely beaten by two Hollywood pimps wearing 'chocolate double-breasted suits'. We see mad Stanley, the ex-Harvard, All-American football star, now in his sixties,

> still hoarding the build of a boy in his twenties,
> as he soaks, a ramrod
> with the muscle of a seal
> in his long tub,
> vaguely urinous from the Victorian plumbing.

Lowell's father was proud of his progressive management of domestic affairs:

> As early as 1928,
> he owned a house converted to oil,
> and redecorated by the architect
> of St. Mark's School. . . . Its' main effect
> was a drawing room, 'longitudinal as Versailles'

Great Aunt Sarah rose from 'her bed of troublesome snacks and Tauchnitz classics'.

This kind of observation can have a terrible sting, as when his father's rendition of 'Anchors Aweigh' is counterpointed to his continuing failure as a business man, or when we are told that he went off 'to loaf in the Maritime Museum',

> loaded with his 'calc' and 'trig' books,
> his clipper ship statistics,
> and his ivory slide rule . . .

The patients all have 'locked' razors in 'Waking in the Blue'. But he maintains the delicate line between genuine irony and fond sentimentality in 'Grandparents' (one of Lowell's greatest poems). It is a loving portrait of an older world, which he had introduced in 'Beyond the Alps':

> I envy the conspicuous
> waste of our grandparents on their grand tours —
> long-haired Victorian sages accepted the universe,
> while breezing on their trust funds through the world.

His grandparents are seen as mildly humorous eccentrics, taking the Pierce Arrow for a 'ritual Friday spin'. Their memory fades in the dry white dust of the road. Their world, the nineteenth century, has gone too, leaving only relics, mementos, and the farm which Lowell has now inherited. He lives there like a guest among his memories, each detail of the house possessed by the lives of his grandparents.

> Never again
> to walk there, chalk our cues,
> insist on shooting for us both.

How precise, and bittersweet is that recollection. It makes possible what follows, where Lowell cries out with the voice of his five-year-old self, 'Grandpa! Have me, hold me, cherish me!', and we see (as in 'Sailing Home from Rapallo') tears in his eyes.

> There
> half my life-lease later,
> I hold an *Illustrated London News*
> disloyal still,
> I doodle handlebar
> moustaches on the last Russian Czar.

The magazine, the Czar, his grandparents, the nineteenth century, belong to a world which is 'altogether otherworldly now'. The handlebar moustache is a superb touch, lowering the tone of the poem, turning his sense of loss into something wryly manageable. Lowell's sense of the past, and our relation to it, lives through details, and lived experience. '91 Revere Street' does not really come alive until the relics, the physical presence of the family, begin to be felt. This suggests something of the weakness of Lowell's historical sense, glaringly visible in *History* (1973): it is difficult to think of any work of the historical sense which is so oblivious of forces, and so obsessed with the character of the major protagonists.

The great set-pieces of 'Waking in the Blue' and 'Skunk Hour', dealing with Lowell's sickness, are tighter constructions. The texture is rougher, the ironies more pointed, the elisions quicker and more telling. Though both poems come out of Lowell's recurrent mental disturbance, his humour and keenness of eye is unimpaired. This sometimes seems surprising, as though being mentally disturbed is the same thing, temporarily, as being dim-witted or mentally deficient. But 'Waking in the Blue' is marked by some extremely funny writing, set in a context of a deeper anxiety which runs throughout:

> Azure day
> makes my agonized window bleaker.
> Crows maunder on the petrified fairway.
> Absence! My heart grows tense
> as though a harpoon were sparring for the kill.
> (This is the house for the 'mentally ill'.)

The sense of these lines is difficult, but not because the syntax or grammatical construction is ambiguous. Lowell is attempting to portray a psychotic state not by description, but by putting together a series of perceptions of the world seen through his window, and of his feelings. We don't (can't) *know* what is wrong, except that the copulas have been suppressed, or don't exist. The window is 'agonized' and the fairway 'petrified' because they are part of *le paysage interieur* of the psychological landscape.[106]   Lowell gave a more precise explanation (and also a disclaimer, to be considered carefully by enthusiasts of extremity):

> I have been through mania and depression; *Life Studies* is about neither. Mania is extremity for one's friends, depression for one's self. Both are chemical. In depression, one wakes, is happy for about two minutes, probably less, and then fades into dread of the day. Nothing will happen, but you know twelve hours will pass before you are back in bed and sheltering your consciousness in dreams, or nothing. I don't think it a visitation of the angels but dust in the blood.[107]

The passage beginning 'Azure day' is as precise a description of depression as, elsewhere, there are descriptions of facts, details, parts of the world; it is no different in kind from the rest of Lowell's poetry.

'Skunk Hour' is burdened with a massive cultural meaning, perhaps more than it can bear. No less than 'Waking in the Blue', it is a description of a state of sickness. Only here the symptoms creep through the whole community: the peculiar heiress who still lives in a Spartan cottage, and who thirsts for the 'hierarchic privacy/of Queen Victoria's century', acts in a curiously passive fashion; the 'summer millionaire', who seemed so well kitted-out he was something out of a mail-order catalogue, has left and his boat has been auctioned off. Lowell's most ambiguous symbol of the sickness conveys a strangely forceful sense of menace, without approaching an explicit statement:

> A red fox stain covers Blue Hill.

The first three stanzas insinuate the idea that there is something wrong, or sick, about the island community. The slight eccentricity of behaviour, the hinted process of social change, the attempt to link the ills of the community with the state of nature, are repressed (as Snodgrass would put it) and concentrated into what are essentially unemphatic details. We are eased, gradually, into unease. 'Skunk Hour' begins properly with the fourth stanza: 'And now our fairy/decorator brightens his shop . . .', but the themes of the rest of the poem seem scarcely related to this tepid social observation. Lowell works characteristically through details towards the re-creation of a state of mind. The observation of 'love-cars' on the 'hill's skull' has an undercurrent of threat; the closest parallel to Lowell's effect is the slight backward and lateral movement of a cine camera from a close shot of two people. The shift in perspective suddenly introduces the *presence* of the observer, with decidedly menacing consequences. Lowell's insistence that 'My mind's not right' does something like this (visions of psychopathic murderers, haunting lovers lane, flash through the consciousness), cutting right through the disconnected and oddly passive 'I', perplexing us as well with his desire to explain, to make explicit what was plentifully obvious. It is a break with tact. Once done, there is no point in drawing back; the point is that the direct statement is *redundant*.

> I hear
> my ill-spirit sob in each blood cell,
> as if my hand were at its throat...
> I myself am hell,
> nobody's here —

At which point the skunks enter, march up the street, nose around in the garbage behind Lowell's house and ignore his presence on the back porch. The skunks are the only creatures in the poem with any resolution. They know what they want, and take it. But the conjunction of the skunks and the local Trinitarian church seems a bit too carefully arranged:

> They march on their soles up Main Street:
> white stripes, moonstruck eyes' red fire
> under the chalk-dry spar spire
> of the Trinitarian Church.

That the church spire is 'chalk-dry' tells us as much as we need to know, theologically, about New England religion; we might also recall from '91 Revere Street' that Lowell's great-grandfather, Charles Lowell, was preacher at West Church, Boston, 'a haven from the Trinitarian orthodoxy'.

Wherever we turn in the poem its meaning is elusive and deep, especially in the central conjunction between personal sickness and communal malaise. There is something in us that wants to resist an idea as monstrous as this, and to say that Lowell has no right. Where would that leave us? Besides, the poem seems too fragile for the burden. It says more about us than it does about Lowell that we feel suspicious and resentful that he should even try to say such a thing.

Even Lowell, for all his prodigal development, seems a dawdler beside Sylvia Plath. The impact of *Ariel* is so great, so indelible, that a retrospective fascination attaches to the whole of Plath's life and work. A more severely focused critical interest, however, finds that it is in her work that the crisis of the 1950s is played out.

Sylvia Plath graduated from Gamaliel Bradford Senior High School in Wellesley, Massachusetts, in June 1950. The *Wellesleyan*, her high school yearbook, describes her as 'Clever with chalk and paints . . . Weekends at Williams . . . Those fully packed sandwiches . . . Basketball and tennis player . . . Future writer . . . Those rejection slips from *Seventeen* . . . Oh, for a license.'[108]   A popular, very bright, highly-ambitious scholarship girl, she entered Smith College in Northampton, Mass., with the freshman class in September 1950. At Smith she was plunged into a remarkable hub of social and intellectual élites. She came into contact with Elizabeth Drew, attended lectures by I. A. Richards, took a course on Hawthorne, Melville and James with Newton Arvin, studied American literature with Alfred Kazin, audited a class by Frank O'Connor; Richard Wilbur was assistant professor of English at Harvard from 1950 to 1954, and was the most celebrated of the younger poets. Plath was competitive and successful. When she won the Irene Glasscock Poetry Contest at Mount Holyoke, the judges were John Ciardi, Wallace Fowlie and Marianne Moore. They all seemed beautifully human and accessible during the several days of dinners and discussions before the main competition in which all six contestants read their work to an enthusiastic audience of over 200. Ciardi was encouraging, and wrote to Plath after the contest with suggestions about where she might send her poems; he even offered to send them along with his own personal endorsement. Plath seems remarkably successful at gaining publication. Her short story, 'Sunday at the Mintons' ', published in *Mademoiselle* in August 1953, won a $500 fiction contest. The money made a difference. Since her father's death when she was nine, Aurelia Plath was left with the sole responsibility for looking after the education of her son Warren and precocious daughter Sylvia. A scholarship to Smith was achieved, but there were other needs for money. In 1954 she was a successful competitor for *Mademoiselle's* 'College Board' — a panel of prize-winning undergraduates invited to join the magazine's staff and produce one issue during the summer. (This period, and its terrible aftermath in her nervous breakdown and attempted suicide, are described in Plath's novel *The Bell Jar*, published in 1963.) From 1952 her poems and stories were appearing regularly in the *Smith Review*, and in *Mademoiselle*. In 1954 she had two poems accepted by *Harper's Magazine* and in the next year poems appeared in the *Atlantic Monthly*, and *The Nation*. At this time she had no luck at all with *The New Yorker*. Nor was she the only brilliant, beautiful poetess in the process of emerging into a major literary career. Adrienne Rich had already published her first book. 'I keep reading about this damn adrienne cecile rich', she wrote to Gordon Lameyer on 28 July 1955, 'only two years older than I, who is a yale younger poet and regularly in all the top mags; and about 23-year-old blondes from radcliffe who are already selling stories plus climbing alps. Occasionally, I retch quietly in the wastebasket.'[109]

Her favourite authors were Yeats and Dylan Thomas, but she decided to write her undergraduate thesis on the theme of the double in Dostoyevsky. She struggled manfully with German: despite her family origin (her father was a first generation German immigrant, and her mother was a second generation American from Austria) it didn't come easily. But her poetry expressed nothing quite so clearly as that it was being written in the age of high formalism. During the summer of 1953 she published 'Poets on Campus' in *Mademoiselle,* containing brief interviews with five American poets (Anthony Hecht, Alastair Reid, Richard Wilbur, F. George Steiner and William Burford).[110] Plath was particularly enthusiastic about Wilbur. Her room-mate during 1954-5, Nancy Hunter Steiner, remembers that she 'talked of him often. She read every word he wrote and showed me every article about him and every photograph of him that appeared anywhere in print.'[111] Plath met Wilbur in 1953, after her attempted suicide, when it was hoped that Wilbur, whose work she intensely admired, might give her some encouragement.[112]   In addition to Ciardi's enthusiasm, Plath found Alfred Kazin extremely helpful (and she liked the close particularity of Kazin's style in his memoir, *A Walker in the City,* 1952). She met Auden, and showed him some of her poems. They were too glib, he said.[113]

She began to keep a manuscript of her poems as early as 1955 (it was then titled 'Circus in Three Rings'). A year later it was titled 'Two Lovers and a Beachcomber' and, according to Ted Hughes, contained forty different poems.[114]   This was the manuscript which Plath submitted for Part Two of the English Tripos at Cambridge in 1957, and which was found, a dozen years later, collecting dust in a cupboard in the English Faculty Library at the Sidgwick Site.[115]   Plath granted that Auden had a valid criticism to make when he said her work was too glib, but adds (in the same letter to Lameyer) that she wasn't trying to be all *that* serious; partly it was just playing around with vowel sounds. The emphasis seems perfectly just. Her early poems were apprentice-work in the best sense. That she was able to publish them, and in such prestigious places, was an indication of how truly skilful she was. It also says a great deal about the standards of even 'good' magazines in the early 1950s that Plath's polished apples went down so well. Her 'success' does not mean that they are wildly interesting as poems. Many of them, able as she unquestionably was, are just exercises. She plays with the length and proper weighting of adjectives in ' "Go Get the Goodly Squab" ': 'fast-feathered eagle', 'galloping antelope', 'purple snails'.[116]   'Circus in Three Rings' is an exercise in the use of extended metaphor or conceit. 'Dialogue en Route' is an exercise in hyperbole. Others, such as 'Danse Macabre', sound like variations on a set theme. Plath won her spurs with 'Lament', a perfectly executed villanelle, which she published in 1955. There is no pressure here actually to say anything, least of all anything 'personal'. Formalism wasn't about that, and Plath was a perfect junior formalist, happily and obliviously caught up in the joyous poeticality and elaborateness of her forms and language. There is this element throughout the whole of her work well up until 1959 or 1960. She attended Robert Lowell's class at Boston University in 1958-9, along with George Starbuck and Anne Sexton, who remembers discussing Plath with Lowell:

> Lowell said, at the time, that he liked her work and that he felt her poems got right to the point. I didn't agree. I felt they really missed the whole point. (These were early poems of hers — poems on the way, on the working way.) I told Mr Lowell that I felt she dodged the point and did so perhaps because of her preoccupation with form. Form was important for Sylvia and each really good poet has one of his own. No matter what he calls it — free verse or what. Still, it belongs to you or it doesn't. Sylvia hadn't then found a form that belonged to her. Those early poems were all in a cage (and not even her own cage at that). I felt she hadn't found a voice of her own, wasn't, in truth, free to be herself. Yet, of course, I knew she was skilled — intense, skilled, perceptive, strange, blonde, lovely Sylvia.[117]

By 'early poems' Anne Sexton certainly meant all of Plath's work up to then. With hindsight, Plath's undergraduate poems 'fit in', show her trying out images, vocabulary, themes, which will reappear in a more highly charged form later. Such as the image of the colossus which first appears in a stance of heroic defiance:

> That grandiose colossus who
> Stood astride
> The envious assaults of sea
> (Essaying, wave by wave,
> Tide by tide,
> To undo him, perpetually). . .   ('Letter to a Purist')

When she published 'The Colossus' in the *Kenyon Review,* Fall 1960, her grasp of the usefulness of metaphor was surer. The colossus is now a ruin, which she is trying, in her feeble manner, to resurrect:

> Thirty years now I have laboured
> To dredge the silt from your throat.
> I am none the wiser.
>
> Scaling little ladders with gluepots and pails of lysol
> I crawl like an ant in mourning
> Over the weedy acres of your brow
> To mend the immense skull-plates and clear
> The bald, white tumuli of your eyes.

Tumuli is one of the many precise, unusual, Latinate words sprinkled through Plath's first book. The usual method of composition, in which Plath wrote very slowly and with constant reference to a thesaurus or dictionary, became a kind of mannerism.[118] The sheer impossibility of resurrection, and her own involvement with the dead figure of her father, is a central complex of ideas and images for Plath, but in 'The Colossus' she is writing about a painful subject in a painless fashion, as though metaphor was a powerful novocaine. When she returns to the image in 'The Stones', the last of the important series which conclude *The Colossus,* it is inverted and transposed from a vehicle for describing her relationship with her long-dead father, to a way of talking about her own state of mind in the period following her marriage. Aspects of this complex of images reappear in 'Lyonnesse' (*Winter Trees*), and 'Lady Lazarus' and 'Gulliver' (*Ariel*). When she finds an image, Plath will work and rework it, discovering implications or possible juxtapositions to deepen and enrich the symbolic meanings she has found.

Part of the way Plath matured as a writer was through a procession of 'influences'. The contributors to *The Art of Sylvia Plath* refer to the following poets: Pasternak, Crane, Stevens, Whitman, Lawrence, Laforgue, Ransom, Rimbaud, Owen, Dickinson, Eliot, Roethke, Lowell, Dylan Thomas, Keats, Anne Sexton; to add to that list would be easy: Marianne Moore, W. D. Snodgrass and Richard Wilbur. And then there is, as George Steiner noted, an Empsonian flavour to many of Plath's early poems. The business of influences is endless, but she could only use what she was ready to use, and we must carefully distinguish between a degree of technical flattery through imitation, and a deeper level of response which comes closer to the imaginative character of Plath's work as a whole. Though the argument needs to be made in greater detail than is possible here, it seems fairly clear that Theodore Roethke was the only poet to operate at the level of a major influence. This expressed itself not so much through Plath's attempt to copy Roethke's style, or his characteristic diction (though there is this), but in a crucial grasp of what Roethke had achieved in metaphor, and of the possibilities of constructing poems solely out of metaphor.

There is only one significant interpretation of the development of Sylvia Plath, that by Ted Hughes, and he places Plath's discovery of Roethke at the crucial moment in late 1959 when she began her sudden process of maturation which was to continue until 1962 and the birth of her second child, and then to resume, on a considerably higher level, for the rest of Plath's life. Hughes finds many interesting things in Plath's poetry up to 1959, but the real stuff comes after that date. No one would seriously argue with this judgment of Plath's work. But Hughes's comments are elusive, and merit a closer inspection.[119] For Hughes, the individuating force that makes a true poet is his unique, personal 'gift'. Without remaining 'infinitely sensitive' to its nature, a poet ran the danger that he would fail to develop, that he might 'lose the feel of its touch in the workings of his mind', and become concerned with things in which his gift had no interest whatsoever. Hughes regards this as a form of psychic suicide. The gift cannot be encouraged, because it visits a poet 'when he is only half suspecting it'. The job of a poet is to bring out, 'without impairment', certain 'memories, images, sounds, feelings, thoughts, and relationships' which have 'become luminous at the core of his mind'. Wendy Campbell, a friend of Plath's at Cambridge, recalled meeting Hughes:

> Ted told us how he felt the process of writing: I don't remember his precise words but he conveyed a clear picture of the process. He sank a shaft into the deepest part of himself and stood aside so to speak, and let the words, the matter, rise up. It was a marvellous image of the process of fishing the unconscious.[120]

This is the meaningful context for one of Plath's most disturbing last poems:

> The sap
> Wells like tears, like the
> Water striving
> To re-establish its mirror
> Over the rock . . .
> Words dry and riderless,
> The indefatigable hoof-taps.
> While
> From the bottom of the pool, fixed stars
> Govern a life.
>
> ('Words')

There were several ways that a poet might resist, or deform, his 'gift'. To 'throw . . . verse into the popular excitement of the time', like Coleridge and Wordsworth, was one way. Another, more typical of an age of formalism, was that of the type of poet formed by a 'highly-disciplined, highly intellectual style of education', and who had, in fact, devoted a lifetime's training, a 'fierce and highly successful effort', in preparation for a career in teaching in a university. This was Sylvia Plath when Ted Hughes met her at Cambridge in 1956. Charles Newman has suggested that Hughes may have been the 'greatest single influence' on Plath — so obvious, indeed, that it has been overlooked.[121] What seems likely — since his idea of the nature of the poet was more highly evolved than Plath's — is that he helped her to acknowledge what he felt to be her 'gift' and to accept 'the invitation of her inner world'. Plath's poem 'Flute Notes from a Reedy Pond' of 1959, Hughes writes, showed a 'sudden enrichment of the texture of her verse', whose shifting focus came as a surprise. 'At this time she was trying to break down the tyranny, the fixed focus and public persona which descriptive or discursive poems take as a norm. We devised exercises of meditation and invocation.' His role, as suggested here, was that he saw what needed to be done, and how to do it. The crucial development of Sylvia Plath was a mutual project between her and her husband.[122] On a visit to the newly-married Hughes family in 1956, Elinor Klein (writing in *Glamour,* November 1966) writes that 'Ted was determined to take us to a witch in the valley below. At the stroke of midnight, with mock apprehension, we left the house, filing, safari fashion, behind Ted. I felt that if fair became foul and if, indeed, we fell in with threatening supernatural forces, Ted, who dwarfed everything around him, could protect us certainly.' The visit ended up an anti-climax. They met the 'gnarled lady in question' and spent a couple of hours talking about farming and the neighbours. There were no supernatural manifestations.

Hughes described Plath as being blessed with 'psychic gifts'. Her early poems were 'bristling hurdles'; 'a lifetime's training' was not to be surrendered so easily. But once the multiple defences of her personality began to allow 'the invitation of her inner world' to be felt, the consequences began to appear in her poems. 'Lorelei', 'Full Fathom Five', 'Flute Notes from a Reedy Pond', and 'The Stones' began the process.

Hughes's theory of Plath's development, presented as an oblique, rather elaborate schema, is made considerably more accessible in the elegant essays of A. Alvarez. On Hughes's part it is based upon a lived experience which outsiders like Elinor Klein and Wendy Campbell can only have glimpsed in fragments. It is doubly hard to assess the interpretation which Hughes makes, because it is so closely related to his relationship to his wife. Hughes's reference to the self 'shattered in 1953' reminds us that Plath had experienced a disastrous psychic collapse while she was an undergraduate. She had climbed back on to the ladder, the only one in her world.[123] Hughes's conception of the nature of the poet seemed to tell her that the ladder (and the highly disciplined drive which made her so academically successful) was working against her. He mentions 'great tactical opposition from individuals she regarded as her benefactors' (were they *not* benefactors, in fact?), when Plath decided to abandon her teaching career in 1958, after one outwardly successful year for Plath at Smith College, which had left them both dissatisfied with academic life. It was only through the abandonment of what Hughes regarded as false goals that he felt she was enabled to recover 'her own centre of gravity'. *Ariel,* in this analysis, was a fulfilment of her 'gift'.

There are other ways to consider Plath's development, but the pattern, the way out of that tight, clever formalism of her early work came through a process of self-questioning, of development and dissatisfaction, which was experienced widely throughout America in the late 1950s. Lowell suggested one way out of a constricting formalism in *Life Studies*; Roethke showed another. Ted Hughes was writing 'with color, splendor, and vigorous music about life, birth, war, animals, hags and vampires, martyrdom, and sophisticated intellectual problems'.[124] In quite different ways, all three might have served to make the point for Plath that the nature of 'reality' included the consciousness of the self, and that the 'central emotions and incidents of life', which, in a letter to her mother of 24 February 1957, she felt Wilbur avoided, were in fact the substance of an art of the real. There was a literary and even a social logic in what Hughes presents too narrowly as a purely personal psychodrama.

In the same analysis, Hughes sees the poems as constituting an *oeuvre*:

> . . . I think it will be a service if I point out just how little of her poetry is 'occasional', and how faithfully her separate poems build up into one long poem. She faced a task in herself, and her poetry is the record of her progress in the task. The poems are chapters in a mythology where the plot, seen as a whole and in retrospect, is strong and clear — even if the origins of it and the *dramatis personae,* are at bottom enigmatic. The world of her poetry is one of emblematic visionary events, mathematical symmetries, clairvoyance and metamorphoses.

(And so Hughes contributes, in no small fashion, to the process of turning Sylvia Plath into a myth. His services in this field are only dwarfed by Lowell, whose foreword to the 1966 American edition of *Ariel* describes Plath as becoming 'something imaginary, newly, wildly and subtly created — hardly a person at all, or a woman, certainly not another "poetess", but one of those super-real, hypnotic, great classical heroines'.) Hughes's emphasis is contradicted by the poems often enough to send us to a comment Plath made to her mother in a letter of 17 December 1960, cautioning her not to take Ted's 'elaborate metaphysical explanations' too seriously. She felt his comments came out of a judgment on a play so adverse that 'he feels a need to invent elaborate disguises as a smoke screen for it'. Precisely the opposite point to Hughes's needs to be made about Plath: that many of her poems describe a very specific occasion, a landscape or relationship, which stands clearly behind the process of metamorphosis into 'emblematic visionary events'. Her 'main difficulty', Plath suggested in a letter to her brother Warren on 11 June 1958,

> . . . has been overcoming a clever, too brittle and glossy feminine tone, and I am gradually getting to speak 'straight out' and of real experience, not just in metaphysical conceits.

Later that summer, Plath and her husband travelled across America, before returning to Saratoga Springs, New York, for a stay at Yaddo, the writer's colony. Out of her camping experience came the story 'The Fifty-Ninth Bear' (published in the *London Magazine,* February 1961), and the poems 'Sleep in the Mojave Desert' and 'Two Campers in Cloud Country', both published in *Crossing the Water.* The landscape in the two poems is different, but come together to make in her mind the same point: that landscape is not consoling, is no place of refuge. Two years earlier, in an angry letter on the British bombing of Suez, Plath wrote that 'the creative forces of nature are the only forces which give me any peace now, and we want to become part of them; no war, after these mad incidents, has any meaning for us'.* The attitude towards nature which she hints at in this letter is profoundly uncharacteristic of her work. In 'Sleep in the Mojave Desert' the dry, hot landscape was supremely indifferent or even hostile to life. The mountainous lake and forest country in Canada described in 'Two Campers in Cloud Country' makes a similar point:

> The horizons are too far off to be chummy as uncles;
> The colours assert themselves with a sort of vengeance.
> Each day concludes in a huge splurge of vermilions
>
> And night arrives in one gigantic step.
> It is comfortable, for a change, to mean so little.
> These rocks offer no purchase to herbage or people:
>
> They are conceiving a dynasty of perfect cold.

There is an inevitable contrast with 'Watercolour of Grantchester Meadows' (*The Colossus*). Nothing here is 'big or far', the birds were 'thumb-sized', the cygnets 'tame':

> It is a country on a nursery plate.
> Spotted cows revolve their jaws and crop
> Red clover or gnaw beetroot
> Bellied on a nimbus of sun-glazed buttercup.
> Hedging meadows of benign
> Arcadian green
> The blood berried hawthorn hides its spines with white.

'Blackgowned' figures (undergraduates wearing academic dress) walk with 'moony indolence', and are 'unaware' of the real nature of the scene through which they move,

---

* One of the minor revelations of *Letters Home* is that Plath was a great deal more 'political' than her husband. Her contribution to the *London Magazine* symposium on 'Context' (February 1962) is her only comment about the relation of literature to politics. The comparison with Hughes's contribution to the same symposium is illuminating.

> How in such mild air
> The owl shall stoop from his turret, the rat cry out.

Life in Cambridge conspired to encourage that 'moony indolence', but in the Mojave Desert or Canadian wilderness the presence of landscape was overwhelming.

> No gesture of yours or mine could catch their attention,
> No words make them carry water or fire the kindling
> Like local trolls in the spell of a superior being.

Nature resists the colonialism of the imagination. The characteristic human response is to create a garden, to tame and civilize, but

> . . . one wearies of the Public Gardens: one wants a vacation
> Where trees and clouds and animals pay no notice;
> Away from the labelled elms, the tame tea-roses.

Between the experience of Grantchester and that of the desert and the mountains, Plath has become hungrier for the real. She sees more clearly the mechanism by which we are fobbed off with the tamed or pacified thing, and wants to substitute for it the 'real experience'. Her description of the optical illusion of seeing a row of poplars 'in the middle distance' of the desert, and the way she describes starlight reflected from the surface of a lake, and the quietness of the forest, become metaphors for her relationship with the landscape as well as precise descriptions of natural phenomena.

There is a perceptible gain in subtlety, and power of metaphor, in Plath's 'Mystic' (*Winter Trees*). This, too, is an 'occasional' poem in that it begins, like so many of Plath's poems, in a real landscape — Mystic seaport on the Connecticut coast, a carefully restored whaling port, whose wood cabins and stiff, preserved sails evoke a memory of a hot uncomfortable summer day. Mystic has been preserved as a monument to the age of whaling, but at great cost: it has lost its suppleness, its feel of life. The scene leads Plath to thoughts of being

> . . . seized up

> Without a part left over,
> Not a toe, not a finger, and used,
> Used utterly in the sun's conflagrations . . .

She asks whether an explanation for that feeling is to be found in 'the pill of the Communion tablet', in prayer (echoing the 'Lord's Prayer'), memory, in a life of spiritual humility, or a diffuse transcendental theism:

> Or picking up the bright pieces
> Of Christ in the faces of rodents,
> The tame flower-nibblers, the ones

Whose hopes are so low they are comfortable —

Meaning does not inhere in such things:

Does the sea

Remember the walker upon it?
Meaning leaks from molecules.

Plath used this image in an earlier poem, 'Wuthering Heights':

Of people the air only
Remembers a few odd syllables.

It is one of the many ways she found to understand the profound distance which lay between herself and the natural world. The values which might serve as a rationale for sacrifice, for her feeling of being totally used up and consumed, do not inhere in things, are not to be found in a world whose otherness is always hostile.

The sun gives you ulcers, the wind gives you TB . . .   ('Lesbos')

This was something to be learned from Auden's 'Musée des Beaux Arts', that tragic sacrifice does not shape a world to its own image.

The ultimate concern in 'Mystic' is for a spiritual communion which is now gone from her world. In quite early poems this emerged as a major preoccupation:

Battle however I would
To break through that patchwork
Of leaves' bicker and whisk in babel tongues.
Streak and mottle of tawn bark,
No visionary lightenings
Pierced my dense lid.   ('On the Plethora of Dryads')

She moved from 'visionary lightenings' and 'luminous shape' to a Christian symbolism in her last work. Plath stated that she was not 'mystical' in the poem 'Pheasant'. Lameyer quotes a letter from Cambridge in which Plath lightly complains of the difficulty of explaining to a Jewish family that she wasn't 'really' a Christian. When she was living in Devon, Plath wrote that 'the Anglican religion seems terribly numb & cold & grim to me . . . All the awful emphasis on our weakness & sinfulness & being able to do nothing but through Christ . . . But I do want Frieda to have the experience of Sunday School, so I may keep up the unsatisfactory practice of going, although I disagree with almost everything.'[125]   The rector called and offered to explain the creed and order of service. 'I'm afraid I could never stomach the Trinity and all that!', she wrote to her mother on 13 October 1961. Plath persisted, to the point of having both children baptized, but ceased attending services after a 'ghastly H-bomb sermon' in which the rector described the 'happy prospect of the Second Coming and how lucky we Christians were compared to the stupid pacifists and humanists and "educated pagans" who feared being incinerated' (letter of 12 March 1962). Plath was very much a ban-the-bomb pacifist. 'I'd really be a church-goer if I was back in Wellesley,' she continued, '— the Unitarian Church is my church. How I miss it!' It would not be wholly justified to conclude that Plath was drawn to Christianity for aesthetic reasons, for the richness and universality of its symbolism, though at times her use of the idea of resurrection has more to do with fertility rites and things she picked up by reading in mythology and collections of folktales, than with any obvious theological meaning.

The most famous of all her attempts to use this theme is 'Lady Lazarus' (*Ariel*), a study in transformation in which Plath sees herself as a feminine Lazarus, reclaimed from the dead and restored to life. The poem is a complex monologue, in which her own suicide becomes a way of shedding an identity which has become reduced to meaninglessness. She becomes, metaphorically, an Egyptian mummy, a striptease artist, a pile of objects, and then the Phoenix rising out of the ashes. There is something deeply disturbing in the way she treats the idea of suicide and death. By turning the process into a spectacle, she aestheticizes it, judging suicide by the style of the attempt:

> Dying
> Is an art, like everything else.
> I do it exceptionally well.
> I do it so it feels like hell.
> I do it so it feels real.
> I guess you could say I've a call.

The word *call* underlines the ironic inversion of the religious meaning of resurrection in the poem. But the idea of spectacle and performance transforms Plath's tone into a lashing irony. She is contemptuous of the spectators, the bystanders, the 'peanut-crunching crowd' which 'shoves in' to see what there is to see. (It took Plath a whole poem, 'Aftermath', to make this same point in *The Colossus*.) There is an interaction between the idea of wholeness and that of dissolution, between the body dehumanized and reduced to a series of objects, and the restoration of the whole self, flesh and living breath, when the resurrection is completed. While her tone is bitterly sarcastic and contemptuous, and her recording of the poem is shatteringly close to the bone, at the same time the poem aches with pathos and longing. She is being transformed from a decayed, death-like visage:

> Peel off the napkin
> O my enemy.
> Do I terrify? —

The nose, the eyepits, the full set of teeth?

which she sardonically flaunts, while feeling herself little more than an object exhibited, for which there is a 'very large charge' to view; she is a shriek, a pile of ashes,

> A cake of soap,
> A wedding ring,
> A gold filling.

And identified herself with the victims of the death camps. By doing so, she returns us to her deeper feeling of loss, of being used up, extinguished, which was her subject in 'Mystic', and which she has now taken to an utmost and terrible conclusion. Yet the jaunty, hostile, ironic tone of her voice serves a different kind of meaning.

> Do not think I underestimate your great concern.

The concern is that of Herr Doktor, Herr Enemy:

> Ash, ash —
> You poke and stir.
> Flesh, bone, there is nothing there —

Suicide promises one way to free herself from the 'great concern', the burden of interest and expectation of that omnibus figure, Doktor-Professor-Father-God-Lucifer, whom she has spent most of her life trying to please, and for whose examination she feels drained, empty, unprepared. Suicide was a form of release from the feeling of being a powerless victim.

The poem ends on a resurgent note. She has found, through dissolution and despair, a new, threatening, power:

> Herr God, Herr Lucifer
> Beware
> Beware.
>
> Out of the ash
> I rise with my red hair
> And I eat men like air.

The echo from Coleridge is unmistakable:

> Could I revive within me
> Her sympathy and song,
> To such a deep delight 'twould win me,
> That with music loud and long,
> I would build that dome in air,
> That sunny dome! those caves of ice!
> And all who heard should see them there,

> And all should cry, Beware! Beware!
> His flashing eyes, his floating hair!

('Kubla Khan')

The dialectic between sickness and health, wholeness and dissolution, is resolved in the figure of the Phoenix, incorporating both thesis and antithesis in a resolving act of aggression and threat. She has ceased to be a passive victim; Mrs Hughes has become Ms Plath; the 'smiling woman' has reappeared as the red-haired Phoenix. 'Lady Lazarus' is a poem that comes out of a particular moment in Plath's life: it is very much an 'occasional' poem. It was written after her husband had abandoned her, and she was left with both children, repeatedly sick, desperately hoping to find a suitable nanny, and in the process of settling into a new flat in London. 'Lady Lazarus' is a defiant gesture of survival — look, I've come through! — which corresponds closely to the tone of her letters home in December 1962. She had been severely depressed and unwell, and her suicide attempt at the age of twenty was on her mind, and appears in 'Lady Lazarus'. (In a letter to her brother Warren on 18 October 1962 she pleaded with him to convince their mother that, 'I am only in danger physically, mentally I am sound, fine, and writing the best ever, free from 4 a.m. to 8 a.m. each day.') 'Lady Lazarus' is not, finally, a poem that glories in death, but is the jubilant, bitter locution of a survivor.

Something like this needs to be said about 'Daddy', a poem about which it is easy to write rather misdirected criticism. 'In this poem,' writes A. R. Jones,

> ... the diseased psyche takes the place of sensibility and the problem is to establish the relations between subconscious psyche and conscious will. Torn between love and violence, the *persona* moves towards self-knowledge, the awareness that she loves the violence or, at least, towards the recognition that the principles of love and violence are so intimately associated one with the other that the love can only express itself in terms of violence.[126]

One understands the poem as an incantation, an attempt to communicate with her long-dead father. At one point she reverts to Shamanism, the use of a bag of bones, to reach his spirit, but as in a farce or a bad dream, it is she who emerges from the bag. Then she tries a little black magic, making a small model of a 'man in black with a Meinkampf look/And a love of the rack and the screw'. Plath's fumbling around with rituals, black magic, and the parodistic bogeyman of a father, are deliberately placed elements in a *comic* poem.

> Every woman adores a Fascist,
> The boot in the face . . .

Unitarians from Wellesley, Mass., graduates from Smith College *summa*

cum laude and Phi Beta Kappa, who are also B.A.(Cantab.) might expect
their well-trained critics to detect some irony in lines like these. The
humour is black, the blackest imaginable, but it is humour. 'Daddy' comes
straight out of Walt Disney or the *marchen* of the brothers Grimm. The
neat moustache, brute heart, black swastika, and 'boot in the face'
suggests a conscious process of exaggeration. The memory of her father,
stern disciplinarian, dying painfully of diabetes mellitus which went
undiagnosed because he felt it was an untreatable case of lung cancer,
became an inner nightmare so smothering and persistent that in the end,
one is tempted to conclude, her only possible response was a kind of
gallows humour. (Lowell's 'Terminal Days at Beverly Farms' betrays little
of Plath's grim involvement, but it was no less an effort to see an agonized
and painful experience without self-pity. It, too, is in the comic mode.)
Plath reverts to the role and voice of a little girl when she says he was 'the
black man who/Bit my pretty red heart in two'. The poem opens with an
image of Plath as a little gnome:

> For thirty years, poor and white,
> Barely daring to breathe or Achoo.

The final stanzas plainly echo memories of 'Frankenstein' and 'Dracula',
with the villagers 'dancing and stamping' on the overthrown monster; it is
comic gothic. The rhythms come from the recalled world of nursery
rhymes, charms and incantations. 'Daddy' is a poem of massively felt
relief at the symbolic murder of her father and husband,

> The Vampire who said he was you
> And drank my blood for a year,
> Seven years, if you want to know.

We see her imagining a break out of the suffocating cycle of subconscious
violence inflicted upon her by both of them. At the end of the poem —

> Daddy, daddy, you bastard, I'm through

— the 'new woman' made her declaration of independence; the 1960s
arrived, angry and exultant.

165

Chapter 3

The 1960s and 1970s

The hegemony of the chatty-vernacular, anti-poetic, corn-porn typical poem of the 1960s and 1970s masks the stealthy emergence of the long poem as the common poetic medium of the day; a *salon des refusés* of untypical poems by Charles Reznikoff, Richard Emil Braun and Basil Bunting, suggests something of the capacious heritage of Ezra Pound; an angry primitivism arrives, led by Gary Snyder; Galway Kinnell from alienation to primitivism; the loose, baggy monsters of John Berryman and Robert Lowell; the final contention between Geoffrey Hill and Ted Hughes.

Selected Chronology

1960

Donald M. Allen, ed., *The New American Poetry*
W. H. Auden, *Homage to Clio*
Gregory Corso, *The Happy Birthday of Death*
James Dickey, *Into the Stone*
Ted Hughes, *Lupercal*
Galway Kinnell, *What a Kingdom It Was*
Seymour Krim, ed., *The Beat*
Denise Levertov, *With Eyes at the Back of Our Head*
W. S. Merwin, *The Drunk in the Furnace*
Frank O'Hara, *Second Avenue*
Charles Olson, *The Maximus Poems*
—*The Distances*
Sylvia Plath, *The Colossus*
Peter Redgrove, *The Collector and Other Poems*
Anne Sexton, *To Bedlam and Part Way Back*
Gary Snyder, *Myths and Texts*

Graham Hough, *Image and Experience*

1961

Donald Davie, *A Sequence for Francis Parkman*
Ed Dorn, *The Newly Fallen*
Robert Fitzgerald, trans., *The Odyssey of Homer*
Allen Ginsberg, *Kaddish and Other Poems*
Thom Gunn, *My Sad Captains*
X. J. Kennedy, *Nude Descending a Staircase*
Denise Levertov, *The Jacob's Ladder*
Louis MacNeice, *Solstices*
Pablo Neruda, *Selected Poems*, trans. Ben Belitt
Thomas Parkinson, ed., *A Casebook on the Beat*
Jerzy Peterkiewicz and Burns Singer, trans., *Five Centuries of Polish Poetry*

The Art of the Real

Richard Wilbur, *Advice to a Prophet*

John Mander, *The Writer and Commitment*
Roy Harvey Pearce, *The Continuity of American Poetry*

1962

A. Alvarez, ed., *The New Poetry*
John Ashbery, *The Tennis Court Oath*
Robert Bly, *Silence in the Snowy Fields*
Gregory Corso, *Long Live Man*
Robert Creeley, *For Love: Poems 1950-1960*
James Dickey, *Drowning with Others*
Roy Fuller, *Collected Poems 1936-1961*
Henry Gifford and Charles Tomlinson, trans., *Versions from Tyutchev*
Donald Hall, ed., *Contemporary American Poetry*
Michael Hamburger and Christopher Middleton, trans., *Modern German Poetry 1910-60*
Leroi Jones, *Preface to a Twenty Volume Suicide Note*
Kenneth Koch, *Thank You and Other Poems*
Thomas McGrath, *Letter to an Imaginary Friend*
George Oppen, *The Materials*
Penguin Modern Poets 1 (Durrell, Jennings, Thomas)
Charles Reznikoff, *By the Waters of Manhattan: Selected Verse*
Anne Sexton, *All My Pretty Ones*
W. C. Williams, *Pictures from Brueghel and Other Poems*
Yevgeni Yevtushenko, *Selected Poems,* trans. Robin Milner-Gulland and Peter Levi, S.J.
Louis Zukofsky, *16 Once Published*

Isaac Rosenfeld, *An Age of Enormity*

1963

Robert Conquest, ed., *New Lines*
Thom Gunn and Ted Hughes, eds., *Five American Poets*
Leroi Jones, ed., *The Moderns*
Philip Levine, *On the Edge*
Edward Lucie-Smith and Philip Hobsbaum, eds., *A Group Anthology*
Louis MacNeice, *The Burning Perch*
Sylvia Plath, 'Ten Poems', *Encounter,* October 1963
— 'The Last Poems of Sylvia Plath', *The Review,* October 1963
Adrienne Rich, *Snapshots of a Daughter-in-Law*
Theodore Roethke, *Sequence, Sometimes Metaphysical*
Louis Simpson, *At the End of the Open Road*

Charles Tomlinson, *A Peopled Landscape*
Georg Trakl, *Twenty Poems*, trans. James Wright
James Wright, *The Branch Will Not Break*
Louis Zukofsky, *Bottom: On Shakespeare*

1964

A. R. Ammons, *Expressions of Sea Level*
John Berryman, *77 Dream Songs*
Donald Davie, *Events and Wisdoms: Poems 1957-63*
James Dickey, *Helmets*
Keith Douglas, *Selected Poems*, ed. Ted Hughes
Geoffrey Hill, *Preghiere*
Galway Kinnell, *Flower Herding on Mount Monadnock*
Denise Levertov, *O Taste and See*
Robert Lowell, *For the Union Dead*
Marianne Moore, *The Arctic Fox*
Frank O'Hara, *Lunch Poems*
Alexander Pushkin, *Eugene Onegin: A Novel in Verse*, trans. Vladimir
    Nabokov
Theodore Roethke, *The Far Field*
Robin Skelton, ed., *Five Poets of the Pacific Northwest*
César Vallejo, *Twenty Poems,* trans. James Wright

Donald Davie, *Ezra Pound: Poet as Sculptor*
James Dickey, *The Suspect in Poetry*
Charles Olson, *A Bibliography on America for Ed Dorn*

1965

A. R. Ammons, *Corson's Inlet*
— *Tape for the Turn of the Year*
Elizabeth Bishop, *Questions of Travel*
Basil Bunting, *The Spoils*
— *Loquitur*
James Dickey, *Buckdancer's Choice*
Roy Fuller, *Buff*
Ian Hamilton, ed., *The Poetry of War 1939-1945*
Randall Jarrell, *The Lost World*
Leroi Jones, *The Dead Lecturer*
Sylvia Plath, *Ariel*
— *Uncollected Poems*
Charles Reznikoff, *Testimony: The United States 1885-1890 Recitative*
Michael Roberts, ed., *The Faber Book of Modern Verse*, Third ed., with a
    new Supplement chosen by Donald Hall

Gary Snyder, *Six Sections of Mountains and Rivers Without End*
Louis Zukofsky, *All: The Collected Short Poems 1923-1958*

Charles Olson, *Human Universe and Other Essays*, ed. Donald M. Allen
Theodore Roethke, *On the Poet and His Craft*, ed. Ralph J. Mills, Jr.

1966

A. R. Ammons, *Northfield Poems*
John Ashbery, *Rivers and Mountains*
Basil Bunting, *Briggflatts*
Ed Dorn, *Geography*
Keith Douglas, *Collected Poems,* ed. John Waller, G. S. Fraser, J. C. Hall
Ford Madox Ford, *Buckshee,* introduction by Robert Lowell
Allen Ginsberg, *Witchita Vortex Sutra*
Thom Gunn, *Positives,* with photographs by Ander Gunn
Ted Hughes, *The Burning of the Brothel*
Denise Levertov, *The Sorrow Dance*
Alun Lewis, *Selected Poetry and Prose,* ed. Ian Hamilton
Louis MacNeice, *Collected Poems*, ed. E. R. Dodds
Marianne Moore, *Tell Me, Tell Me*
Pablo Neruda, *The Heights of Macchu Picchu,* trans. Nathaniel Tarn
David Ray and Robert Bly, eds., *A Poetry Reading Against the Vietnam War*
Adrienne Rich, *Necessities of Life*
Theodore Roethke, *Collected Poems*
Stevie Smith, *The Frog Prince and Other Poems*
George Steiner, ed., *The Penguin Book of Modern Verse Translation*
Gary Snyder, *A Range of Poems*
Charles Tomlinson, *American Scenes*
Andrei Voznesensky, *Selected Poems,* trans. Herbert Marshall
Peter Whigham, trans., *The Poems of Catullus*
Yevgeni Yevtushenko, *Poems Chosen by the Author,* trans. Robin Milner-Gulland
Wholly Communion: Poetry at the Royal Albert Hall, June 11th 1965
Louis Zukofsky, *All: The Collected Short Poems 1956-64*

1967

John Ashbery, *Selected Poems*
Stephen Bann, ed., *Concrete Poetry*
John Berryman, *Berryman's Sonnets*
Robert Bly, *The Light Around the Body*
Joseph Brodsky, *Elegy to John Donne and Other Poems,* trans. Nicholas Bethell
Basil Bunting, *Two Poems*

Robert Creeley, *Words: Poems*
Ed Dorn, *The North Atlantic Turbine*
Thom Gunn, *Touch*
Ted Hughes, *Wodwo*
Robert Lowell, *Near the Ocean*
Edward Lucie-Smith, ed., *The Liverpool Scene*
W. S. Merwin, *The Lice*
Marianne Moore, *Complete Poems*
Charles Olson, *Selected Writings,* ed. Robert Creeley
Carl Rakosi, *Amulet*
Adrienne Rich, *Selected Poems*
Anne Sexton, *Live or Die*
Gary Snyder, *The Back Country*
Lucien Stryk, ed., *Heartland: Poets of the Midwest*
Andrei Voznesensky, *Antiworlds*, trans. W. H. Auden *et al.*

Roland Barthes, *Writing Degree Zero*, trans. Annette Lavers and Colin
    Smith
R. P. Blackmur, *A Primer of Ignorance*
The Letters of Wallace Stevens, ed. Holly Stevens
Cecil Woolf and John Bagguley, eds., *Authors Take Sides on Vietnam*
Louis Zukofsky, *Prepositions*

1968

A. R. Ammons, *Selected Poems*
John Berryman, *His Toy, His Dream, His Rest*
Basil Bunting, *Collected Poems*
e. e. cummings, *Complete Poems*
Ed Dorn, *Gunslinger, Part I*
Roy Fisher, *Collected Poems*
Roy Fuller, *New Poems*
Zbigniew Herbert, *Selected Poems*, trans. Czeslaw Milosz and Peter Dale
    Scott
Geoffrey Hill, *King Log*
Galway Kinnell, *Body Rags*
Philip Levine, *Not This Pig*
Pablo Neruda, *Twenty Poems*, trans. James Wright and Robert Bly
Sylvia Plath, *Three Women*
Robin Skelton, ed., *Poetry of the Forties*
W. D. Snodgrass, *After Experience*
Georg Trakl, *Selected Poems*, trans. Christopher Middleton
James Wright, *Shall We Gather at the River*

A. Alvarez, *Beyond All This Fiddle*
Walter Benjamin, *Illuminations*, trans. Harry Zohn

Selected Letters of Theodore Roethke, ed. Ralph J. Mills, Jr.
Charles Tomlinson, *The Poem as Initiation*

1969

Anna Akhmatova, *Selected Poems,* trans. Richard McKane
Elizabeth Bishop, *Complete Poems*
Robert Bly, *The Morning Glory*
André Breton, *Poems,* trans. Kenneth White
Robert Creeley, *Pieces*
Donald Davie, *Essex Poems 1963-67*
Ed Dorn, *Gunslinger, Part II*
Douglas Dunn, *Terry Street*
Juan Ramon Jiminez, *Forty Poems,* trans. Robert Bly
David Jones, *The Tribune's Visitation*
X. J. Kennedy, *Growing into Love*
Kenneth Koch, *The Pleasures of Peace and Other Poems*
Robert Lowell, *Notebook 1967-68*
Pablo Neruda, *A New Decade: Poems 1958-1967,* trans. Ben Belitt
— *Twenty Poems and a Song of Despair,* trans. W. S. Merwin
Charles Olson, *Maximus IV, V, VI*
Adrienne Rich, *Leaflets*
Anne Sexton, *Love Poems*
Charles Tomlinson, *The Way of a World*
Richard Wilbur, *Walking to Sleep*

Richard Howard, *Alone With America*
Charles Olson, *Letters for Origin 1950-1956,* ed. Albert Glover

1970

John Ashbery, *The Double Dream of Spring*
Alexander Blok, *The Twelve and Other Poems,* trans. Jon Stallworthy and
    Peter France
Alan Bold, ed., *The Penguin Book of Socialist Verse*
Robert Bly, *The Teeth-Mother Naked at Last*
Robert Creeley, *The Charm: Early and Uncollected Poems*
Ted Hughes, *Crow*
David Ignatow, *Poems 1934-1969*
Denise Levertov, *Relearning the Alphabet*
W. S. Merwin, *The Carrier of Ladders*
Pablo Neruda, *Selected Poems,* ed. Nathaniel Tarn
Charles Olson, *Archaeologist of Morning*
Laura Riding, *Selected Poems: In 5 Sets*

Robert Creeley, *A Quick Graph: Collected Notes & Essays,* ed. Donald
    Allen

Michael Hamburger, *The Truth of Poetry*
Charles Newman, ed., *The Art of Sylvia Plath*
Selected Essays of Delmore Schwartz, ed. D. A. Dike and D. H. Zucker
Selected Letters of Edith Sitwell, ed. John Lehmann and Derek Parker

1971

A. R. Ammons, *Uplands*
John Berryman, *Love and Fame*
Richard Emil Braun, *Bad Land*
Robert Desnos, *22 Poems*, trans. Michael Benedikt
Ed Dorn, *The Cycle*
Ford Madox Ford, *Selected Poems*, ed. Basil Bunting
Ted Hughes, *A Choice of Shakespeare's Verse*
—*Mercian Hymns*
X. J. Kennedy, *Breaking & Entering*
Galway Kinnell, *The Book of Nightmares*
Philip Levine, *Red Dust*
Neruda and Vallejo: Selected Poems, trans. Robert Bly and James Wright
Frank O'Hara, *Collected Poems*, ed. Donald Allen
Octavio Paz, Jacques Roubaud, Edouardo Sanguinetti and Charles
        Tomlinson, *Renga*
Sylvia Plath, *Crossing the Water*
—*Crystal Gazer*
—*Fiesta Melons*
—*Winter Trees*
Carl Rakosi, *Ere-Voice*
Jeremy Robson, ed., *The Young British Poets*
Louis Simpson, *Adventures of the Letter I*
Dylan Thomas, *The Poems*, ed. Daniel Jones
Marina Tsvetayeva, *Selected Poems*, trans. Elaine Feinstein
James Wright, *Collected Poems*

1972

A. R. Ammons, *Collected Poems 1951-1971*
John Ashbery, *Three Poems*
John Berryman, *Delusions, Etc*
Richard Emil Braun, *The Foreclosure*
Paul Celan, *Nineteen Poems*, trans. Michael Hamburger
Donald Davie, *Collected Poems 1950-1970*
Douglas Dunn, *The Happier Life*
H.D., *Hermetic Definition*
Allen Ginsberg, *The Fall of America*
Ted Hughes, *Selected Poems 1957-1967*
Peter Jones, ed., *Imagist Poetry*

Denise Levertov, *Footprints*
Philip Levine, *They Feed They Lion*
Pablo Neruda, *Extravagaria*, trans. Alastair Reid
George Oppen, *Collected Poems*
—*Seascape: Needle's Eye*
Adrienne Rich, *The Will to Change*
Anne Sexton, *The Book of Folly*
—*Transformations*
Charles Simic, *Dismantling the Silence*
John Wheelwright, *Collected Poems*, ed. Alvin H. Rosenfeld

1973

Poems of Akhmatova, trans. Stanley Kunitz and Max Hayward
Robert Bly, *Sleepers Joining Hands*
Joseph Brodsky, *Selected Poems*, trans. George L. Kline
H.D., *Trilogy*
Roy Fuller, *Tiny Tears*
Reiner Kunze, *With the Volume Turned Down and Other Poems*, trans. Ewald Osers
Philip Larkin, ed., *The Oxford Book of Twentieth Century Verse*
Robert Lowell, *The Dolphin*
—*For Lizzie and Harriet*
—*History*
Osip Mandelstam, *Selected Poems*, trans. Clarence Brown and W. S. Merwin
William Plomer, *Collected Poems*
Pierre Reverdy, *Selected Poems*, trans. Kenneth Rexroth
Adrienne Rich, *Diving into the Wreck: Poems 1971-2*
Gary Snyder, *The Fudo Trilogy*
Charles Tomlinson, *Written on Water*
Anthony Thwaite, *Inscriptions*
Whitman, selected by Robert Creeley
James Wright, *Two Citizens*

Donald Davie, *Thomas Hardy and British Poetry*
The Notebooks of David Ignatow, ed. Ralph J. Mills, Jr.
Denise Levertov, *The Poet in the World*

1974

Alexander Blok, *Selected Poems*, trans. Jon Stallworthy and Peter France
Robert Bly, *Old Man Rubbing His Eyes*
Tony Connor, *The Memoirs of Uncle Harry*
Donald Davie, *The Shires*
Douglas Dunn, *Love or Nothing*
Thom Gunn, *To the Air*

Peter Huchel, *Selected Poems*, trans. Michael Hamburger
David Jones, *The Sleeping Lord*
X. J. Kennedy, *Emily Dickinson in Southern California*
Galway Kinnell, *The Avenue Bearing the Initial of Christ into the New World: Poems 1946-64*
Stanley Kunitz, *The Terrible Threshold: Selected Poems 1940-1970*
Philip Larkin, *High Windows*
Philip Levine, *1933*
W. S. Merwin, *Writings to an Unfinished Accompaniment*
Charles Reznikoff, *By the Well of Living & Seeing: New & Selected Poems 1918-1973*, ed. Seamus Cooney
Jerome Rothenberg, *Poland/1931*
Anne Sexton, *The Death Notebooks*
Charles Simic, *Return to a Place Lit by a Glass of Milk*
C. H. Sisson, *In the Trojan Ditch: Collected Poems and Selected Translations*
Gary Snyder, *Turtle Island*
Anthony Thwaite, *New Confessions*
Charles Tomlinson, *The Way In*
Daniel Weissbort, ed., *Post-War Russian Poetry*
Andrew Young, *Complete Poems*

Roma Gill, ed., *William Empson: The Man and His Work*

1975

Kenneth Allott, *Collected Poems*
John Ashbery, *Self-Portrait in a Convex Mirror*
Charles Causley, *Collected Poems: 1951-1975*
Roy Fuller, *From the Joke Shop*
Ted Hughes, *Cave Birds*
—*Season Songs*
David Ignatow, *Facing the Tree*
Denise Levertov, *The Freeing of the Dust*
Charles Olson, *The Maximus Poems: Book Three*
Carl Rakosi, *Ex Cranium, Night*
Charles Reznikoff, *Holocaust*
Adrienne Rich, *Poems: Selected and New 1950-1974*
Adrienne Rich's Poetry, ed. Barbara Charlesworth Gelpi and Albert Gelpi
Alan Ross, *Open Sea*
Anne Sexton, *The Awful Rowing Toward God*
Stevie Smith, *Collected Poems*
The Collected Books of Jack Spicer, ed. Robin Blaser
Tristan Tzara, *Selected Poems*, trans. Lee Harwood

Roland Barthes, *The Pleasure of the Text*, trans. Richard Miller

Hugh Kenner, *A Homemade World*
Stanley Kunitz, *A Kind of Order, A Kind of Folly: Essays and Conversations*
Sylvia Plath, *Letters Home*, ed. Aurelia S. Plath
W. D. Snodgrass, *In Radical Pursuit*

The 1960s and 1970s

At the end of *Notebook 1967-68*, Robert Lowell printed a list of dates of events which occurred during the composition of the poem. It is a terrible accumulation of war, riots, deaths, demonstrations, politics and revolution, bracketed by Vietnam. The last two years of Lyndon Johnson's presidency telescoped the horrors of the decade, public and private, into a list which takes up less than a page in Lowell's book, but which is still of a nightmarish actuality.

The literature of the decade partakes directly of the confusions of the society. In poetry there was a profusion of scenes, public readings, styles and poetics, translations, and hoop-la, which made for great excitement, but also for more enthusiasm than judgment in the editorial direction of publishing houses, and in the response of critics. It is difficult to say anything about readers: like everyone else, they got the big sell, the heavy cultural manipulation or the anti-cultural manipulation. Books were sold, but who knows how much was read, or thought over. Poetry became a commodity, like toilet paper. The gap between academic verse and its opposite — call it 'naked' or whatever — became a permanent feature of the landscape, to the consequent impoverishment of both. There was no end to the cant, posturing, self-promotion, cabals and logrolling. It was, one supposes, the way things always had been, only more so. Charming mystifiers like John Ashbery built formidable reputations upon their contempt for the presumption that poetry is meant to be read, and even enjoyed. Culture became Balkanized, with new 'scenes' emerging in Liverpool, Newcastle, New York, the Pacific North-West, and the Heartland of the Midwest. A new meaning was given to the cultural pluralism which was characteristic of the age. The intermingling of styles of life and styles of verse, begun in earnest in the 1950s with the Beats, spread rapidly throughout both countries. There was a lot of protest poetry, poems which sounded like song lyrics (and vice versa), and critics who wrote like Raymond Chandler but who had the taste and sensibility of an Ernest Dowson. It was a great period for translation. Four or five poets established themselves in the 1960s — James Dickey, Robert Bly,

James Wright, Galway Kinnell, Adrienne Rich — and a group of older poets came in from the cold: Kunitz, Reznikoff, Rakosi, Oppen, and Zukofsky in America, Bunting, Jones and MacDiarmid in Britain.

England proved remarkably receptive to certain kinds of American poetry in the 1960s. Lowell and Berryman, and then Sylvia Plath, found many enthusiastic readers who were hoping for something reputable to use against the boring epigone of the Movement. (A. Alvarez's campaign against the Movement was the wittiest, and most effective, and Ian Hamilton, editor of *The Review* and later *The New Review*, also made a contribution, although he lacked Alvarez's range.) Williams, Olson and Zukofsky were published in England in a remarkably lavish fashion. From the point of view of the publishers, it was very much pearls before the swine, and they gave up trying. The receptiveness did not extend to Frank O'Hara, or Ashbery (his *Selected Poems* published by Jonathan Cape was not reviewed), or for that matter to William Stafford, Maxine Kumin, John Logan, Mark Strand or James Tate. But in the decade 1964-74 there must have been close to fifty volumes by individual American poets published in England. Very few sold as well as Lowell or Plath, but the interest was sustained and intelligent — and, it seems, very much one way. A number of British academics found ready audiences in America for the flattering message that the only poetry worth reading was by American poets. There was always a condescending exception granted for Philip Larkin, and for Ted Hughes, often made an honorary American for the occasion. It remains true that no British poet since Dylan Thomas has made a significant impact on American taste. It is also true, and perhaps is not unrelated, that there is no anthology of contemporary British poetry worth the name in America today.

In the 1950s the little presses thrived in England: the Marvell Press in Hessle, Yorkshire, and the Fantasy Press near Oxford, led a generation of younger poets to the glories of the metropolis and Faber and Faber. Little presses again made the running in the 1960s, though as avant-garde influences. Remarkably high standards of production were set by Fulcrum, Trigram and Goliard. The lists of Anvil and Carcanet were catholic and progressive. Perhaps the largest single publishing contribution to the poetry boom of the 1960s in England came from Penguin Books, who, under the editorial influence of Nikos Stangos, published a distinguished series of volumes in translation. The three-in-one volumes of the Penguin Modern Poets series were transformed into an aggressively contemporary list. The Modern Poets began in 1963 with a selection of the poems of Durrell, Jennings and R. S. Thomas. By 1970 some fifty-four poets had been included, a fair number of whom had not at that time been published in England. The role of poetry readings in America, linked initially with the *éclat* of the Beats, was taken to a more serious level by the mid-1960s when poets led the public struggle against the war in Vietnam. Poetry was turned into a political weapon in a fashion unknown since the 1930s, but the importance of the event rapidly outstripped that of the poem. It is inconceivable to place Auden's 'Spain' side by side with something like Ginsberg's 'Witchita Vortex Sutra' in a public performance. Very little poetry of enduring interest came out of the struggle against the war for this reason: the circumstances which gave poets a public importance robbed the poetry of its proper function. When the war began to wind down in the early 1970s the poetry bubble burst, just as it had after World War II. This, combined with the recession and inflation which followed, turned the clock back to the situation in the late 1940s. Publishers have reduced the number of new books of poetry on their lists; some, such as Macmillan in London, have given up on poetry altogether; others, such as Secker and Warburg, have a general rule of thumb to the effect that no new volumes of American poetry should be accepted. It seems likely that the little presses, run along non-commercial lines and often with support from public or foundation resources, will have to pick up the pieces. Michael Schmidt's Carcanet Press is the biggest publisher of new poetry in Britain today. His American counterpart is the Black Sparrow Press in Santa Barbara, California.

In both England and America the situation is much the same. There is, in fact, something of a uniform tone and style in contemporary poetry in both countries. The typical poem is immediately identifiable by its resolute resistance to the idea of the poetic, its narrow range of subject-matter, by its chatty-vernacular diction, and the poet's self-absorption and indifference to social concerns. An example, from Edward Lucie-Smith in *The Well-Wishers* (1974):

> Clothes on a chair, torn off
> pell-mell, in a hurry
> to be joined, and to get to
> Our business.

Whereas Fleur Adcock, nice lady that she is, spent an evening

> ... avoiding the sweet obvious act
> as if it were the only kind of indulgence.
> Silly, perhaps.   (*The Scenic Route*, 1974)

Sandra Hochman is rather more inventive:

> He entered the bathroom elegantly
> His dyed hair smoothed by pomade, the shiny strands greased black
> Over gray his mustache
> Waxed for this special occasion. To improvise: he joined me
> In the tub, where I awaited him

> Under the detergent.
> How easy! The ecstasy —
> Our electrical field of water and shock,
> The short-distance field
> Exposing us to
> Washcloth and soap.
>
> Somehow I want to say — to get it 'across to you' — how moving
> That bath was ...   (*The Vaudeville Marriages*, 1966)

It sounds like great fun, but not great poetry. We have now a decorum of indecorum, a kind of corn-porn, in Marjorie Perloff's apt phrase.

To write about the literature of the present, and the immediate past, inevitably becomes speculative. History has a way of making monkeys of critics. In 1930 Charles Williams published a sober volume, *Poetry at Present*, containing essays on sixteen living poets. Two years later F. R. Leavis published *New Bearings in English Poetry*. Other than Yeats and Eliot (of whom Williams wrote: 'I feel a real apology is due to Mr Eliot, for whose work I profess a sincere and profound respect, though I fail to understand it'), one would scarcely gather that both critics were involved in the same national literature. Williams wrote at length on the senior poets (Hardy, Bridges, Housman, Kipling, Yeats), and upon an assortment of Georgians (de la Mare, Hodgson, Gibson, Abercrombie). Leavis, of course, saw that the crucial new bearings would be taken from Hopkins, Pound and Eliot. It was a remarkably speculative book, vindicated and still in print forty years later, and an incitement to what must seem equally arbitrary decisions to ignore Gunn, Dickey and Creeley, in order to discuss an unknown poet like Richard Emil Braun. I suspect that the justification for this is to be found, if anywhere, in the suggestion that it is the long poem alone which challenges the novel as an adequate reflector of our own times.

There have always been long poems. Those of the twentieth century which come to mind most promptly ('The Waste Land', *The Cantos*, 'The Bridge', 'Notes Towards a Supreme Fiction'), the modernist long poem, were closely identified with a particular argument with traditional (that is nineteenth-century) poetry. Modernist poets doubted the very possibility of narrative. Forms were fractured, poetry became more difficult and obscure, because the world itself was incoherent. People continued, however, to tell stories in verse. Edgar Lee Masters's *Spoon River Anthology* (1915), Robinson Jeffers's *Tamar* (1924) and *Roan Stallion* (1925) and Stephen Vincent Benet's *John Brown's Body* (1929) exemplified the more conventional narrative virtues. Auden published *The Orators* in 1932; his 'Letter to Lord Byron' (1937) and Louis MacNeice's *Autumn Journal* (1939), were quite consciously not in the symbolist or modernist tradition, but aspired towards the discursive social ease of neo-classic verse. (The motive has re-emerged as one of the least engaging qualities of contemporary formalism in John Wain's *Letters to Five Artists*, 1969; Davie's *Six Epistles to Eva Hesse*, 1970; James Fenton's 'Open Letter to Richard Crossman', 1971; the mutual reviews by Fenton and John Fuller in *The Review*, Spring-Summer 1972; John Fuller's *Epistles to Several Persons*, 1973; and Clive James's 'To Pete Atkin: A Letter from Paris', 1974.)

In the 1940s Delmore Schwartz revived the narrative mode with *Genesis, Book One* (1943), and Karl Shapiro wrote a neo-classical discursive poem in his *Essay on Rime* (1945). Auden's *New Year Letter* appeared in 1941, and *For The Time Being* three years later. As we have seen, the long poem played a crucial role in the 1950s, either as narrative, written by formalists (Lowell's *The Mills of the Kavanaughs*, 1951, and Robert Penn Warren's *Brother to Dragons*, 1953), or as vehicles for explicitly modernist viewpoints in Williams, Olson and Jones. John Berryman's *Homage to Mistress Bradstreet* (1956) is very much in a category of its own. Despite Kenneth Koch's mock-heroic *KO, or A Season on Earth* (1959), the impulse towards narrative weakened in the 1960s, as though people's confidence in their ability to understand and explain the world around them was also weakened. A narrative sonnet-sequence could still win the Newdigate Prize at Oxford (James Fenton's *Our Western Furniture*, 1968), but long narrative poems or sequences like Hyam Plutzik's *Horatio* (1961) and James Schevill's *Stalingrad Elegies* (1964) attracted little interest. Quite different kinds of long poems began to be written in the 1960s, and it is this work which will be our primary concern. The persistence of a double or triple tradition of modernist-discursive-narrative long poems did not wholly disappear. The discursive mode re-emerged as the verse letter, part of an enervated formalism. Richard Emil Braun's *Bad Land* (1971) is an interesting adaptation of the narrative. What remains are the long sequences: Berryman's *Dream Songs*, Lowell's *Notebook*, Hughes's *Crow*, Hill's *Mercian Hymns*, Thwaite's *New Confessions,* and others, such as Robert L. Peters's *Songs for a Son* (1967). These are sequences built upon small, discrete poems, linked by subject, tone or opportunity, but obeying no structural imperative other than a not-too-strictly enforced chronology. There are other long poems, such as Basil Bunting's *Briggflatts* and Galway Kinnell's *The Book of Nightmares*, which reflect a greater sense of construction. In this great array of long poems written in the past decade and a half we see the way the modernist impulse has been accepted, without the pretensions of an Olson, and transformed into the *common* poetic medium of the day. It has been a subtle insinuation of what, twenty years ago, would have seemed remarkably ambitious poetic ventures, into the developing work of ex-formalists, disciples of Black Mountain, and others of various persuasions.

Let us begin, then, with three poets whose work is likely to be unfamiliar: Charles Reznikoff, Richard Emil Braun and Basil Bunting. (Despite the appearance of Bunting's *Collected Poems* in 1968, and Roger Guedalla's bibliography in 1973, one looks in vain for any substantial assessment of his work.)

Charles Reznikoff (1894-1976) first emerged as a poet in 1918, when he published *Rhythms*, a collection of slight imagist verse. As the son of Russian Jewish immigrants to New York, Reznikoff encompassed in his early years the traumatic experience of assimilation into American life. His parents, whose story he lovingly tells in *Family Chronicle* (1969), became hat manufacturers on lower Broadway. He graduated from New York University Law School, and was admitted to the bar in 1916. Reznikoff never practised law, though he worked in the 1920s for a publisher of legal encyclopaedias. For most of his life his verse appeared in numerous privately published small editions. Samuel Roth, soon to achieve a kind of immortality as the pirate of *Ulysses*, printed a group of Reznikoff's poems in an edition of 250 copies in 1920. His general indebtedness to Pound's imagism was combined with an almost uninterrupted residence in New York, to produce an urban imagism, fully accepting Pound's insistence upon seeing the details of the object or situation with a pure observing eye, uncluttered by 'comment':

> On the kitchen shelf the dusty medicine bottles;
> She in her room heaped under a sheet,
> And men and women coming in with clumsy steps.[1]

Reznikoff's true subject is the loneliness, small ironies, deaths and numbness of the immigrant in the urban tenement.

> The yards and fire-escapes were glinting with
> sunlight, and the tall fences,
> Dirtied by rain, their rows of nails on top
> bleeding rust.[2]

The best of his early poems reveal an unwillingness to moralize, to draw back from experience and try to understand it in other terms. Experience, the real, possesses an integrity which Reznikoff instinctively respected. It gives his poems the feeling of an earned clarity. It is almost as though uncertainty, ambiguity, a clouded perception, the admission of things which exhorted or transcended the real, were a betrayal of the poet's responsibility:

> He showed me the album. 'But this?' I asked, surprised
> at such beauty.

I knew his sister, her face somewhat the picture's —
    coarsened.
'My mother before marriage.'
Coming in, I had met
Her shrivelled face and round shoulders.
Now, after the day's work, his father at cards with friends
Still outshouted the shop's wheels.
Afterwards, when I left, I had to go through their candy store
With its one showcase of candy,
In little heaps in little saucers, ever so many for a penny.
They kept no lights in the window. A single gas jet
    flared in the empty store.[3]

Reznikoff was preoccupied with the writing of prose in the late 1920s and early 1930s. A volume entitled *By the Waters of Manhattan: An Annual* appeared in 1929. It contained a quasi-fictional autobiography, a first-person narrative of his mother, Sarah's, life in Russia and her early experiences in New York, and a long sequence in verse on biblical themes. The first two narratives were revised and published as *By the Waters of Manhattan*, with an introduction by Louis Untermeyer, by Charles Boni in 1930. It was Reznikoff's first 'commercial' publication, and his last for over thirty years. Reznikoff was familiar with Williams's brilliant *In the American Grain* (1925), and shared Williams's sense of the betrayed promise of American life, a feeling widely held by the literary intelligentsia in the 1920s. Reznikoff attempted in the prose volume *Testimony* (1934) to present the 'facts' of common life in America (or at least *some* of the facts) with the authority of testimony in a court of law. Kenneth Burke, in his introduction to *Testimony*, quotes a letter from Reznikoff:

> A few years ago I was working for a publisher of law books, reading cases from every state and every year (since this country became a nation). Once in a while I could see in the facts of a case details of the time and place, and it seemed to me that out of such material the century and a half during which the United States has been a nation could be written up, not from the standpoint of an individual, as in diaries, nor merely from the angle of the unusual, as in newspapers, but from every standpoint — as many standpoints as were provided by the witnesses themselves.[4]

Testimony contains some fifty episodes or incidents, in a deliberately factual, understated style. Reznikoff's legal training helped him to see that the intrinsic forcefulness of the material did not need an elaborate stylistic presentation. The content utterly dominates his prose. Consider his description of a case of smallpox aboard a steamship on the coastal rivers of Oregon:

Tomlinson, a seaman on board the steamship Pacific was sick of the smallpox. The ship was then on the Umpqua River. The captain told him he had seen to it that he would be taken care of at a village about fifteen or twenty miles up the river, where there was a doctor, and he had a boat ready to take him there. Tomlinson went into the boat and was rowed to the village. He asked the man who rowed him where the doctor was and was told there was none in the place, or nearer than Oakland, sixty miles or so away.

The sick man went to the store – the principal building of the village – and the storekeeper also told him there was no doctor there. The sight of Tomlinson with smallpox broken out on his face, frightened every one. The storekeeper advised him to go back and, down the river, about six miles below the steamer, he could get a horse to take him to Coos Bay.

They reached the steamer about nine o'clock at night. The boatman called to the master and asked if he should take the sick man down the river. The master, angered and cursing, answered that he might put him ashore anywhere. Tomlinson was landed at dead of night and began to crawl over rocks and driftwood to the only house for miles around. He reached it late at night and found a young man who, unaware of his sickness, let him sleep in the house, and in the morning gave him a horse to ride to Coos Bay. (The young man was dead of the smallpox in a few weeks.)

Toward night, Tomlinson came to the river across which the town is reached by a ferry. Here, as directed by a man he met on the road, he tried to get to the flag-staff and raise the flag as a signal for the ferry-boat, but, worn out, he fell from the horse in a faint. The man, shortly afterwards, came back and, keeping safely away, told Tomlinson that he would cross the river in his boat and tell the authorities about him.

This was Sunday night. Until Tuesday morning Tomlinson lay upon the beach, blind, unable to move, without anybody coming near him to give him even a cup of water.[5]

This does not cease to be a simple narrative when its meanings are pondered; but it has become, in Reznikoff's hands, literature, a bitter *conte* which takes us to the heart of the meaning of community. Reviewers in 1934, such as Babette Deutsch, complained of Reznikoff's 'cold impartiality': *Testimony* was 'a sometimes disturbing, sometimes terrifying picture of human cruelty and human callousness'. An anonymous reviewer in *The Nation* said that 'for sheer brutality there is nothing in literature quite like this little volume'.[6] Even by our own lights, these comments are not far off the mark, but the brutality is implicit in the subject-matter. Though the law does not encompass the whole of life, it concentrates and pares down certain kinds of fundamental human experiences. The book is brutal and cruel, but this is to be complained of, theoretically, only if literature is expected to play a moral role in our culture. Reznikoff has no need to press for indictments, retribution, or justice: the testimony he presents will do that without extraneous appeals on his part. The reader of the book is quite explicitly set to be the jury, listening dispassionately to accounts of nearly inconceivable violence and cruelty. Reznikoff alters the process of the law to the extent of eliminating both prosecution and defence, in preference for the Continental office of the investigating magistrate (the poet) who assembles the 'facts' of the case as completely as he is able, without reference to the points of view of plaintiff or defendant. It is a work that bends over backward to be objective, impartial, and yet, ironically, the judgments made by the reader are intense. In *Testimony* Reznikoff has extended the technique and desired objectivity of imagism into prose literature. At a time when it had virtually disappeared as a movement in verse, Reznikoff demonstrated that the imagist principles of 1912, as formulated by Ezra Pound, had a continued and unexpected usefulness.

At some point in the 1950s Reznikoff returned once again to legal material. Only this time he chose to discipline the material even further by the use of an economical free verse. He projected a three-volume history of the United States between 1885 and 1910, based on verse paraphrase of courtroom testimony. The first volume, covering the years 1885-90, appeared in 1965. A second volume, for 1891-1900, was privately printed in 1968, and a third, covering the years 1901-10, remains in manuscript. One cannot fail to be gripped by the sheer human drama of the material:

> One of the hands on the oyster boat
> was sick, He tried to work
> but, unable to do so,
> the captain beat him across the back and sides
> with a shovel or handspike —
> whatever was handy.
>
> Next morning, too weak to wind up the anchor,
> one of the other hands jerked it up,
> and he fell on the deck. The captain came up to him
> and kicked him; when he cried out,
> pressed a foot heavily on his throat.
> The captain then tied a rope about his body
> and, fastening the rope to a hook on the port rail,
> dragged him from side to side of the boat
> until he said he would work.
>
> But he was too weak.
> Trying to turn the crank of the dredge,
> he again fell flat on the deck.

> The captain tied his thumbs with a rope
> and, by means of a hook fastened to the rope,
> hoisted his body
> until his feet swung above the deck.
>
> He was finally put into a yawl-boat
> and taken ashore. As he was lying there,
> the captain for good measure
> stamped on his neck.
> In a few hours he was dead.
> The doctor, moving his head, could hear
> the crackling of the bones
> in the broken neck.[7]

A young girl has her hand crushed in an accident in a steam laundry; a man is shot and robbed in a swamp; six drunk boys kill a Negro with a stone; a husband kicks his wife out of their home and she is found the next day frozen to death; a skeleton is found with a bullet hole in the back of the skull; a poor Irish immigrant becomes the Madame of the largest whorehouse in New Orleans; a family squabble leads to a shooting.

These are not the kinds of facts which, in themselves, interest the historian — or are they? 'By the end of the nineteenth century,' writes Michael Lesy at the end of *Wisconsin Death Trip* (1973),

> ... country towns had become charnel houses and the counties that surrounded them had become places of dry bones. The land and its farms were filled with the guilty voices of women mourning for their children and the aimless mutterings of men asking about jobs. State, county, and local newspapers consisted of stories of resignation, failure, suicide, madness and grotesque eccentricity. Between 1900 and 1920, 30 percent of the people who lived on farms left the land.

Lesy's full argument, and its relationship to revisionist work in American history, is too involved to summarize here. He relies upon the evidence (the testimony) of the photographs of Charles Van Schaick, originally amounting to 30,000 glass negatives, and the newspaper articles of Frank and George Cooper in the *Badger State Banner* from the 1890s. Lesy also uses the records and case histories of the Mendota State Hospital. *Wisconsin Death Trip* is a collection of photographs, and other evidence, assembled to suggest a new understanding of the psychic crisis in rural America in the 1890s. Lesy approaches the basic assumption of Reznikoff's *Testimony,* namely that at least a part of the history of America is only explicable in terms of the experience and behaviour of very ordinary people. Hayden Carruth described the point of view in *Testimony* as 'one of relentless, absorbing, cold, bitter contempt:

contempt for the society in question. Whether or not this is a reasonable attitude is something to be decided elsewhere if at all.'[8] Carruth has certainly got Reznikoff wrong: what Reznikoff feels is what any 'reasonable' man might feel when faced with the reality (a selected and intensified reality, but no less important for that) of what he has collected together. It is extremely hard to make a straightforward literary appreciation of this book. It comes to us with a harsh clarity, so harsh, in fact, that it seems an impertinence (but a necessary one) to deflect attention to its nature as *mere* literature. It is a work of art wholly at the service of the real.

A book like Richard Emil Braun's *Bad Land* (1971) seems to come out of nowhere, fully formed, a mature and achieved work of art. He was born in 1934 and studied Latin at the University of Michigan in the 1950s. A first book of poems, *Children Passing*, was published in 1962 by the Humanities Research Center of the University of Texas, where Braun was a student from 1960 to 1962. Since then he has taught classics at the University of Alberta. *Bad Land*, published by Jonathan Williams in his gathering of fugitives for the Jargon Society, tells a story. Braun writes about two families, the Harlans and Greers, in Osseola, Kansas, from the late depression through to the postwar prosperity of the 1950s. It is one of the few poems to use the parodic meaning of homosexuality in contemporary verse, yet that seems almost incidental to Braun's interest in the possibility of using narrative, of telling a story, without feeling that he has to sacrifice the possibility of the complex manipulation of sequence and understanding which is customarily the prerogative of the experimental novel. *Bad Land* is divided into seven sections of which the last, the story of John Greer, composes two-thirds of the fifty-five page text. The first six sections introduce the Greer and Harlan familes. John Harlan, a widower with a young daughter, is ambiguously involved with John Greer, eight years his junior, and with Greer's sister Joan. Two men who meet in a Mexican gaol discover that they share the mutual acquaintance of the Greers and Harlans, thus constructing a neat Edwardian frame for the story which unfolds at first through their recollection, and then in its own right. The first section begins in jail, and is the monologue, and interspersed dialogue, of a man who recalls once seeing Greer and Harlan naked by a pool. In the next section a narrator describes seeing Harlan on board a train, in the company of the two Greers. It was 1940. 'We just love to bicker,' they say, 'but all we/truly want is always to be together.' Braun then shifts back in time to Harlan's nervous habit of building bottled ships after the death of his wife, and introduces the local gossip linking Harlan and Joan Greer, and also the hinted attachment of Joan Greer to her brother. In the fifth section

Harlan's marriage is described as little short of a disaster: his wife was slowly going mad. The crisis is described by yet another narrator, the family doctor. The scene suddenly moves forward to Harlan's daughter Ellie, grown up, preparing to go to college.

> Out of the windy center, gloomy West
> where the prairie is crossed arbitrarily
> by Main and Market and these are paralleled
> and crossed fourteen times further in a square
> until the creek on the north and the rails
> to the west are met and east and south are left
> as Catfish Town (in the shape of an L) —
> out of the West, I say, came Ellie Harlan
> abandoning riches, hunting wisdom.[9]

After a series of affairs, Ellie 'found/the end of her tremendous tether' and was brought home by her father.

The narrative now picks up John Greer, who is also returning home (though our attention does not remain fixed upon Osseola, Greer's presence there perceptibly heightens our sense of expectation). His puzzled thoughts about his identity on the way home are interrupted by the free-verse monologues of Greer's scatty boyfriend left behind to look after the apartment on Bleeker Street in Greenwich Village. The story of his past life is gradually unfolded through a confusing process of recollection and dramatized experience. Greer had attended university at Ann Arbor in the late 1930s, and returned home, a dangling man, to await the draft. We see him on board a jammed troop train inordinately sensitive to the smell of the men, thinking how glad he was to have been born a man. There is a tantalizing memory of a vow to marry his sister, and a superb evocation of the colours and odours of his mother's cosmetics, perfumes, and clothes. He also recalls his youthful idea of womanhood:

> Those were the days I thought the suburb of my school
> was or was animated by a tall Lady
> whom one might spy in the fog of early morning
> as a moving parting of the fog only, who
> might hold a man in the hook of her unknown arm,
> until, diminishing at every turning, when town
> was circumambulated, near the dawn, he would be
> shrunken and spiney and light as a broken bird.[10]

It constitutes a portrait of the artist as a young homosexual. Greer received news of his sister's death while in the Army in 1945. After the war he returned to Osseola, borrowed $500 from Harlan, and moved to Los Angeles where he was set up in a very comfortable, luxurious apartment with a boyfriend. A couple of Mexican thieves wiped out their new prosperity, leaving them both bound in the emptied apartment, where they are found by a boy bringing the news that Greer's father has died. He decides to travel east, to New York, to live and paint. The atmosphere in the Greenwich Village flat is bitchy and rather funny:

'I'll step downstairs and buy myself a quart of milk.
I think I'll do just that. Calcium, don't you know?
for the nerves.' But he waits. 'I don't think I'd
quite like to face those steps just now: too uncompromising.
Besides I fear my tread might crack the world. Lord, Lord!'
Instead, he fills a hot tub around himself, taking
comfort in its billowing, then, buoyant, murmurs:
'There'll come a morning sometimes when hot water won't
help you, honey.' And later: 'You can stay in the tub
two hours. You can take a dozen showers.' And then,
intoning over the doorbell: 'But when you emerge,
Baby, you won't be pink; no, Baby, you'll be white
as a toilet. So you'll drink some of that red wine,
like every day all afternoon till the street lights shine.'[11]

A letter from his older brother Will eleven years later, asking John to return to Osseola and look after their mother, brings us back to the present. John is living with his mother, and has rehabilitated his father's pre-war car. Greer meets John Harlan again, and tries in long discussions with Ellie to explain the changes he sees at home. 'There's less of her left than I remember, or less of me than can remember.' Random conversations with ugly German farmers in Wernig's café are interrupted by passages from John's letters to New York, which are interspersed with the cynical comments of his 'Friend'. The experience of being home is pushing Greer towards a nervous breakdown. Osseola is the 'bad land' of the title:

Any country such
as this and much of the nation, that does not, can not,
could never have made do for man who is the jabber
and seeder of soil, is bad; as what is good is
what is good for him.[12]

The objects around him begin to take on a hostile life of their own:

The rug seethed.
The padded chair near him moved its lap excitedly.

'I haven't had a drink in seven weeks', he said.
He saw the ceiling was liquid but unperturbed.
He heard, around him on the floor, something he reckoned
was flat and black go fluttering.
He felt his cheeks

> sag and pulse. He groped his chin. A tongue caressed his
>   palm.
>
> Between his knees next grew a balloonish head, eyes
> and nose sucked shut. It jutted its tongue at him.
>   Then,
> on the floor, he actually saw a thing twitching,
> black, that partook categorically of qualities
> of a mummified woman and of a ruined bird.

(Thus connecting his nightmare with his childhood fantasies of the 'tall Lady', and his sense of himself as a 'broken bird'.)

> Secret familiarity excited him.
> He drooled. He wept. He ground his pelvis toward the thing.
> It rose. It plunged through the ceiling as if diving
> into milk.
>   He waded into the hall. The head yawned
> between shanks and knees like a basketball.
>   His mother's
> room was empty. Candles spat. Incense fumed. Dust powdered
> everything. Silk hose thrown in bookcases were flapping.
> Iron trays of powders hummed among cans of liquids.
> 'What a cold wind', he said.
>   He puked milk.
>   He passed out.[13]

Perhaps fearing that this was more than a fantasy (how else explain the candles and incense in his mother's room?), Greer calls upon a local woman reputed to be a witch, who gives him a root and the advice to stand up to his mother. He returns home to confront his mother, seizing his father's heavily symbolical 'gilded umbrella' as he walks in the door. She has been using black magic against him, sticking steel pins into his childhood toys. 'You need the past,' she tells him, relenting. 'I don't. I'll set/poor childhood free.' We next see Greer waiting at the bus station. He talks with Ellie Harlan and gently refuses her offer of sex, and returns to 'my lolloping bailiwick', New York.

The intensely charged atmosphere, the hinted (and explicit) sexual meanings, the confused chronology, the ambiguous net of relationships, contribute to a complex literary experience of homosexual American gothic. Braun's manipulation of the sequence of events creates some unnecessary difficulties which most readers will unscramble on a first or second reading. What Braun has gained is a powerful and ironic juxtaposition of scene against scene, one journey balanced by another, one tone of voice or state of mind counterpointed against another, showing that he grasps the possibilities of construction in a poem which stands in relation to the *Odyssey* as a parody or metatext. His decision not to describe the central relationship of Harlan and Greer shows a Jamesian restraint. *Bad Land* is that unusual thing, a verse novel. It is closer in tone to David Storey's *Radcliffe* (1963) than to anything else in contemporary writing. *Bad Land* is an interesting example of the possibilities of a long narrative poem, which owes nothing to the modernist revolution.[14]

We can complete our inspection of this *salon des refusés* with Basil Bunting's *Briggflatts* (1966), received with the uncharitableness which was at that time characteristic of the *Times Literary Supplement*: 'The successes of *Briggflatts* . . . are all local — physically energetic passages, lyrical moments, sudden flashes of strange perception ('Asian vultures riding on a spiral/column of dust'). As a whole it is a failure; lacking any theme other than the poet's sense of home after much travel, it has no forward driving movement. It's exoticism is attractive, but finally unsatisfying' (16 February 1967).[15] Bunting has, if anything, encouraged his critics in their incomprehension and disapproval. On the publication of *Briggflatts* he wrote that

> Poetry is seeking to make not meaning, but beauty; or if you insist on misusing words, its 'meaning' is of another kind, and lies in the relation to one another of lines and patterns of sound, perhaps harmonious, perhaps contrasting and clashing which the hearer feels rather than understands; lines of sound drawn in the air which stir deep emotions which have not even a name in prose. This needs no explaining to an audience which gets its poetry by ear.[16]

It is one of the oldest abuses of analogy to treat language as though its referential content was an annoying distraction. There are no great Dada nonsense poems. Bunting *faute de mieux* must actually say something in his poems, and of course he does; it is all a matter of tactics, of literary politics, that he should pile mystifications like Pelion upon Ossa, and no less amazing that his supporters should take comments like this at face value. Herbert Read, after quoting this comment by Bunting, writes: 'Since we are not to look for meanings in this poem, I will not attempt to explain its progression or narrative evolution: it may not have one. The movements are clearly distinguished in sound and rhythm.'[17] Charles Tomlinson goes one better than Read:

> . . . the pattern is music, twining like the lines of illumination from the Lindisfarne Gospel whose decoration, margining this edition, was elaborated on the holy island that lies in the poem's northern geography. Technically the music relies on a:
>
> Flexible, unrepetitive line

> to sing, not paint; sing, sing,
> laying the tune frankly on the air...

The music Bunting refers to for his imagery (Byrd, Monteverdi, 'Schoenberg's maze') suggests voice against voice, line against line — madrigal and canon, not impressionistic sound-painting.[18]

Despite his own comments, Bunting is no Mallarmé, *de la musique avant toute chose*, but the disciple of Ezra Pound who has fastened on to a part of the Poundian legacy (in the name of refining it); but it is certain that Pound, growing more furiously committed as he grew older, could never regard 'meaning' as a meaningless abstraction. His meaning was often unclear or difficult, but always *there*. And *Briggflatts*, too, has a meaning. It is as great a poem as any written in England since 1939.

Bunting describes the poem as an autobiography, but it is one which eliminates the external apparatus of dates, personalities, literary gossip, history itself, in favour of a meditation upon the meaning of place and the intersection of the sensibility and memory of the poet with that sense of place. *Briggflatts* begins in the Northumbria of his Edwardian childhood, a world of stonemasons, horse-drawn carts, sounds, and a memory of a delicate adolescent love:

> Gentle generous voices weave
> over bare night
> words to confirm and delight
> till bird dawn.
> Rainwater from the butt
> she fetches and flannel
> to wash him inch by inch,
> kissing the pebbles.
> Shining slowworm part of the marvel.
> The mason stirs:
> Words!
> Pens are too light.
> Take a chisel to write.

The memory is immediate, sensuous; pure 'gist', as Pound might have put it. When he compares the mason's chisel with the poet's pen, and decides that the former is preferable, Bunting begins the parallel argument in the poem which runs within the course of recollection, about the nature of poetry itself. The Northumbrian scene collapses in his memory into uncertainty, recrimination and disillusionment, which is the subject of part two: the poet in the modern world. There are certain tasks which a poet must now accept. It is not that he is, any longer, asked to chronicle the present ('Name and date/split in soft slate/a few months obliterate') but to write of the forms of the natural world. The alternatives have beguiled too many:

Secret, solitary, a spy, he gauges
lines of a Flemish horse
hauling beer, the angle, obtuse,
a slut's blouse draws on her chest,
counts beat against beat, bus conductor
against engine against wheels against
the pedal, Tottenham Court Road, decodes
thunder, scans
porridge bubbling, pipes clanking, feels
Buddha's basalt cheek
but cannot name the ratio of its curves
to the half-pint
left breast of a girl who bared it in Kleinfeldt's.
He lies with one to long for another,
sick, self-maimed, self-hating,
obstinate, mating
beauty with squalor to beget lines still-born.

The symbolism is oblique, but not inaccessible. The functions suggested
by decoding thunder, scanning porridge, feeling a 'Buddha's basalt cheek'
are, by hyperbole, recognizable poetic modes (romantic, domestic,
aesthetic), but all lack a certain kind of precision, 'the ratio of its curves';
the indictment is extended by a quite different kind of image of
degradation ('He lies with one to long for another'), and its consequences,
the 'sick, self-maimed, self-hating' modern poet who can only 'beget lines
still-born'.

Bunting's quarrel with the modern world, and with modern poetry, is
deeply felt. But as with Pound, his grasp of contemporary reality is not
very profound. The passage just quoted seems rather presumptuous:
Bunting does not bother to earn the judgments, they just emerge. Take it
or leave it: Bunting may no longer care one way or the other.

There is a transition at this point in the poem to a ship, and to a richer
sense of the alternatives in nature, in both balance and form, to a
civilization which he feels has gone desperately wrong. He discovers in the
sea, and especially in tidal basins, a natural imagery:

Unscarred ocean
day's swerve, swell's poise, pursuit,
he blends, balances, drawing leagues under the keel
to raise cold cliffs where Tides
knot fringes of weed.

It is the idea of form which comes directly out of nature — the weeds
knotted and turned into a fringe by the tide — which is the cutting edge of
Bunting's understanding of the alternatives to the false art of our own

civilization. When he writes upon the harsh magnificence of the northern sea, he fastens upon this same idea of natural form:

> Summer is bergs and fogs, lichen on rocks.
> Who cares to remember a name cut in ice
> or be remembered?
> Wind writes in foam on the sea . . .

When the ship turns south, towards the Mediterranean, Bunting comes to define his own songs in lines already quoted by Tomlinson:

> Flexible, unrepetitive line
> to sing, not paint; sing, sing
> laying the tune on the air,
> nimble and easy as a lizard . . .

It is that fourth line, which Tomlinson does not quote, which ties Bunting's idea of song to the pattern-making of nature, rather than to the specific instances of song (Byrd, Monteverdi) which appear later in the poem. The distinction seems to me not inconsiderable. The discovery of form in nature gives him one way of judging 'men/driven by storm fret' who 'gloried in unlike creation':

> Starfish, poinsettia on a half-tide crag,
> a galliard by Byrd.
> Anemones spite cullers of ornament
> but design the pool
> to their grouping.

The third section of *Briggflatts*, a kind of Inferno, describes two climbers making their way up a cliff face. It is obscenely covered with dung, but there seems no point in killing the birds (or the poets and others who foul up the world). One climber halts, concluding that the climb is impossible. The other completes the ascent and catches a glimpse of the angel Israfel. He rests, exhausted, and momentarily becomes a slow-worm. (Roethke did this kind of transformation, only earlier and less self-consciously.) The poem in the fourth and fifth sections is less clearly located. There is an obscure procession of images of actions that suggest a concluding process. These images yield finally to the loving couple from part one, saying goodbye. It is now winter, with snow, ice and mist, and Bunting returns to his poetic mission:

> Sing,
> strewing the notes on the air
> as ripples in a shallow. Go
> bare, the shore is adorned
> with pungent weed loudly
> filtering sand and sea.

The modern world is summed up in one savage image:

> . . . runts murder the sacred calves of the sea by rule
> heedless of herring gull, surf and the text carved by waves
> on the skerry.

We have now returned to Northumbria,

> where the fells have stepped aside
> and the river praises itself,
> silence by silence sits
> and Then is diffused in Now.

The poem ends with images of light, water, stars, the 'bleached sky', Bunting's memories of the past deliquesce into beautiful images of song and wind and boats, celebrating the translation of the past into the future.

Bunting combines a savage rancour against mankind with a passionate devotion to nature. But he is not, like Gary Snyder, a romantic primitivist: he is too pessimistic, has been around too long. To place him is to say he is the lone surviving heir to Pound, save the objectivists *pur sang*. Like Reznikoff, Bunting was a contributor to Louis Zukofsky's *An 'Objectivists' Anthology* (1932). A volume of his was announced, but never published, by the Objectivist Press. (His first volume, *Redimiculum Matellarum*, was published in Milan in 1930.) Pound included Bunting in *Profile* (1932), and *Active Anthology* (1933), but in the work of the objectivists there is a quite different sense of the most usable part of Pound's capacious heritage. In this I think Reznikoff was the wiser pupil, though he has never written anything which rises to the heights of Bunting's long masterpiece.

There are squads of contemporary poets who think, with Bunting, that our so-called civilization stinks. They are convinced that modern man has lost his roots, and the possibility of any non-exploitative relationship with the natural world. The complaint is age-old: a spiritual hunger, unappeased by modern materialism, transforming itself into prophecy. In *Howl* the prophetic mode is still caught up with the texture and rhythms of a decayed urban scene; in Gary Snyder, in an even more radical form, we see a prophetic primitivism which has grown more strained. In a recent poem the Great Sun Buddha speaks:

> In that
> future American Era I shall enter a new form: to cure
> the world of loveless knowledge that seeks with blind hunger;
> and mindless rage eating food that will not fill it.'

> And he showed himself in his true form of
> SMOKEY THE BEAR.[19]

(Smokey the Bear, for the benefit of English readers, is the symbol of camping and forestry lore in advertisements warning against starting forest fires.) Snyder has increasingly found it difficult to restrain his own rage at the 'mindless rage' of others:

> The jets crack sound overhead, it's OK here;
> Every pulse of the rot at the heart
> In the sick fat veins of Amerika
> Pushes the edge up closer —
>
> A bulldozer grinding and slobbering
> Sideslipping and belching on top of
> The skinned-up bodies of still-live bushes
> In the pay of a man
> From town.[20]

This is a saddening dispersal of Snyder's enormous powers of concentration and observation; it is simply propaganda poetry, no more interesting because it is ecological propaganda than other kinds of things which he is pushing. Snyder's 'Mid-August at Sourdough Mountain Lookout', published in *Riprap* in 1959, is a demonstration of his ability to strip away 'culture', the past, his own personality, to return to the sheerness of simple perception. 'Piute Creek' from the same volume is a deeper-textured conception of the self in nature. He describes hill and forest country as something complicated, packed-in, vast, timeless. He is radically sceptical about the power of reason: the mind can encompass a small hunk of nature, a ridge, tree, rock — but no more. 'Words and books', the instruments of reason, evaporate, disappear, along with 'All the junk that goes with being human'. The only relationship that he can imagine is that between the seen and the man who sees; all human relations are ultimately reduced to the act of perception. The despoilers of nature are the quintessence of evil in Snyder's eyes, particularly when compared to the way primitive people lived with nature, and not against it. (Snyder's essay 'Poetry and the Primitive' in *Earth House Hold*, 1969, argues that the world-view of the primitive peoples, with their elaborate rituals for celebrating the interconnectedness of nature, is precisely what modern man needs now.) Though he sees the traditional cultures as irrevocably doomed, Snyder does not imagine we can suddenly transform ourselves into being primitives. Rather, because 'whatever is or ever was in any other culture can be reconstructed from the unconscious',[21] our ability to reach the unconscious becomes the most immediate problem. Snyder recommends the traditional means of meditation. Other writers who basically share Snyder's position have tried drugs (peyote, yage, hash, opium, marijuana, LSD), surrealism, Jungian archetypal images and the mandala, black magic, tarot, astrology, totemism, shamanism, and various kinds of animistic rites to reach back through the corrupted self of the mid-twentieth century to the undefiled inner nature of primitive man and the archaic past of the race. Snyder is an aggressive visionary, hectoring the gentiles with a vision of 'a totally integrated world culture with matrilineal descent, free-form marriage, natural-credit communist economy, less industry, far less population and lots of national parks'.[22]

The primitivism of modern poetry is traditional in the rather narrow sense that as modernization proceeded in Western Europe and America there were poets, thinkers, artists, who understood that the scientific revolution, rationalism, and industrialization came with a psychic toll; that these things have cost us something; that certain aspects of human nature were being repressed in the need for quite different patterns of behaviour, thought and relations of production. Though driven into the subconscious, these hungers or traits could be tapped, were potentially free to erupt into the modern world in the work of visionaries like Blake and Melville. These submerged sides of human nature were those things which asserted mankind's oneness with the world of natural creation, as opposed to the objectivity of the scientific outlook. Freud provided terms for the psychic struggle in his division of the energies of the subconscious into id and ego. And it is the ego, as Galway Kinnell writes, 'which separates us from the life of the planet, which keeps us apart from one another, which makes us feel self-conscious, inadequate, lonely, suspicious, possessive, jealous, awkward, fearful, and hostile; which thwarts our deepest desire, which is to be one with all creation'.[23] There is a hostility or indifference towards religious orthodoxy associated with this position. The feeling is reciprocated. Donald Davie has rebuked Kinnell for his failure to seize the 'disciplines' that might have 'opened him up to the spiritual apprehensions he hungers for'. The disciplines being self-evidently (for Davie) those of Christian worship. He condemns Kinnell for a blasphemous willingness to make 'great play' with Jesus, while rejecting the faith and its 'disciplines'.[24] Thus the dialogue between orthodoxy and the heretics.

In contemporary primitivism the characteristic alienation of advanced industrial society has experienced a dialectical movement from quantitative changes to a decisive qualitative shift. For primitivism is the end of the line. Its roots are old, as old as our culture's distrust of the mind, but the implications are stark: when primitivism ceases to be an eccentric response of individuals, but becomes the general state of the literary intellectuals, the effort to sustain our historic connection with the culture of the past will have been abandoned.[25] Primitivism is inimical to the historical sense, for if ritual and custom are the only arbiters of social behaviour there is no meaningful escape from their tyranny. The

199

world-view of the neolithic tribesman may have sustained him in ecological harmony with the world, but that is not, I suppose, going to help us deal with the problems of the real world. The primitivists promise a long holiday from reality; it is a measure of our social crisis that they speak with such unmerited assurance.

Kinnell's contribution does not lie in his intellectual grasp of the new primitivism — his essays seem remarkably fatuous — but in the tension within his verse between the desire for an inner liberation and an impulse towards narrative which he has struggled against with great gusto. He wants to discard convention, to dump narrative overboard, to abandon rationality, and to write from the 'deep sources' within. Somehow the ego intervenes, stops Kinnell at the edge of the cliff, and the poems never quite command, or are at the command of, that incoherence that he regards as the test of the genuine. But like Bunting, the poems seem a great deal more interesting than the ideas which have emerged in their wake.

Kinnell has written two long poems, the first being 'The Avenue Bearing the Initial of Christ into the New World' which appeared in *What a Kingdom It Was* in 1960. The poem is 'about' the lower East Side of New York — not the bustling immigrant ghetto of the turn of the century, where Charles Reznikoff's family lived and worked, but the dying neighbourhood of the 1930s or 1940s, when the promise of American society had broken, when people merely survived, 'roots/Hooked in any crevice they can find'. Kinnell senses a withdrawal into a purely private experience:

> ... merchants infold their stores
> And the carp ride motionlessly sleeplessly
> In the dark tank in the fishmarket,
> The figures withdraw into chambers overhead —
> In the city of the mind, chambers built
> Of care and necessity, where hands lifted to the blinds,
> They glimpse in mirrors backed with the blackness of the world
> Awkward, cherished rooms containing the familiar selves.   (Part 8)

His landscape here is urban, but quite unlike Auden's decaying industrial world which expresses symbolically the inner sickness of English society. Nor is Kinnell trying to reach those who are 'lecturing on navigation while the ship is going down'.[26] He does not view the dispossessed with the reformist's zeal. And so he is without that very specific sense of constituency that gives early Auden such distinctness. Kinnell writes here of an alien world, which he views with repugnance. He has the tourist's fascination with the picturesque: the bizarre crone selling newspapers on the corner, an old chassid, an Orthodox Jew, trailed by children, walking down the street, the names on the shops:

Nathan Kugler Chicken Store Fresh Killed Daily
Little Rose Restaurant
Rubinstein the Hatter Mens Boys Caps Furnishings
J. Herrmann Dealer in All Kinds of Bottles
Natural Bloom Cigars
Blony Bubblegum
Mueren las Cucaraches Super Potente Garantizada de
    Matar las Cucarachas mas Resistentes   (Part 3)

Precisely the kind of curiosity that might encourage a sympathetic visitor
to jot down a list of names in a notebook stands behind this passage.
Kinnell wants to say some strong things about the scene before him:
looking at vegetables on sale, it runs through his mind that they are not
particularly exotic, or even interesting, are not redolent of exotic places;
they are as common as the villages and hamlets of the Old Country.
Kinnell then names fourteen places where the Nazis built concentration
camps in an obscure and violent attempt to transfer the *frisson* associated
with the camps to the places themselves, all rather small villages, and to
attach that emotion to the commonness of the pushcart market and the
goods on sale. Elsewhere in the poem he links dead fish on a counter of a
fishmonger's shop with a death announcement from which would be sent
by the Camp Commandant. It doesn't work in either case, the
juxtaposition being too wilfully staged. But it does suggest that Kinnell's
relationship to the scene before him is fundamentally uncertain: he grasps
at this meaning because he does not know whether the world of Avenue C
will bear any 'meaning' at all.

Kinnell is at his best when he is alive to the insistent presence of the
detritus of ordinary life. At one point he asks why he was on Avenue C,
among 'bedbugged mattresses, springs/The stubbornness has been loved
out of ', but it is not until the tenth part that a meaningful answer is
possible. He writes of 'the black/Irreducible heap, mausoleum of what we
were'. The garbage trucks, pushcart markets, East River, noises of the
city, were part of the common experience of the urban poor, the
immigrants, a generation ago. Lessons were learned there, but which now
seem to come through in the attractive sepia tones of nostalgia:

> You stood on Houston, among panhandlers and winos
> Who weave the eastern ranges, learning to be free,
> To not care, to be knocked flat and to get up clear-headed
> Spitting the curses out.   (Part 4)

The lower East Side has a particular vivid symbolic meaning to American
Jews. This was *their* ghetto, where they struggled against an urban
environment that allowed no pause in the effort merely to survive. By the
1950s a second and third generation looked back at the lower East Side

with mingled relief and nostalgia. They had made it, had entered the mainstream of American life. The old neighbourhood gradually became a Black and Puerto Rican ghetto. Kinnell comes to Avenue C as an outsider, moved to sympathy at the degraded poor, the common lot; he would like it to somehow be more heroic until, at the end of the poem, he contemplates the human capacity to endure:

> The heart beats without windows in its night,
> The lungs put out the light of the world as they
> Heave and collapse, the brain turns and rattles
> In its own black axlegrease —
>
> In the nighttime
> Of the blood they are laughing and saying,
> Our little lane, what a kingdom it was!

oi weih, oi weih (Part 14)

The uncertainties of 'The Avenue Bearing the Initial of Christ into the New World', and its failures of tone, betray that characteristic dilemma of modern avant-garde writing, the alienation of the artist from his society. In this poem Kinnell looks back to 'what we were', in order to understand what we have become. He ends the poem lamely, without having fully understood either.

Kinnell's second major long poem, *The Book of Nightmares* (1971), moves significantly towards the state of freeing himself completely from narrative. In the process his language has lost some of the pressure of specificity. The poem is mysterious, abstract, metaphysical. Fragments of narrative survive, including one fine sequence describing a stay in a down-and-out hotel. The first part of the poem (it is constructed of ten parts, each made up of seven shorter poems), 'Under the Maud Moon', describes the birth of Kinnell's daughter Maud, and her first year. But the existence of thematic or chronological sequences in *The Book of Nightmares* does not of itself contribute to the structure of the whole. The form is elaborate, precise, mathematical, and I do not see how Kinnell can describe the arrangement of the poem as something that 'wasn't made entirely rationally, and so it isn't explicable rationally' (*Ohio Review*, XIV, No. 1). He may mean by arrangement the placing of material within the given structure. If so, it is a fiddling way to write from the 'deep sources' within himself. The poem is an obscure, symbolic presentation of two years of Kinnell's life. Like Bunting's *Briggflatts*, it contains the essential autobiography of that period, and may come to be seen much more clearly after the appearance of a biography, or collected letters, and of course in the light of the future direction of Kinnell's work. In his transformation from alienation to primitivism, Kinnell has sacrificed verbal energy for a metaphysical depth of meaning, yet it is not clear that the poem would repay the sustained attention it demands of its readers — towards whom he seems perfectly oblivious.

The elaborate symbolism and the ritualized formalism of *The Book of Nightmares* contrasts vividly with the relaxed, rambling character of the two major poetic enterprises of this period: Berryman's *Dream Songs* and Lowell's *Notebook*. The similarity of these poems has often been noticed, but there seems to be no tone (other than the elegiac) or style common to both. The crucial resemblance lies in the structural principal (or lack of principle) informing them: the idea of a verse sequence composed of an infinitely expansible number of discrete shorter poems. Lowell's poem is constructed with fourteen-line verse sonnets; Berryman uses an irregularly rhymed eighteen-line poem. They proved to be supremely *workable* forms: both men rattled off poems at a great pace month after month. The combination of personal and public concerns is one of the most distinctive common elements. *Dream Songs* and *Notebook* were written by poets of the same generation, by old friends who were educated at élite institutions (Harvard, Kenyon, Columbia, Cambridge) and who were themselves teachers in universities. The period of composition overlaps in 1967. Berryman was writing before the full crisis of American society in the 1960s was visible, and unlike Lowell made full use of the *persona* of Henry and a large cast of characters. His poem betrays less clearly than Lowell's the particular moment of its composition. Lowell erected the fortuitous into a structural principle:

> . . . I wished to describe the immediate instant. If I saw something one day, I wrote it that day, or the next. Things I felt or saw, or read were drift in the whirlpool . . .[27]

Berryman, too, seizes upon the headlines with a sick euphoria:

> A buddhist, doused in the street, serenely burned.
> The Secretary of State for War,
> winking it over, screwed a redhead whore.
> Monsignor Capouilla mourned. What a week.
> (*Dream Songs*, No. 66)

Both poets mourn the death of friends, the venality and corruption of American life, the paralysing dilemmas of the artist in a materialist society. In an acute but unfeeling phrase of Cyril Connolly's, Lowell and Berryman write about the events of the day 'as viewed by the liberal élite'.

The structural resemblance is overwhelmingly the most important, but one which needs to be approached circuitously. In 1934 George Oppen, a contributor to *An 'Objectivists' Anthology,* published *Discrete Series.* Explaining the title, he remarked:

> A discrete series is a series of terms each of which is empirically

derived, each one of which is empirically true. And this is the reason for the fragmentary character of those poems. I was attempting to construct a meaning by empirical statements . . .[28]

Oppen emphasizes the integrity of each term but it has come at the cost of the copulas of narrative. The relations between the poems can never be accidental or casual, yet each term can and does stand in its own right, linked only by the integrity of the poet's perception of the world. Of course that perception is always subjective, not so much in the sense of bearing an idiosyncratic personal meaning, but in being the expression of a particularly intense commitment to the task of poetry. That Oppen might have decided upon a form to be used in *Discrete Series*, and then written up the events of the day (the stockmarket crash, Hitler, Stalin, the comings and goings of old friends, Oppen's marriage and his political involvement) is frankly inconceivable. *Discrete Series* comes from another world of theoretical severity and artistic seriousness than *Dream Songs* and *Notebook*. There are thirty poems in Oppen's book: enough for him to say what he could say. He was a young man, and did not publish another book for twenty-eight years (*The Materials*, 1962). The prolixity of Berryman and Lowell, and their complacency before their gift, gives an impression of something scarcely controllable, of something that rendered them prisoners of their own facility.

Lowell, in an afterthought to *Notebook 1967-68* (1969), remarked that 'as my title intends, the poems in this book are written as one poem, jagged in pattern, but not a conglomeration or sequence of related materials'. He goes on to say that the book was not a chronicle or a diary, but contained a plot which 'rolls with the seasons': 'The separate poems and sections are opportunist and inspired by impulse. Accident threw up subjects, and the plot swallowed them — famished for human chances.' But with each successive manipulation of the sequence (the fourth, but not, given Lowell, necessarily the last, leaves us with *History* and *For Lizzie and Harriet*, with *The Dolphin* obviously coming from the same impulse) the idea that the book was a single poem has clearly been abandoned. 'My old title,' he writes in *History*, 'was more accurate than I wished, i.e. the composition was jumbled. I hope this jumble or jungle is cleared — that I have cut the waste marble from the figure.' Lowell may have been helped to this judgment by some of his English critics. Ian Hamilton's review of *Notebook* in the *Times Literary Supplement* of 25 December 1970 makes an unanswerable case against the informing structural principle ('the accumulative strategy'), and savagely dismisses the majority of poems as being simply shoddy. Having drawn blood so effectively, it is not surprising that Hamilton was mollified, possibly flattered, by Lowell's massive revisions. In a review in *The Observer* of 24 June 1974 he praised the changes ('immensely successful') in detail and design: 'Suddenly Lowell discovers a sequence which has what *Notebook* altogether lacked: a dramatic shape, a centre of intensity.' And how has Lowell found that dramatic shape and centre of intensity? By putting his sonnets into *chronological* order! A great help, if you are in a hurry, looking for Lowell's thoughts on Cleopatra or Stalin, Sir Thomas More or Colonel Charles Russell Lowell. He has added eighty new sonnets, filling in some of the gaps. The consequent shape is that of a procession, and it is less interesting than any of the three earlier versions. Certain groupings and sequences stand out, such as the revised versions of Rimbaud and Baudelaire which he has borrowed from *Imitations* (1962); nine sonnets on America in the nineteenth century; a group on Lowell's early mentors (Tate, Ransom, Ford); a moving group of elegies for his own 'tragic generation': Matthiessen, Jarrell, Roethke, MacNeice, and Berryman. But the surprises and ironies of juxtaposition which play so strongly within *Notebook* have been sacrificed. The famous poem on the march on the Pentagon in 1967 is cheek-by-jowl in *Notebook* with 'Charles Russell Lowell 1835-1864', giving a deeper meaning to Lowell's use of the myth of the Civil War. The Dutch courage of the notables on the march is ironically measured by the genuine heroism of Lowell's ancestor. Colonel Lowell is now on page 88 of *History*, and 'The March' some sixty pages later. In a crude sense 'history' has gained, but the haunting, poetic effect has been lost. The sequence of poems written about the terrible summer and fall of 1968 take us from Miami and the Republican Convention busy nominating Richard M. Nixon:

> Insects and statesmen grapple on the carpet
> Saying, 'You will swallow me. I you.'   ('Five-Hour Rally')

to the Democratic Convention in Chicago:

> The police weren't baby-sitting at 5 a.m.;
> in our staff headquarters, three heads smashed, one club.
> For five days the Hilton was liberated by cops and troops –
> fall of a government. The youth for McCarthy
> knew and blew too much on their children's crusade.
>   (' "We Are Here to Preserve Disorder" ')

and on to election eve, and political disaster:

> We must rouse our broken forces and save the country:
> we often said this, now the beaten player
> opens old wounds and hungers for the blood-feud
> hidden like contraband and loved like whiskey.   ('November 6')

Closely following this sequence is 'Winter', a poem about Dante, politics and exile:

> All comes from a girl met at the wrong time:

205

> God and her love that called him forth to exile
> in midwinter time cold and lengthening days . . .

Lowell's relationship with Caroline Blackwood, his political defeat, and 'exile' in England, give these lines an extraordinary personal resonance. He revised the title to 'Dante 1' for *History*, and substituted 'Dante' for the pronoun. A level of meaning, one of the ways the personal and the public concerns of the poem were held together, has been silently eliminated.

His revisions are inconsistent and annoying. In the sonnet 'Alexander' he substitutes 'Demosthenes' for 'the pundit'. In 'The New York Intellectual' the 'old critic' stands revealed as just plain 'Irving' (Irving Howe, editor of *Dissent*). But in the sonnet on Colonel Lowell, 'Phil Sheridan' is changed to 'his general'. In 'Caracas 1' he omits 'as hideous/as' before 'Los Angeles', without any explanation. Is L.A. less hideous in 1973 than it was in 1969? It would be nice to know why Hitler, Mussolini, Daladier and Chamberlain 'lost' in 'Munich 1938', when in the earlier version they had 'won'.

If too many of the revisions are trivial, what of the 'figure' now that the 'waste marble' has been cut away? By settling for a procession, an historical pageant, Lowell assembles quirks, habits, voices — bits of personality — of the great and the famous. It is difficult to think of any historical sense so oblivious to the role of economic or political forces, and which is so obsessed by character. In *History* Lowell's presiding genius is Plutarch, whose *Parallel Lives* (Alexander and Caesar, Demosthenes and Cicero, Pericles and Fabius Maximus) exhibit character, models of virtue, slaves of passion.

> Untouched,
> Alone in my Plutarchan bubble, I miss
> you, you out of Plutarch, made by hand —
> forever approaching our maturity.   ('R.F.K.')

An obsession with character helps to explain Lowell's passion for anecdote:

> A month from his death, we stood by Epstein's bust
> of Bertrand Russell; Louis said, 'It's better
> to die at fifty than lose my pleasure in terror.'
>
> ('The House-Party')

> 'When I talked that nonsense about Jews on the Rome
> wireless, she knew it was shit, and still loved me.'   ('Ezra Pound')

Lowell has also allowed himself a latitude for moralizing which, alas, reveals a tedious banality:

> ... this life too long for comfort and too brief
> for perfection...
>
> ('Long Summer 15')

> We are here for such a short time,
> we might as well be good to one another.
>
> ('In the Family')

Ian Hamilton's original verdict is too harsh: the vast majority of poems in *Notebook* are not shoddy, but there is enough bad writing, and finicky, inconsequential revisions, to make the whole rather less than the sum of its parts.

It is possible, sated as we are with a quite different kind of incoherence in explicitly modernist long poems, that Berryman and Lowell are blamed for what is the fault of the age. The resistance to Lowell's latest work and to *Dream Songs* on the part of some critics looks suspiciously like a formalist taste in the process of reasserting itself. Berryman and Lowell are renegade formalists, applying the old dispensation to what are modernist and post-modernist conceptions of decreation and aleatory form. Accident and chance are the name of the game. But neither Berryman nor Lowell are sufficiently interesting, page by page. One skips, looking for an interesting anecdote, a sympathetic portrait, a clever verbal trope, and forgets that this is supposed to be (in Lowell's case) a single poem. It is hard to abandon the idea, even after Pound, Eliot, Williams and Olson, that a poem is somehow different from a verse journal or notebook. It is not that they write about unpoetical things:

> — I can't read any more of this Rich Critical Prose,
> he growled, broke wind, and scratched himself & left
> that fragrant area.
> When the mind dies it exudes rich critical prose ...
>
> (*Dream Songs*, No. 170)

as if there was a kind of experience that was 'poetic', and another which was not; or that their fund of ideas seems rather 'safe' and somehow familiar:

> Renoir, paralyzed, painted with his penis,
> did naked women, not Michelangelos.
>
> ('Redskin')

> 'I paint'
> (Renoir said) 'with my penis.'
> A picture in Philadelphia proves it.
>
> (*Dream Songs*, No. 221)

What is ultimately unsatisfactory in *Dream Songs* and *Notebook* is that undirected, explosive verbal facility, a poetic diarrhoea. These poems are a perfect expression of the society in which they were written, juddering from disaster to disaster, swamped by abundance, saddened, tense, eloquent, frustrated. The connection between Lowell's jumbled hotel room, his prescription 'for nervousness' and the police riot during the Democratic Convention in 1968, which are held together in one sonnet, must have some meaning in the proximate relations he establishes. But Lowell, hurrying on to the next sonnet ('After the Convention'), does not stop to figure it out. Berryman somehow seems more kindly and patient:

> About that 'me'. After a lecture once
> came up a lady asking to see me. 'Of course.
> When would you like to?'
> Well, *now*, she said. 'Yes, but I have a lunch-
> eon—' Then I saw her and shifted with remorse
> and said 'Well; come on over'.
>
> So we crossed to my office together and I sat her down
> and asked, as she sat silent, 'What is it, miss?'
> 'Would you close the door?'
> Now Henry was perplexed. We don't close doors
> with students; it's just a principle. But this
> lady looked beyond frown.
>
> So I rose from the desk & closed it and turning back
> found her in tears — apologizing — 'No,
> go right ahead,' I assur-
> ed her, 'here's a handkerchief. Cry.' She did, I did.
>   When she got control, I said 'What's the matter — if
>   you want to talk?'
> 'Nothing. Nothing's the matter.' So.
> I am her.
>   (*Dream Songs*, No. 242)

The only appropriate Rich Critical Prose is: yes. Yes to writing like this, despite a thousand reservations about the *Dream Songs* and about the idea that a long poem can be made this way:

> Q. Is there any ulterior structure to the *Dream Songs*?
> A. Ah — you mean, somebody can get to be an associate professor or an assistant professor by finding it out? Mr Plotz, there is none. Il n'y en a pas! There is not a trace of it. Some of the Songs are in alphabetical order; but, mostly, they just belong to areas of hope and fear that Henry is going through at a given time. That's how I worked them out.[29]

One hopes that Mr Plotz had the temerity to tell Berryman that even an associate professor might find that a wilful and obscure way to go about a long poem.

Between Lowell and Gary Snyder there is little common ground about the ways to apprehend the present. Lowell established a relation with the past — at least that part of the past which he finds 'interesting' — yet seems to have no particular historical sense. The past is embedded in the present, absorbed into our collective sensibility, thus making irony our characteristic voice, but not transcendence. For Lowell the past is not conceived as the bearer of meanings for the present, and certainly not as a source of political alternatives. Snyder, on the other hand, lives in a continuous present. Writing in his journal in December 1956, he posed two alternatives for the poet. The first implied an immersion into the deep stream of 'his people, history, tradition, folding and folding himself in wealth of persons and pasts'. The alternative, which Snyder preferred, was 'to step beyond on to the way out, into horrors and angels, possible madness or silly Faustian doom, possible utter transcendence'.[30] For Snyder, transcendence has nothing to do with history or society: it was a personal and mystical possibility whose roots lay in the timeless nature of man, and in the wilderness around him. A sense of the developing ecological crisis led Snyder to a practical engagement with the why and how of social change.[31] But his attitude to the present is unequivocal: he approves of society only in so far as it encouraged handcrafts, is ecological, communal, and anti-materialistic. Otherwise, the 'criminal waste' of capitalism 'must be halted totally with ferocious energy and decision'.[32] When the question of agency is posed, Snyder drifts off into the clouds. The 'children's crusade', observed so ambivalently by Lowell at the Democratic Convention in Chicago in 1968, was the only vehicle in sight, but was not, in its fuzzy world of drugs, mysticism, ecology and communalism, much to base one's hopes on. That the students were a source of 'ferocious energy and decision' was a delusion widely shared among the intelligentsia. Snyder's practical intervention into the politics of ecology turns out to be thoroughly utopian.

If the demarcations are not clearly drawn between Lowell and Snyder, they at least suggest the kind of fundamental opposition which seems to define the contemporary cultural moment. Very little poetry is being written which commits itself to that world of 'people, history, tradition', and even less about the public life of either country. A poem on the E.E.C. referendum? Watergate? Gerald Ford? History seems to be happening somewhere else (Portugal, Greece, Spain, Argentina, Angola); poetry in England and America shares the numbness that has given the 1970s its insubstantial, styleless quality. We have gone into a period of the most severe privatization of meaningful experience, and there is no knowing how long this cultural vacuum is going to last. It seems unlikely that important literature is going to come out of it. One might have said the same, writing in 1947 or in 1953, with an equally gloomy feeling about the way the world was going. The continual political and cultural ferment since 1956 has addicted a generation to those big, horrific headlines, and unfitted us for the long littleness of political decline and social disintegration. Inevitably nostalgia dominates our cultural life, contributing its share to the process of emptying the present of its reality. Certain moments of the past seem more real to us than the present, which seems alien, hostile and which so conclusively betrays our social stagnation and cultural sterility.

The forms of that contention between Lowell and Snyder have a precise counterpart in English poetry: between Geoffrey Hill and Ted Hughes. That there should be such a starkly presented choice between history and transcendence or myth is perhaps our inheritance from the crisis of the 1960s, when the men of the centre (whoever they were), were displaced by a more polarized, dire cultural struggle — although if there is a cultural struggle today in England, it is not very visible on the streets. Unlike Snyder, Hughes sees no 'cause' worth fighting for. He is anti-rational, a conservative mystic who doubts whether any action which men take will make the slightest difference to that world 'of war and wastefulness and woe', as Auden put it in *New Year Letter*. Hill, with his laboured, erudite religiosity (who else would quote Simone Weil in an essay on Yeats?), is unlikely to join a 'children's crusade'. The contention, then, is taking place solely within the intellectual and literary community. Snyder alone possesses a sense of his constituency: he knows for whom he speaks. He was taken up by the students, but their return to quiescence has not pushed Snyder towards a re-evaluation of the ecological crisis. He writes as if 1968 will never end.

Hill is not at all the poet one would have expected to shoulder the burden of history. There are two distinct views about his work which emerged in reviews of *For the Unfallen* (1959). G. S. Fraser described Hill as writing with 'a chillingly distinguished formality', and of being 'a master rhetorician' (*New Statesman*, 31 October 1959). John Seymour remarked 'the almost frigid air of formality' (*Outposts*, 1959). On the other hand, Alvarez described Hill in *The Observer* as a myth-maker who was 'in an oblique way, religious'. Anthony Thwaite described Hill as 'a powerful religious poet', as does Elizabeth Jennings.[33] There is more a difference in emphasis than a contradiction between the idea of Hill as a mystic or religious poet, and Hill as a formalist's formalist. With *Mercian Hymns* (1971) the skills of the formalist and the inclinations of the myth-maker are harnessed to a poetry whose full meaning is historical. The book contains thirty hymns or prose meditations whose central figure is the Mercian king Offa, 'the presiding genius of the West Midlands'. The notes which Hill adds to the text are mostly unnecessary, and give the sequence an air of something worked up, when the prose poems have a freshness and intensity which does all the work that has to be done. Offa, then, was an eighth-century Mercian ruler, but the *Mercian Hymns* are only intermittently designed to convey a picture of Offa, or his times. Hill wittily uses anachronisms to say something about the continuities of the place, and its life. Offa is the 'overlord of the M5', who plays with a toy airplane, and in whose realm there are 'Merovingian car-dealers'. He manipulates the time-sequence freely within poems, and from poem to poem, to mingle our own age with Offa's. In part, he wants to find a timeless core of experience, unchanged from the eighth century to our own time, and does so in Offa's pride and violence, and in the picture of men at work:

> The men were paid to caulk water-pipes. They brewed
>   and pissed amid splendour; their latrine seethed its
>   estuary through nettles.   (XII)

Alongside images of continuity, there are those of change:

> Primeval heathland spattered with the bones of mice and
>   birds; where adders and bees made provision, mantling
>   the inner walls of their burh:

> Coiled entrenched England: brickwork and paintwork stalwart
>   above hacked marl. The clashing primary colours —
>   'Ethandune', 'Catraeth', 'Maldon', 'Pengwern'. Steel
>   against yew and privet. Fresh dynasties of smiths.   (XX)

The diminution of historic battles to suburban house-names speaks of one kind of judgment, as does 'Steel against yew and privet'. When Hill writes of the present in *Mercian Hymns* it is through the texture of memories (as in poem XXIII, a childhood recollection of World War II, and the bombshelters, camouflaged Nissen huts, and the 'wireless'). Memory plays an important role in connecting us with the past:

> I speak this in memory of my grandmother, whose child-
>   hood and prime womanhood were spent in the mailer's darg.

> The nailshop stood back of the cottage by the fold. It
>   reeked stale mineral sweat. Sparks had furred its low
>   roof. In dawn-light the troughed water floated a
>   damson-bloom of dust —

> not to be shaken by posthumous clamour.   (XXV)

Hill's prose is closely written. The language in his hands is chunky, specific, not a fluent medium but laboured, careful. The slangy tone in poem IX is not quite plausible. He shifts levels of diction uncertainly, as though the colloquial was about to explode in his face. The strongest and most characteristic passages are slightly over-elaborate and even mannered. Sometimes the ironies come too easily, as in poem XVIII,

211

describing Offa's visit to Boethius's dungeon. 'He strolled back to the car, with discreet souvenirs for consolation and philosophy.' But the achievement of the whole sequence is considerable.

The most interesting progeny of *Mercian Hymns* is Anthony Thwaite's *New Confessions* (1974), a series of meditations upon the life and work of Augustine. Like Hill, Thwaite moves easily between Augustine's world and our own. The combination of prose and verse, of jogging popular rhythm (in poem XXXV) and a more powerful prophetic voice, adds variety and interest which is sometimes missing in *Mercian Hymns*. Thwaite is, if anything, quicker than Hill to insist upon the contemporary reference of Augustine's life:

> Among small ancient farms where every day
> Morning enlists fields to be ploughed, stones to be cleared,
> Fences mended, brushwood burnt, cattle and goats
> To be herded from sparse patch to sparse patch,
> And each day has its discipline and pattern —
> From such ancestral narrowness I come
> To find elsewhere no such conscripted labour
> But talents scattered in a city gutter
> And idleness proliferating like weed
> In ways untended and unprofitable.
>
> (XVII)

Behind this poem is a childhood in the 1930s, and National Service, and the experience of middle age observing the children of Albion without amusement. But Thwaite finds that the clothes fit too well. Augustine's *angst* and disillusionment, his spiritual cravings notwithstanding, seems too thoroughly of our world. Maybe that is the point. But it makes the historical sense some perilously close to playing Shakespeare in lounge suits.

Hughes, alas, is a problem. Not the violence (Reznikoff makes him seem a gentler figure altogether), but the world-view, the sense of things as embodied in *Crow*. Our taste for the primitive must go deeper than anyone supposed, or at least a taste for the slick version of the primitive which we find in *Crow*. His sense of the failure of our culture is complete and unquestioning. In his much-discussed interview with Egbert Faas in the *London Magazine* (January 1971) he talks of the whole population sitting before their television sets, in 'a sort of anaesthetized unconcern', watching 'perpetual tortures and executions'. And this he presents as the 'dream' of a whole society: 'We are dreaming of a perpetual massacre.' The problem is, you really can't argue with this. There are no surveys of viewing habits, lists of most-popular programmes, studies of the effects of exposure to violence on television, which would earn Hughes's qualification for this assertion. It is an item of faith. As is his contempt for reason:

The laws of Creation are the only literally rational things, and we don't yet know what they are. The nearest we can come to rational thinking is to stand respectfully, hat in hand, before this Creation, exceedingly alert for a new word. We no longer so readily make the grinding funicular flights of cerebration from supposed first principles. On all points of uncertainty we give the Universe the benefit of doubt.
(*New Statesman*, 2 October 1964)

He has a strong belief in the efficacy of violence. His comments to Faas seem closer to a fascistic exaltation of violence for its own sake, as in Marinetti and Mussolini, than to any other tradition of thought. It does not quite amount to a worship of the will. But the 'elemental power circuit of the Universe' which, in the past, was restricted by rituals and dogma, but which today frightens the rationalist and humanist, is now suppressed. It would appear that Hughes does not mean this allegorically or symbolically. He is our purest instance of primitivism. James Baird discusses in his book *Ishmael: A Study of the Symbolic Mode of Primitivism* (1956) the powerful atavistic impulse behind certain forms of primitivism, and this helps us somewhat with Hughes. He is utterly dependent as a writer upon an extremely elaborate myth of the nature of the primitive. His response to that myth involves the creation of another structure of myth about the nature of modern Western society (he wildly exaggerates its rationalism) which confirms and justifies the first.

In a review Hughes describes socialism as 'the great "cooperatives" of non-competitive mutual parasitism' (*New Statesman*, 6 September 1963), revealing how little he sympathizes with any social or political development designed to ameliorate the condition of ordinary people. Socialism is one of the expressions of the intense and reasonable desire to abate that 'elemental power circuit of the Universe' which regularly swept people into misery, sickness and death. That Hughes can so confidently dismiss it as part of the hubris of an aggressive rationalism tells us something about the place that the sympathetic instinct occupies in his world-view. None — at least in theory. (There must not be any cheap gibes at the discrepancy between raising a family in good old secure welfare-state Britain while worshipping the dark gods and invoking their fierceness.)

Hughes has immersed himself in folktales, ritual literature, primitive cultures, and in anthropological studies of primitive societies. He feels that their world of ritual and dogmas make it possible to accept the world of natural energy:

> If you refuse the energy you are living in a kind of death. If you accept the energy, it destroys you. What is the alternative? To accept the energy and find methods of turning it to good, of

keeping it under control — rituals, the machinery of religion. The old method is the only one.

(London Magazine, January 1971).

This is the theme of Hughes's *Cave Birds,* performed at the Ilkley Festival in 1975, and published by the Scolar Press in a limited edition for £125. It begins with an arraignment of a 'defendant' who has murdered his 'demon', his inner gift through which alone we can accept that energy. It is a surprisingly passive psycho-drama and quest, and is part of the ongoing work begun with *Crow.* It is impossible to guess at the eventual shape of the completed poem, but Hughes has indicated the existence of an Ur-myth behind *Crow* (which is clearly not reached in that poem) [34] which may inform the whole. A mysterious prisoner of God ventures a wager with his keeper, that 'mancreated, broken down, corrupt despot of a ramshackle religion'. He creates Crow and accompanies him through a series of misadventures, metamorphoses and temptations, designed to destroy Crow. Hughes sees the sequence as enacting Crow's quest for God, but this appears more in *Cave Birds* than in *Crow* itself. The sequence reads less like an expressive symbolic presentation of myth than the presentation of instances of the archaic and the primitive, assembled and contrived in what Baird calls 'academic primitivism'. The sexual symbolism is striking, at first reading, but quickly loses its power to shock. Only the desire to do so remains:

> And woman's vulva dropped over man's neck and tightened.
>
> ('Crow's First Lesson')

> Words came in the likeness of a wreathed vagina pouring out Handel —
>
> ('The Battle of Osfrontalis')

The same is true of Hughes's heavily underlined attitude towards religion of the non-animistic sort:

> ... man's and woman's knees melted, they collapsed
> Their neck muscles melted, their brows bumped the ground
> Their tears evacuated visibly
> They whispered 'Your will is our peace'.
>
> ('A Horrible Religious Error')

And of Hughes's attitude to intelligence:

> Crow thought of intelligence —
> It turned the key against him and he tore at its fruitless bars.
>
> ('Magical Dangers')

A persuasive argument by David Lodge in the *Critical Quarterly* in 1971 tries to explain *Crow* as a cartoon character, utterly violated and resilient. But cartoons are usually deeply conservative in their careful balance of aggressions. The biter is bitten, the plotter unmasked, the schemer foiled: cartoon characters inhabit an elaborate and common-sense moral universe. The distance would appear to be substantial between the amoral world of Crow, and that of the cartoon in which the disturbances in the moral order are invariably righted. Crow's world is one of utter nihilism:

> People were running with bandages
> But the world was a draughty gap
> The whole creation
> was just a broken gutter pipe.   ('The Smile')

Hughes can (and does) go on like this for pages. His invention of metaphor is prodigal:

> When he burst out in rage
> She fell back with an awful gash and a fearful cry.
>
> When he stopped she closed on him like a book
> On a bookmark...   ('Crow and Mama')

In reaction to a nerveless poetry, critics have praised Hughes's 'admirable violence'.[35] But it is all violence in the head, 'academic primitivism'. Pound was lucky: when the ideas began to be translated into action, there was time to say 'Pull down thy vanity', to say 'I'm sorry'. Hughes is the voice of that part of our culture whose disaffection is so complete that they couldn't care less, one way or the other. I don't number myself among them. MacNeice wanted an art that would acknowledge the existence of contingent values, other people, history itself. That is what an *art of the real* is about.

Notes

PREFACE

1. The Eliot lecture is quoted by F. O. Matthiessen, *The Achievement of T. S. Eliot: An Essay on the Nature of Poetry*, 2nd ed. (New York: Oxford University Press, 1947), p. 90. I am grateful to Mr Lucien Stryk for calling this passage to my attention.
2. M. L. Rosenthal, *The New Poets: American and British Poetry Since World War II* (New York: Oxford University Press, 1967).

THE 1940s

1. Maurice Bowra, *Memories 1898-1939* (London: Weidenfeld & Nicolson, 1966), p. 178.
2. Louis MacNeice, *The Strings are False: An Unfinished Autobiography* (London: Faber & Faber, 1965), pp. 97, 98, 103.
3. Cyril Connolly was at first assigned to 'watch deserted buildings', which wasn't much fun, but when he was told to keep the crowd moving at Marble Arch, he wrote to Noel Blakiston that it was much more interesting. Connolly to Blackiston, 8 and 10 May 1926, *A Romantic Friendship: The Letters of Cyril Connolly to Noel Blakiston* (London: Constable, 1975), pp. 123, 125.
4. Julian Bell, letter in *New Statesman*, 9 December 1933, quoted by Samuel Hynes, 'Introduction', *Romance and Realism: A Study in English Bourgeois Literature*, by Christopher Caudwell (Princeton: Princeton University Press, 1970), p 7n.
5. MacNeice, *The Strings Are False*, op. cit., p. 133.
6. Ibid., p. 143.
7. D. E. S. Maxwell, *Poets of the Thirties* (London: Routledge & Kegan Paul, 1969), p. 179.
8. Caudwell, *Romance and Realism*, op. cit., pp. 135-6.
9. George Orwell, *Collected Essays, Journalism and Letters, Vol. 1 An Age Like This 1920-1940*, ed. Sonia Orwell and Ian Angus (London: Secker & Warburg, 1968), p. 257.
10. Auden, Poem VIII, *Another Time* (London: Faber & Faber, 1940).

p. 27. This poem was first published as 'Song for the New Year' in *The Listener*, 17 February 1937.

11. MacNeice's review of Laura Riding's *The Life of the Dead, New Verse*, No. 6 (December 1933), p. 19. Cf. MacNeice's 'In Defence of Vulgarity', *The Listener*, 29 December 1937.

12. MacNeice, *The Strings Are False*, op. cit., p. 53.

13. Orwell, *CEJL*, I, pp. 499-500.

14. John Lehmann, *New Writing in Europe* (Harmondsworth: Penguin Books, 1940), p. 116.

15. Julian Symons, *Notes from Another Country* (London: Alan Ross, 1972), pp. 92-3.

16. William Plomer, 'The Playboy of the Demi-World: 1938', *Collected Poems* (London: Jonathan Cape, 1973), p. 120.

17. Henry Reed, *A Map of Verona* (London: Jonathan Cape, 1946), p. 28.

18. Sir Hugh Walpole, quoted in John Lehmann, *I Am My Brother* (London: Longman, 1960), p. 103; *In My Own Time: Memoirs of a Literary Life* (Boston: Little, Brown, 1969), p. 284.

19. Sir Harold Nicolson, diary entry, 2 April 1940. *Diaries and Letters*, ed. Nigel Nicolson (New York: Atheneum, 1967), II (The War Years 1939-1945), p. 65.

20. As late as October 1938 Auden enthusiastically praised Malraux's *Days of Hope*: 'if you choose to call it so, *Days of Hope* is propaganda — propaganda for the truth' (*Town Crier*, 14 October 1938, p. 2). See Philip Toynbee's contribution to *Leaving School* (London: Alan Ross, 1966), pp. 5-18, on how Auden found himself reviewing Malraux in an obscure Birmingham Labour paper.

21. Auden quoted in *Poetry of the Thirties*, ed. Robin Skelton (Harmondsworth: Penguin Books, 1964), p. 41.

22. Anne Fremantle, 'Reality and Religion', *W. H. Auden: A Tribute*, ed. Stephen Spender (London: Weidenfeld & Nicolson, 1975), p. 89. In 1956 Auden wrote, 'On arriving in Barcelona I found as I walked through the city that all the churches were closed and there was not a priest to be seen. To my astonishment, this discovery left me profoundly shocked and disturbed', quoted by Edward Mendelson, *W. H. Auden: A Tribute*, op. cit., p. 10.

23. Spender, comments on Book Programme, B.B.C., 1 April 1975.

24. Cyril Connolly, 'Some Memories', *W. H. Auden: A Tribute*, op. cit., p. 70.

25. Stephen Spender, *World Within World* (London: Hamish Hamilton, 1951), p. 247.

26. George Orwell, 'Inside the Whale' (1940), *CEJL*, I, p. 516.

27. Spender, *World Within World*, op. cit., p. 247.

28. E. P. Thompson, 'Outside the Whale', *Out of Apathy*, ed. E. P. Thompson (London: Stevens & Sons for New Left Books, 1960), p. 148.

29. Ursula Niebuhr, 'Memories of the 1940s', *W. H. Auden: A Tribute*, op. cit., p. 105.
30. *Eight Oxford Poets*, ed. Michael Meyer and Sidney Keyes (London: George Routledge & Sons, 1941). The Foreword continues with a reference to Auden: 'we are all . . . *Romantic* writers, though by that I mean little more than that our greatest fault is a tendency to floridity; and that we have, on the whole, little sympathy with the Audenian school of poets'. Bernard Bergonzi must ignore this comment, and others to this effect, in his 'Auden & the Audenesque', *Encounter*, XLVI, No. 2 (February 1975), an article in which he argues for the 'Audenesque' as the 'collective idiom' of the 1930s, and which was 'still viable' at the end of the war.
31. Allen Tate, 'Young Randall', *Randall Jarrell 1914-1965*, ed. Robert Lowell, Peter Taylor and Robert Penn Warren (New York: Farrar, Straus & Giroux, 1967), p. 231.
32. See Clement Greenberg's review of *Blood for a Stranger, Partisan Review*, IX, No. 6 (November-December 1942), pp. 532-3.
33. Orwell, *CEJL*, II, p. 335.
34. John Lehmann, 'The Armoured Writer', *New Writing and Daylight*, I (Summer 1942), p. 153.
35. D. J. Enright, 'The Muse in Confusion', *Focus One* (London: Denis Dobson, 1945), pp. 86-9. Enright extended his analysis in 'The Significance of "Poetry London" ', *The Critic*, I, No. 1 (Spring 1947), pp. 3-10.
36. Some useful documentation is provided by Jack Salzman in *The Survival Years: A Collection of American Writing of the 1940's* (New York: Pegasus, 1969). See also Geoffrey Perrett, *Days of Sadness, Years of Triumph: The American People 1939-1945* (Baltimore: Penguin Books, 1974), pp. 87-103.
37. Brooks's lecture at Hunter College was published as *On Literature Today* (New York: E. P. Dutton, 1941). The lecture delivered at Columbia is printed in revised form in Brooks's *The Opinions of Oliver Allston* (New York: E. P. Dutton; London: J.M. Dent, 1941).
38. Lord Elton, *Notebook in Wartime* (London: Collins, 1941) and *St. George or The Dragon: Towards a Christian Democracy* (London: Collins, 1942). The Conservative case was put with great vehemence by Douglas Jerrold in *The Lie About the War* (London: Faber & Faber, 1930).
39. Dorothy L. Sayers, 'The English War', *Times Literary Supplement*, 7 September 1940, p. 445.
40. Anne Ridler, 'Now as Then', *Poetry in Wartime*, ed. M. J. Tambimuttu (London: Faber & Faber, 1942), pp. 122-3. See also 'For This Time' in Mrs Ridler's *A Dream Observed and Other Poems* (London: Poetry London, 1941), p. 20. I am grateful to Mrs Ridler for answering my query about the provenance of 'Now as Then'. On

the consequences of the war during the inter-war years, see Paul Fussell, *The Great War and Modern Memory* (New York: Oxford University Press, 1975).

41. Nicolson, *Diaries and Letters*, II, p. 36.
42. Sidney Keyes, 'The Artist in Society' (1942), *Minos of Crete: Plays and Stories*, ed. Michael Meyer (London: Routledge, 1948), p. 140.
43. Peter Ure, journal entry, September 1942, quoted by Frank Kermode, 'Peter Ure, 1919-1969', *Yeats and Anglo-Irish Literature: Critical Essays* by Peter Ure, ed. C. J. Rawson (Liverpool: Liverpool University Press, 1974), pp. 15-16.
44. Keith Vaughan, *Journal & Drawings 1939-1965* (London: Alan Ross, 1966), pp. 86-7. Vaughan's anonymous contributions to *Penguin New Writing* ('From a Painter's Notebook') deserve careful study.
45. Alun Lewis, *Letters from India*, with a note by Mrs Alun Lewis and a Preface by A. L. Rowse (Cardiff: Penmark Press, 1946), pp. 41-2. All further references to Lewis's correspondence are from this source.
46. Roy Fuller, *Professors and Gods: Last Oxford Lectures on Poetry* (London: Andre Deutsch, 1973), pp. 132-4.
47. Ibid., p. 147.
48. Compare the experience of a slightly older poet, Geoffrey Grigson, in *The Crest on the Silver: An Autobiography* (London: Cresset, 1950), pp. 119ff.
49. Fuller, *Professors and Gods,* op cit., p. 148.
50. Henry Reed, *A Map of Verona*, op. cit., p. 25.
51. Roy Fuller, 'Mood of the Month', *London Magazine*, V, No. 11 (November 1958), p. 74.
52. The dilemma of Philip Witt, poet and solicitor for a building society, in *Image of a Society* (London: Andre Deutsch, 1956) has an interesting personal resonance:

> The enormity of his offence consisted not only in the revelation of his fallibility, but also — and even more acutely — in its evidence of the failure of the duty he owed to the society that relied on his skill, maintained him and gave him his status. It became clear to him that his errors arose out of his divided life — that he could not hope to serve the society as he should if he cared more for the imaginative creations of his leisure. And it was plain, too, that whatever he thought privately of the society, its functions, its ruling caste, its aims, since it had in good faith engaged his loyalty and skill, his error was an offence against a morality which he could not confine to his business life (pp. 214-15).

As Fuller put it in 'Spring Song', '. . . still the poet in his rhyme/ "Accept, accept", cries from his tower'.

THE 1950s

1. Delmore Schwartz, 'T. S. Eliot as the International Hero', *Partisan Review*, XII (Spring 1945), pp. 199-206; reprinted in *Selected Essays of Delmore Schwartz*, ed. Donald A. Dike and David H. Zucker (Chicago: University of Chicago Press, 1970).

2. Wrey Gardiner, 'Editorial', *Poetry Quarterly*, X, No. 1 (Spring 1948), p. 3.

3. Parsons, quoted in Joel Roache, *Richard Eberhart: The Progress of an American Poet* (N.Y.: Oxford University Press, 1971), pp. 183-4.

4. Lehmann, *In My Own Time*, op. cit., pp. 446-8.

5. Philip Larkin, 'Introduction', *Jill: A Novel* (London: Faber & Faber, 1975), p. 12.

6. J. B. S. Haldane, 'Cancer's a Funny Thing' in *The Oxford Book of Twentieth-Century Verse*, chosen by Philip Larkin (Oxford: Clarendon Press, 1973), pp. 271-2.

7. See Walter Benjamin, 'The Work of Art in the Age of Mechanical Reproduction', *Illuminations*, ed. Hannah Arendt (N.Y.: Schocken, 1968).

8. Philip Larkin, 'Introduction', *All What Jazz: A Record Diary 1961-68* (London: Faber & Faber, 1970), p. 17.

9. Donald Davie, *Purity of Diction in English Verse* (1952; London: Routledge & Kegan Paul, 1967), p. 97.

10. See the reviews in *Ezra Pound: The Critical Heritage*, ed. Eric Homberger (London: Routledge & Kegan Paul, 1972).

11. The crucial year was 1953, when Wain's *Contemporary Reviews of Romantic Poetry*, Hough's *The Romantic Poets*, John Holloway's *The Victorian Sage*, and Abrams's *The Mirror and the Lamp* were published.

12. Davie, *Purity of Diction*, op. cit., p. 99.

13. Hobsbaum, letter in *The Listener*, 21 December 1961.

14. John Wain, 'Oxford and After', *Outposts*, No. 13 (Spring 1949), pp. 21-3.

15. John Wain, 'Ambiguous Gifts: Notes on a Twentieth-Century Poet', *Penguin New Writing*, No. 40 (1950) pp. 116-28; reprinted in Wain's *Preliminary Essays* (London: Macmillan, 1957).

16. Alan Ross, 'A Lament for the 'Thirties Poets', *Poetry Quarterly*, X, No. 2 (Summer 1948), p. 71. This poem was not collected in Ross's *Poems 1942-67* (London: Eyre & Spottiswoode, 1967). Donald Davie, 'Remembering the 'Thirties', *Brides of Reason* (1955); *Collected Poems 1950-1970* (London: Routledge & Kegan Paul, 1972), pp. 20-1.

17. Charles Tomlinson, 'Poetry Today', *The Modern Age: Volume 7 of the Pelican Guide to English Literature*, ed. Boris Ford (Harmondsworth: Penguin Books, 1961), p. 458.

18. A. Alvarez, review of *The Whitsun Weddings* in *The Observer*, 1964;

reprinted in *Beyond All This Fiddle* (London: Allen Lane, The Penguin Press, 1968), pp. 85-6.

19. Donald Davie, 'Poetry & Landscape in Present England', *The Granta*, 19 October 1963, pp. 2-4; reprinted in *Thomas Hardy and British Poetry* (London: Routledge & Kegan Paul, 1973), pp. 64-72.

20. See Larkin's comment in D. J. Enright's *Poets of the 1950s* (1955), and Frank Kermode's 'The Myth-Kitty', *Puzzles and Epiphanies* (London: Routledge & Kegan Paul, 1962), pp. 35-9.

21. Donald Davie, 'The Varsity Match', *Poetry Nation*, No. 2 (1974), p. 77.

22. Kingsley Amis in *Poetry of the 1950s*, ed. D. J. Enright (Tokyo: Kenkyusha, 1955), p. 17.

23. Davie, *Ezra Pound: Poet as Sculptor* (New York: Oxford University Press, 1964), pp., 151, 163, 204, 243.

24. Davie, *Purity of Diction in English Verse*, op. cit., pp. 92-9, 197.

25. G. S. Fraser, 'Sober Livery', *The New Statesman and Nation*, LI (14 January 1956), p. 48.

26. Davie, 'In the Pity', *New Statesman*, LXVIII (28 August 1964), p. 282. In this category we presumably should include 'Stevens is really a naive writer . . .' in Davie's 'Great or Major?', *The New Statesman and Nation*, LI (14 January 1956), p. 48.

27. The word 'civil' took on a distinct political meaning in the 1950s, when it was picked up in the 'end of ideology' debate. Edward Shils's 'Ideology and Civility: On the Politics of the Intellectual' in the *Sewanee Review,* Summer 1958, makes an impassioned defence of 'civil politics', now that Marxism has been tarnished by events, and the fires have cooled between capitalists and socialists. 'There seems to be no more grounds for ideological politics . . . civil politics entail judging things on their own merits . . . and they also require respect for tradition.'

28. Roy Fuller noted this in his review of Davie's *Collected Poems* in *London Magazine*, n.s. XII, No. 6 (February-March 1973), pp. 132-3. The most important discussion of the poem is John Fuller's review of *The Forests of Lithuania* in *Tomorrow*, No. 3 (February-March 1960), pp. 24-9.

29. Davie, *Collected Poems*, p. 86; and the passage in the Marvell Press edition, pp. 60-1.

30. *Thomas Hardy and British Poetry*, op. cit., p. 72.

31. Davie in *Poets of the 1950s*, p. 48.

32. Sources for the material in the cento: Derwent May in *Poetry from Oxford*, ed. Martin Seymour-Smith (London: Fortune Press, 1953), p. 47; Sanford Friedman, 'An Interview with Richard Howard', *Shenandoah*, XXIV, No. 1 (Fall 1972), p. 14; Anthony Thwaite, 'The Young Poet in the University', *The Listener* (16 December 1954), p. 1069; William Carlos Williams, 'Wallace Stevens', *Poetry*, 87, No. 4 (January 1956), p. 238; Richard Wilbur, 'The

Genie in the Bottle', *Mid-Century American Poets*, ed. John Ciardi (New York: Twayne, 1950), p. 7; Donald Hall in *Poetry from Oxford*, 1953, p. 17; Marius Bewley, 'Aspects of Modern American Poetry', *Scrutiny*, XVII, No. 4 (March 1951), pp. 335-6; John Lehmann, 'The Other T. S. Eliot', *The Listener* (28 January 1954), pp. 179-182; Herbert Read, 'The Drift of Modern Poetry', *Encounter*, IV, No. 1 (January 1955), p. 10; G. S. Fraser, 'The New British Poets', *New World Writing*, No. 7 (1955), p. 107; William Phillips, 'American Writing Today', *The Twentieth Century*, 160 (July 1956), p. 11; Adrian Mitchell's comment from a debate with Gabriel Pearson in *Oxford Left* (Michaelmas 1954), p. 34; Muir in a letter to Janet Adam Smith (26 September 1956), *Selected Letters of Edwin Muir*, ed. P. H. Butter (London: Hogarth Press, 1974), p. 187.

33. Randall Swingler, 'History and the Poet', *New Writing*, n.s. III (Christmas 1939), p. 50.
34. Ezra Pound, 'America: Chances and Remedies. VI', *The New Age*, XIII (5 June 1913), p. 143.
35. Marius Bewley, 'Aspects of Modern American Poetry', op. cit., p. 341.
36. Donald Davie, 'Eliot in One Poet's Life', *Mosaic*, VI, No. 1 (Fall 1972), p. 232.
37. Richard Eberhart, 'Strong, Sensitive and Balanced', *New York Times Book Review*, CV (24 June 1956), p. 5.
38. Simpson, *Air with Armed Men*, pp. 159-60.
39. Diana Trilling, *Claremont Essays* (London: Secker & Warburg, 1965), p. 171.
40. Richard Wilbur, 'On My Own Work' in *Contemporary American Poetry*, ed. Howard Nemerov (Voice of America Forum Lectures, n.d., n.pp.), p. 213.
41. Philip L. Gerber and Robert J. Gemmett, 'The Window of Art: A Conversation with Richard Wilbur', *Modern Poetry Studies*, I, No. 2 (1970), p. 65.
42. Wilbur, 'On My Own Work', op. cit., p. 204.
43. Richard Wilbur, 'The Bottle Becomes New, Too', *Quarterly Review of Literature*, VII, No. 3 (1953), p. 192.
44. Ralph J. Mills, Jr., *Cry of the Human: Essays on Contemporary American Poetry* (Urbana: University of Illinois Press, 1975), p. 194. This essay usefully surveys Hall's recent work.
45. 'A New Aestheticism? A. Alvarez talks to Donald Davie', *The Modern Poet: Essays from 'The Review'*, ed. Ian Hamilton (London: Macdonald, 1968), pp. 157-8.
46. Charles Tomlinson, 'Yeats and the Practising Poet', *An Honoured Guest: New Essays on W. B. Yeats*, ed. Denis Donoghue and J. R. Mulryne (London: Edward Arnold, 1965), p. 1.
47. Ian Hamilton, 'Four Conversations: Charles Tomlinson', *London Magazine*, n.s. IV, No. 6 (November 1964), p. 83.

48. Charles Tomlinson, review of *Literary Essays by Ezra Pound*, *The Spectator*, CXCII (19 February 1954), p. 212; reprinted in *Ezra Pound: The Critical Heritage*, pp. 422-4, with a statement indicating that he very decidedly no longer approves of this review.

49. Charles Tomlinson, 'Poets and Mushrooms', *Poetry*, C, No. 2 (May 1962), p. 109.

50. Charles Tomlinson, *The Poem as Initiation* (Hamilton, N.Y.: Colgate U.P., 1967), n.p.

51. Roethke to Dorothy Gordon, February 1934, *Selected Letters of Theodore Roethke*, ed. Ralph J. Mills, Jr. (Seattle and London: University of Washington Press, 1968), p. 13. Further references to Roethke's letters will be incorporated by date into the text.

52. Williams to Robert McAlmon, 9 March 1947, *The Selected Letters of William Carlos Williams*, ed. John C. Thirlwall (New York: McDowell, Obolensky, 1957), p. 254.

53. *Straw for the Fire: From the Notebooks of Theodore Roethke 1943-63*, selected by David Wagoner (Garden City, N.Y.: Doubleday & Co., 1972), p. 181. Further references will be incorporated in the text.

54. *On the Poet and his Craft: Selected Prose of Theodore Roethke*, ed. Ralph J. Mills, Jr. (Seattle and London: University of Washington Press, 1965), p. 15.

55. W. D. Snodgrass, *In Radical Pursuit: Critical Essays and Lectures* (New York: Harper & Row, 1975), pp. 103-4.

56. Sylvia Plath, 'OCEAN-1212-W', *The Listener*, LXX (29 August 1963), pp. 312-13; reprinted in *The Art of Sylvia Plath*, ed. Charles Newman (London: Faber & Faber, 1970).

57. Roethke's comments are from a talk on 'Identity', February 1963, printed in *On the Poet and his Craft*, pp. 23-4. The 'longish dry period' followed the sequence from 'The Lost Son' to 'O, Thou Opening, O', and may have been its cost in terms of creative energy.

58. Sylvia Plath, 'Lorelei', *The Colossus* (1960; Faber & Faber, 1967), p. 22.

59. *The Selected Letters of William Carlos Williams*, pp. 138-9. Further references will be incorporated by date in the text.

60. *Selected Essays of William Carlos Williams* (New York: Random House, 1954), p. 212. Abbreviated in the text as *Essays*.

61. William Carlos Williams, *Paterson Books I-V* (New York: New Directions, 1963), pp. 50-1. Abbreviated in the text as *Paterson*.

62. Quoted in Robert Creeley, *A Quick Graph: Collected Notes & Essays*, ed. Donald Allen (San Francisco: Four Seasons Foundation, 1970), p. 185.

63. Noticed by Robert von Hallberg, 'Olson, Whitehead and the Objectivists', *Boundary 2*, II, Nos. 1-2 (Fall 1973-Winter 1974), p. 86.

64. David Jones, *The Anathemata* (London: Faber & Faber, 1952), p. 60.

65. David Jones, 'Past and Present', *Epoch and Artist: Selected Writings*, ed. Harman Grisewood (London: Faber & Faber, 1959), pp. 139-40.
66. Jones, *Epoch and Artist*, op. cit., pp. 124-5.
67. G. S. Fraser, 'On the Interpretation of a Difficult Poem', *Interpretations*, ed. John Wain (London: Routledge & Kegan Paul, 1955), p. 221. The comments by Alvarez are on p. 3, and by Gillie on p. 77.
68. Jones, *The Anathemata*, op. cit., p. 90.
69. Martin Duberman, *Black Mountain: An Exploration into Community* (New York: Dutton, 1972), p. 399.
70. Charles Olson, 'Letter to Elaine Feinstein', May 1959, *The Human Universe and Other Essays*, ed. Donald Allen (New York: Grove Press, 1967), pp. 96-7.
71. Ibid., p. 11.
72. Ibid., pp. 59-60.
73. Charles Olson, *The Maximus Poems* (London: Cape Goliard [1970]), pp. [14-15].
74. See, for example, Irving Howe's 'The Sentimental Fellow-Travelling of F. O. Matthiessen', *Partisan Review*, XV, No. 10 (October 1948), pp. 1125-9.
75. Surveyed in Malcolm Cowley, *The Literary Situation* (New York: Viking Press, 1955).
76. C. Wright Mills, 'The Decline of the Left', *Power, Politics and People*, ed. Irving Louis Horowitz (New York: Oxford University Press, 1963), p. 225.
77. See Ann Charters's excellent *Kerouac: A Biography* (London: Andre Deutsch, 1974).
78. Ginsberg in an interview with Allen Young, *International Times*, No. 148 (23 February-8 March 1973), pp. 17-20.
79. For Cassady's initial reaction to Ginsberg, see *The First Third & Other Writings* (San Francisco: City Lights, 1971), pp. 118-21. See also Ginsberg's 'Elegy for Neal Cassady', *The Paris Review*, No. 53 (Winter 1972), pp. 76-9.
80. A selection of Cassady's letters are reprinted in *The First Third*, pp. 124-57; see also Charters, *Kerouac*, pp. 113-16.
81. Allen Ginsberg, *Kaddish and Other Poems 1958-1960* (San Francisco: City Lights, 1961), p. 14.
82. See Ginsberg's comic 'History of the Jewish Socialist Party in America' in *Airplane Dreams: Compositions from Journals* (San Francisco: House of Anansi/City Lights, 1969), pp. 1-3. The entry is dated 1961, i.e. the year when *Kaddish* was published.
83. Allen Ginsberg *Howl and Other Poems* (San Francisco: City Lights, 1956), p. 11.
84. Big Men on Campus at Columbia at the time included John Hollander, Jason Epstein and Norman Podhoretz. Hollander's cutting remark on Ginsberg is quoted by Morris Dickstein, 'Allen

Ginsberg and the 60's', *Commentary*, XLIX, No. 1 (January 1970), pp. 64-70, a notably sympathetic treatment of Ginsberg's place in recent American life. Ginsberg's contemporaries were much less sympathetic, particularly those associated with the *Partisan Review*, such as Norman Podhoretz, whose 'The Know-Nothing Bohemians' appeared in the Spring 1958 issue. The distaste felt by Hollander and Podhoretz was shared by Diana Trilling, whose 'The Other Night at Columbia' describes a reading which Ginsberg gave at his *alma mater*. It appeared in the *Partisan Review*, Spring 1959, and was collected in Mrs Trilling's *Claremont Essays* (New York: Harcourt Brace Jovanovich, 1964).

85. Louis Simpson, 'Poets of the "Silent Generation"', *New World Writing*, No. 11 (1957), p. 111; 'Poetry Chronicle', *Hudson Review*, XVI (Spring 1963), p. 132; 'Dead Horses and Live Issues', *The Nation*, CCIV, No. 17 (24 April 1967), pp. 520-2.

86. George Santayana, 'Genteel American Poetry', *The New Republic*, 29 May 1915; reprinted in *George Santayana's America: Essays on Literature and Culture*, ed. James Ballowe (Urbana and London: University of Illinois Press, 1967), pp. 147-9.

87. *The Nation*, 19 September 1959, reprinted in *Critics on Robert Lowell*, ed. Jonathan Price (London: George Allen & Unwin, 1974), pp. 71-5.

88. W. D. Snodgrass, *In Radical Pursuit: Critical Essays and Lectures* (New York: Harper & Row, 1975), p. 28.

89. Ibid., p. 55.

90. Philip L. Gerber and Robert J. Gemmett, 'No Voices Talk to Me: A Conversation with W. D. Snodgrass', *Western Humanities Review*, XXIV (Winter 1970), pp. 66-7.

91. 'W. D. Snodgrass: An Interview', *Contemporary Poetry in America*, ed. Robert Boyers (New York: Schocken Books, 1974), p. 175.

92. Richard Howard, *Alone with America: Essays on the Art of Poetry in the United States Since 1950* (New York: Atheneum, 1969), p. 474.

93. Robert Creeley, contribution to a symposium on 'The Writer's Situation: II', *New American Review*, No. 10 (August 1970), p. 227.

94. Snodgrass, *In Radical Pursuit*, pp. 20-1.

95. Ibid., p. 176.

96. T. S. Eliot, *The Waste Land: A Facsimile and Transcript . . .*, ed. Valerie Eliot (London: Faber & Faber, 1971), p. [1].

97. Frederick Seidel, 'Writers at Work: Robert Lowell', *The Paris Review*, No. 25 (Winter-Spring 1961), pp. 65-95; reprinted in *Writers at Work: The Paris Review Interviews, Second Series* (New York: Viking Press, 1963), p. 366.

98. *Writers at Work*, op. cit., p. 349.

99. Ian Hamilton, 'A Conversation with Robert Lowell', *The Review*, No. 26 (Summer 1971), p. 26.

100. Marjorie G. Perloff, *The Poetic Art of Robert Lowell* (Ithaca and London: Cornell University Press, 1973), pp. 80-99.
101. See Eric Homberger, 'Pound, Ford and "Prose": The Making of a Modern Poet', *Journal of American Studies*, V (January 1972), pp. 281-92.
102. Glauco Cambon, *The Inclusive Flame: Studies in Modern American Poetry* (Bloomington: Indiana University Press, 1963), p. 245.
103. *Writers at Work*, op. cit., p. 353.
104. Ibid., pp. 355-6.
105. 'A Conversation with Robert Lowell', op. cit., p. 14.
106. See Marshall McLuhan's 1951 essay, 'Tennyson and Picturesque Poetry', *The Interior Landscape: The Literary Criticism of Marshall McLuhan*, ed. Eugene McNamara (New York: McGraw-Hill, 1971), pp. 135-55.
107. 'A Conversation with Robert Lowell', op. cit., p. 26.
108. Harriet Rosenstein, 'Reconsidering Sylvia Plath', *Ms*, I, No. 3 (September 1972), p. 46.
109. Gordon Lameyer, *Who Was Sylvia? A Memoir of Sylvia Plath During 'The Bell Jar' Days*, manuscript, p. 110.
110. Lois Ames says the interviews with the poets were conducted by correspondence, 'Notes Toward a Biography', *The Art of Sylvia Plath*, ed. Charles Newman (London: Faber & Faber, 1970), p. 162. George Steiner writes that 'In the summer of 1952 a young woman came to interview me in London. She was writing an all-too-predictable article on 'Poets on Campus' for *Mademoiselle* . . . I recall little of the occasion, except the young lady was poised and conventionally inquisitive . . .', 'In Extremis', *The Cambridge Review*, 90, No. 2187 (7 February 1969), p. 247.
111. Nancy Hunter Steiner, *A Closer Look at Ariel: A Memory of Sylvia Plath*, with an Afterword by George Stade (London: Faber & Faber, 1974), p. 32.
112. Richard Wilbur, 'Cottage Street, 1953', *American Poetry Review* (November-December 1972), p. 13.
113. Plath quotes Auden in a letter to Lameyer, p. 38.
114. Ted Hughes, 'Sylvia Plath's *Crossing the Water*: Some Reflections', *Critical Quarterly*, XIII (Summer 1971), p. 165.
115. Four poems from this manuscript were published in *The Cambridge Review* on 7 February 1969.
116. For the publication of Plath's early poems, see Eric Homberger, *A Chronological Checklist of the Periodical Publications of Sylvia Plath* (Exeter: University of Exeter American Arts Documentation Centre, 1970).
117. Anne Sexton, 'The Barfly Ought to Sing', *The Art of Sylvia Plath*, op. cit., p. 177.
118. Ted Hughes describes Plath's method of composition in the *Poetry Book Society Bulletin*, No. 44 (February 1965), p. 1.
119. Sources for Hughes's views are: the *Poetry Book Society Bulletin*,

1965; the article on the chronology of Plath's poems in *The Art of Sylvia Plath*, 1970; and the radio talk on *Crossing the Water*, printed in *The Critical Quarterly*, 1971. By far the most useful source has been his contribution to the symposium on 'Context' in the *London Magazine*, February 1962.

120. Wendy Campbell, 'Remembering Sylvia', *The Art of Sylvia Plath*, op. cit., p. 184.

121. Charles Newman, 'Candor is the only Wile – The Art of Sylvia Plath', ibid., p. 52n.

122. Plath wrote to her mother on 2 August 1956: 'He is educating me daily, setting me exercises of concentration and observation'; on 11 June 1958: 'Ted says simply to produce work, produce, read not novels or poems only, but books on folktales, fiddler crabs and meteorites – this is what the imagination thrives on', *Letters Home: Correspondence 1950-1963*, ed. Aurelia Schober Plath (New York: Harper & Row, 1975), pp. 267, 342.

123. Early in 1957, Plath's letters home are filled with her desire to teach. It was closely involved with her need for self-respect, and to 'give out', perhaps out of a deeper sense of indebtedness to those who had encouraged her academic career (*Letters Home*, op. cit., pp. 290, 301); but she found the atmosphere at Smith 'airless', and was disillusioned by her colleagues (pp. 329, 341). On 28 November 1957 she wrote 'I see too well the security and prestige of academic life, but it is Death to writing' (p. 331).

124. Plath, *Letters Home*, op. cit., p. 298.

125. Lameyer, p. 119; Plath, quoted by Ames, *The Art of Sylvia Plath*, op. cit., pp. 170-1.

126. A. R. Jones, 'On "Daddy" ', ibid., p. 234.

THE 1960s AND 1970s

1. Charles Reznikoff, *Five Groups of Verse* (New York: Charles Reznikoff, 1927), p. 9.

2. Ibid., p. 17.

3. Ibid., pp. 30-1.

4. Charles Reznikoff, *Testimony* (New York: The Objectivist Press, 1934), p. xiii.

5. Ibid., pp. 35-6.

6. Babette Deutsch, 'Heirs of the Imagists', *New York Herald Tribune Books*, 1 April 1934, section VII, p. 16; 'Shorter Notices', *The Nation*, CXXXVIII, No. 3593 (16 May 1934), p. 572.

7. Charles Reznikoff, *Testimony: The United States 1885-1890: Recitative* (New York: New Directions-San Francisco Review, 1965), p. 41.

8. Hayden Carruth, 'A Failure of Contempt', *Poetry*, CVII (March 1966), p. 396.

9. Richard Emil Braun, *Bad Land* (Pentland, North Carolina: The Jargon Society, 1971), p. [15].

10. Ibid., p. [24].

11. Ibid., p. [21].

12. Ibid., p. [29].

13. Ibid., p. [44].

14. Braun has published a translation of *Antigone* (New York: Oxford University Press, 1973), and has a version of Euripides' *Rhesos* forthcoming. *The Foreclosure*, a volume of dramatic lyrics, appeared in 1972.

15. Bunting arouses fierce passions. Writing on a theme close to the core of Bunting's work, see W. E. Parkinson in 'Poetry in the North East' in *British Poetry Since 1960: A Critical Survey*, ed. Michael Schmidt and Grevel Lindop (South Hinksey, Oxford: Carcanet Press, 1972), p. 111.

16. Bunting, quoted by Herbert Read, 'Basil Bunting: Music or Meaning?', *Agenda*, IV, Nos. 5-6 (Autumn 1966), p. 4.

17. Ibid., p. 8.

18. Charles Tomlinson, 'Experience into Music', ibid., p. 15.

19. Gary Snyder, 'Smokey the Bear Sutra', *The Fudo Trilogy* (Berkeley: Shaman Drum, 1973), n.p.

20. Gary Snyder, 'Front Lines', *Turtle Island* (New York: New Directions, 1974), p. 18.

21. Gary Snyder, *Earth House Hold* (New York: New Directions, 1969), pp. 92-3.

22. Ibid., p. 93.

23. Galway Kinnell, 'Poetry, Personality, and Death', *Field*, No. 4 (Spring 1971), p. 61.

24. Donald Davie, 'Slogging for the Absolute', *Parnassus*, III, No. 1 (Fall/Winter 1974), p. 17.

25. James Baird's *Ishmael: A Study of the Symbolic Mode in Primitivism* (Baltimore: The Johns Hopkins Press, 1956) is of some usefulness, but needs to be revised in the light of developments in structural anthropology. Baird's discussion of the 'nostalgia for the primitive' and 'cultural failure' has been revised, in a different guise, in the series of studies of intellectual fascism by John R. Harrison (*The Reactionaries*, 1966), Alastair Hamilton (*The Appeal of Fascism*, 1971), Tarmo Kunnas (*Drieu la Rochelle, Céline, Brasillach et la tentation fasciste*, 1972), and William M. Chace (*The Political Identities of Ezra Pound and T. S. Eliot*, 1973). Primitivism is perhaps the only thing that left intellectuals and fellow-travellers have not been accused of (see David Caute, *The Fellow-Travellers*, 1973).

26. W. H. Auden, Poem XXII, *Poems* (London: Faber & Faber, rev. ed. 1933), p. 76.

27. Ian Hamilton, 'A Conversation with Robert Lowell', *The Review*, No. 26 (Summer 1971), p. 14.

28. Oppen, in an interview in *Contemporary Literature*, X (Spring 1969), p. 161.
29. 'An Interview with John Berryman', *Harvard Advocate*, CIII, No. 1 (Spring 1969), p. 5. He has rather more to say about the 'sometimes rigid and sometimes plastic, structural notions' behind *Dream Songs* in an interview in *The Paris Review*, No. 53 (Winter 1972), p. 191.
30. Snyder, *Earth House Hold*, op. cit., p. 39.
31. See 'Four Changes' in *Turtle Island*, op. cit.
32. Ibid., pp. 97-8.
33. Anthony Thwaite, *Contemporary English Poetry: An Introduction* (London: Heinemann, 1959; second ed. 1961), pp. 158-9; Elizabeth Jennings, *Poetry To-Day (1957-60)* (London: Longman for the British Council, 1961), pp. 44-5.
34. Keith Sagar, *The Art of Ted Hughes* (Cambridge: Cambridge University Press, 1975), p. 118. Hughes's comments were made during a recording of *Crow* in 1973.
35. Edwin Muir, review of *The Hawk in the Rain*, *New Statesman*, LIII (28 September 1957), p. 392. This comment must be seen in the light of Muir's letter to Janet Adam Smith, 26 September 1956 (chapter 2, note 32).

Select Bibliography

This is meant to provide a list of general titles on contemporary poetry in England and America, and, as well, on the wider social and historical ambience. The editions given are those which I have used. Titles have not usually been repeated from the chronologies. The bibliography is divided into a section of reference works, of varying usefulness, and a list of general works. The volume *Contemporary Poets of the English Language*, edited by Rosalie Murphy, is as near as we are likely to get to a comprehensive and accurate list of the major publications of contemporary poets, though even here there are absences which one notices from time to time. Ms Murphy's book is the place where a student of contemporary poetry should begin.

REFERENCE

Kinsman, Claire D., ed., *Contemporary Authors: A Bio-Bibliographical Guide to Current Authors and their Works* (Detroit: Gale Research Co., 1962-19—). 56 parts in 19 vols, with revisions, to date.

Kunitz, Stanley J., ed., *Twentieth Century Authors: A Bibliographical Dictionary of Modern Literature.* First Supplement. (New York: H. H. Wilson Co., 1955.)

Malkoff, Karl, *Crowell's Handbook of Contemporary American Poetry* (New York: Thomas Y. Crowell, 1973).

Murphy, Rosalie, ed., *Contemporary Poets of the English Language* (London: St. James Press; New York: St. Martin's Press, 1970).

The Penguin Companion to Literature, vol. 1 (Britain and the Commonwealth), ed. David Daiches; vol. 2 (United States and Latin America), ed. Eric Mottram, Malcolm Bradbury and Jean Franco. (Harmondsworth: Penguin Books, 1971.)

Seymour-Smith, Martin, *Guide to Modern World Literature* (London: Wolfe, 1973).

Spender, Stephen and Donald Hall, eds., *The Concise Encyclopaedia of English and American Poets and Poetry* (London: Hutchinson, 1963).

Willison, I. R., ed., *The New Cambridge Bibliography of English*

Literature, vol. 4 (1900-1950). (Cambridge: Cambridge University Press, 1972.)

GENERAL

Allen, Donald M. and Warren Tallman, eds., *The Poetics of The New American Poetry* (New York: Grove Press, 1973).

Alvarez, A., *Beyond All This Fiddle: Essays 1955-1967* (London: Allen Lane, The Penguin Press, 1968).

Anon., 'On the Shelf: Poetry in the Public Library', *Times Literary Supplement*, No. 3393 (9 March 1967), pp. 177-8.

Auden, W. H., 'Criticism in Mass Society', *The Intent of the Critic*, ed. D. A. Stauffer (Princeton: Princeton University Press, 1941).

Banerjee, A., *Spirit Above Wars: A Study of the English Poetry of the Two World Wars* (London: Macmillan, 1976).

Barrett, William, 'The Truants: *Partisan Review* in the 40's', *Commentary*, LVII, No. 6 (June 1974), pp. 48-54.

Bedient, Calvin, *Eight Contemporary Poets* (London: Oxford University Press, 1974).

Bergonzi, Bernard, 'Auden & the Audenesque', *Encounter*, XLIV, No. 2 (February 1975), pp. 65-75.

Bewley, Marius, 'Aspects of Modern American Poetry', *Scrutiny*, XVII, No. 4 (March 1951), pp. 334-52.

Bly, Robert, 'Five Decades of Modern American Poetry', *The Fifties*, No. 1 (1958), pp. 36-7.

—'On English and American Poetry', *The Fifties*, No. 2 (1959), pp. 45-7.

—'Poetry in an Age of Expansion', *The Nation*, 192 (22 April 1961), pp. 350-4.

Bogdanor, Vernon and Skidelsky, Robert, eds., *The Age of.Affluence 1951-1964* (London: Macmillan, 1970).

Boundary 2, II, Nos. 1 and 2 (Fall 1973/Winter 1974). Charles Olson: Essays, Reminiscences, Reviews, ed. Matthew Corrigan.

Boyers, Robert, ed., *Contemporary Poetry in America: Essays and Interviews* (New York: Schocken Books, 1974).

Bradbury, Malcolm, '*Horizon* and the English Nineteen-Forties', *Gemini*, II, No. 6 (Spring 1959), pp. 20-4.

—*The Social Context of Modern English Literature* (Oxford: Basil Blackwell, 1971).

Butscher, Edward, *Sylvia Plath: Method and Madness* (New York: Seabury Press, 1976).

Cambon, Glauco, *The Inclusive Flame: Studies in Modern American Poetry* (Bloomington, Indiana: University of Indiana Press, 1963).

Charters, Samuel, *Some Poems/Poets* (Berkeley: Oyez, 1971).

Cook, Bruce, *The Beat Generation* (New York: Charles Scribner's Sons, 1971).

Cowley, Malcolm, 'What the Poets are Saying: 1941', *Think Back on Us*, ed. Henry Dan Piper (Carbondale: Southern Illinois University Press, 1967), II (The Literary Record), pp. 372-7.

Craig, David, ed., *Marxists on Literature: An Anthology* (Harmondsworth: Penguin Books, 1975).

——'The New Poetry of Socialism', *The Real Foundations* (London: Chatto & Windus, 1973), pp. 215-23.

Denney, Reuel, *The Astonished Muse: Popular Culture in America* (Chicago: University of Chicago Press, 1957).

Dickins, Anthony, 'Tambimuttu and Poetry London', *London Magazine*, n.s. V (December 1965), pp. 53-60.

Dickstein, Morris, 'Cold War Blues', *Partisan Review*, XLI, No. 1 (1974), pp. 30-55.

——'Allen Ginsberg and the 60's', *Commentary*, XLIX, No. 1 (January 1970), pp. 64-70.

Dike, Donald A. and Zucker, David H., eds., *The Selected Essays of Delmore Schwartz* (Chicago and London: University of Chicago Press, 1970).

Dodsworth, Martin, ed., *The Survival Of Poetry* (London: Faber & Faber, 1970).

Donadio, Stephen H., 'Some Younger Poets in America', *Modern Occasions*, ed. Philip Rahv (London: Weidenfeld & Nicolson, 1966), pp. 226-46.

Donoghue, Denis, *The Ordinary Universe: Soundings in Modern Literature* (London: Faber & Faber, 1968).

Duberman, Martin, *Black Mountain: An Exploration in Community* (New York: E. P. Dutton & Co., 1972).

Edwards, Thomas R., *Imagination and Power: A Study of Poetry on Public Themes* (London: Chatto & Windus, 1971).

Ehrenpreis, Irvin, ed., *American Poetry* (Stratford-Upon-Avon Studies 7). (London: Edward Arnold, 1965.)

Eisinger, Chester, ed., *The 1940s: Profile of a Nation in Crisis* (Garden City, N.Y.: Anchor Books, 1969).

Enright, D. J., 'The Significance of "Poetry London"', *The Critic*, I, No. 1 (Spring 1947), pp. 3-10.

——'Robert Graves and the Decline of Modernism', Inaugural Lecture, University of Singapore, 17 November 1960, reprinted in *Conspirators and Poets* (London: Chatto & Windus, 1966), pp. 48-67.

Frankenberg, Lloyd, *Pleasure Dome: On Reading Modern Poetry* (Boston: Houghton, Mifflin, 1949).

Fraser, G. S., *The Modern Writer and His World* (London: Derek Verschoyle, 1953).

——'Some Notes on Poetic Diction', *Penguin New Writing*, No. 37 (1949), pp. 115-28.

——'Towards Completeness', *Seven*, No. 8 (Spring 1940), pp. 27-31.

——*Vision and Rhetoric: Studies in Modern Poetry* (London: Faber & Faber, 1959).

Gardner, Wrey, 'Poetry Quarterly 1939-1953', *Stand*, VIII, No. 3 (1966-7), pp. 51-60.

Glover, Jon, ' "Person and Politics": Commitment in the Forties', *Poetry Nation*, No. 3 (1974), pp. 69-80.

Graham, Desmond, *Keith Douglas 1920-1944: A Biography* (London: Oxford University Press, 1974).

Graves, Robert, 'War Poetry in this War', *The Listener* (23 October 1941), pp. 566-7.

Grubb, Frederick, *A Vision of Reality: A Study of Liberalism in Twentieth-Century Verse* (London: Chatto & Windus, 1965).

Guenther, John, *Sidney Keyes: A Biographical Inquiry* (London: Alan Ross, 1967).

Gunn, Thom, Review of *Collected Poems* by Wallace Stevens, *London Magazine*, III, No. 4 (April 1966), pp. 81-4.

—Review of *Collected Poems* by William Empson, *London Magazine*, III, No. 2 (February 1956), pp. 70-5.

—'The New Music', *The Listener*, LXXVIII, No. 2001 (3 August 1967), pp. 129-30.

—'Waking with Wonder – Thom Gunn writes about the poetry of Gary Snyder', *The Listener*, LXXIX (2 May 1968), pp. 576-7.

—'William Carlos Williams', *Encounter*, XXV, No. 1 (July 1965), pp. 67-74.

Hall, Donald, 'The New Poetry: Notes on the Past Fifteen Years in America', *New World Writing*, No. 7 (1955), pp. 213-47.

Hall, Stuart, 'Inside the Whale Again?', *Universities and Left Review*, No. 4 (Summer 1958), pp. 14-20.

Hamburger, Michael, *A Mug's Game: Intermittent Memoirs 1924-1954* (Cheadle Hulme: Carcanet Press, 1973).

—*The Truth of Poetry: Tensions in Modern Poetry from Baudelaire to the 1960s* (London: Weidenfeld & Nicolson, 1969).

Hamilton, Ian, *A Poetry Chronicle: Essays and Reviews* (London: Faber & Faber, 1973).

—ed., *The Modern Poet: Essays from 'the Review'* (London: Macdonald, 1968).

Hill, Donald, *Richard Wilbur* (New Haven, Conn.: College & University Press, 1967).

Hill, Geoffrey, 'Robert Lowell: Contrasts and Repetitions', *Essays in Criticism*, XIII (April 1963), pp. 188-97.

Homberger, Eric, 'Dictatorship of the conversational', *Times Higher Education Supplement*, No. 78 (13 April 1973), p. 15.

—ed., *Ezra Pound: The Critical Heritage* (London and Boston: Routledge & Kegan Paul, 1972).

—' "Surviving" Poetry', *Cambridge Review*, 95 (31 May 1974), pp. 150-3.

—'The Uncollected Plath', *New Statesman*, LXXXIV (22 September 1972), pp. 404-5.

Howard, Richard, *Alone With America: Essays on the Art of Poetry in the*

United States Since 1950 (New York: Atheneum, 1969).

Ironwood, No. 5 (1975). George Oppen: A Special Issue.

Jarrell, Randall, 'Poetry in a Dry Season', *Partisan Review*, VII, No. 2 (1940), pp. 166-7.

——'Poetry in War and Peace', *Partisan Review*, XII (1945), pp. 120-6.

Jennings, Elizabeth, *Poetry To-Day (1957-60)* (London: Longman for the British Council, 1961).

——'The Poet To-Day', *The Isis*, No. 1228 (2 June 1954), p. 19.

Kenner, Hugh, *The Art of Poetry* (New York: Holt, Rinehart & Winston, 1959).

——*Gnomon: Essays on Contemporary Literature* (New York: McDowell, Obolensky, 1958).

——*A Homemade World: The American Modernist Writers* (New York: Alfred A. Knopf, 1975).

——*The Pound Era* (Berkeley and Los Angeles: University of California Press, 1971).

Kinnell, Galway, 'Poetry, Personality, and Death', *Field*, No. 4 (Spring 1967), pp. 56-75.

Koestler, Arthur, 'The Yogi and the Commissar', *Horizon*, V, No. 30 (June 1942), pp. 381-91.

Kuby, Lolette, *An Uncommon Poet for the Common Man: A Study of Philip Larkin's Poetry* (The Hague: Mouton, 1974).

Levertov, Denise, 'Anne Sexton: Light Up the Cave', *Ramparts*, XII, No. 5 (December 1974-January 1975), pp. 61-3.

——*The Poet in the World* (New York: New Directions, 1973).

Lindsay, Jack, *After the 'Thirties* (London: Lawrence & Wishart, 1956).

Lowell, Robert, 'Digressions from Larkin's 20th-Century Verse', *Encounter*, XL, No. 5 (May 1973), pp. 66-8.

——*et al.*, eds., *Randall Jarrell 1914-1965* (New York: Farrar, Straus & Giroux, 1967).

Maclaren-Ross, Julian, *Memoirs of the Forties* (London: Alan Ross, 1965).

Madge, Charles and Harrisson, Tom, *Britain, by Mass Observation* (Harmondsworth: Penguin Books, 1939).

Mander, John, *The Writer and Commitment* (London: Secker & Warburg, 1961).

Manvell, Roger, *Films and the Second World War* (London: J.M. Dent, 1974).

Maps, No. 5 (1973). Louis Zukofsky number.

Meltzer, David, ed., *The San Francisco Poets* (New York: Ballantine Books, 1971).

Mersmann, James F., *Out of the Vortex: A Study of Poets and Poetry against the War* (Lawrence, Kans.: University of Kansas Press, 1974).

Miles, Jospehine, *The Primary Language of Poetry in the 1940s* (Berkeley and Los Angeles: University of California Press, 1951).

——'American Poetry in 1965', *Massachusetts Review*, VII, No. 2 (Spring

1966), pp. 321-35.

Miller, J. Hillis, *Poets of Reality: Six Twentieth-Century Writers* (Cambridge, Mass.: Harvard University Press, 1965).

Mills, Ralph J., Jr., *Contemporary American Poetry* (New York: Random House, 1965).

—*Cry of the Human: Essays on Contemporary American Poetry* (Urbana: University of Illinois Press, 1975).

Mitchell, Julian, *et al.*, *Light Blue, Dark Blue: An Anthology of Recent Writing from Oxford and Cambridge Universities* (London: Macdonald, 1960).

Mottram, Eric, 'Sixties American Poetry, Poetics and Poetic Movements', *American Literature Since 1900*, ed. Marcus Cunliffe (London: Barrie & Jenkins, 1975), pp. 271-311.

Nemerov, Howard, ed., *Contemporary American Poetry* (N.p.p.: Voice of America Forum Lectures, n.d.).

—*Poetry & Fiction: Essays* (New Brunswick: Rutgers University Press, 1963).

Newman, Charles, ed., *The Art of Sylvia Plath: A Symposium* (London: Faber & Faber, 1970).

Nuttall, Jeff, *Bomb Culture* (London: MacGibbon & Kee, 1968).

Orr, Peter, ed., *The Poet Speaks* (London: Routledge & Kegan Paul, 1966).

Ossman, David, ed., *The Sullen Art: Interviews* (New York: Corinth Books, 1963).

Ostroff, Anthony, ed., *The Contemporary Poet as Artist and Critic* (Boston: Little, Brown, 1964).

Owen, Guy, ed., *Modern American Poetry: Essays in Criticism* (Deland, Fla.: Everett/Edwards, 1972).

Pelling, Henry, *Britain and the Second World War* (London: Fontana, 1970).

Phillips, Robert, *The Confessional Poets* (Carbondale: Southern Illinois University Press, 1973).

Phoenix, Nos. 11/12 (Autumn and Winter 1973/4). Philip Larkin Issue.

Plath, Sylvia, *Letters Home: Correspondence 1950-1963*, ed. Aurelia Schober Plath (New York: Harper and Row, 1975).

Poetry Wales, X, No. 3 (Autumn 1975). Alun Lewis Special Number.

Press, John, 'English Verse Since 1945', *Essays by Divers Hands*, n.s. XXXI (London: Oxford University Press, 1962), pp. 143-84.

—*Rule and Energy: Trends in British Poetry Since the Second World War* (London: Oxford University Press, 1963).

Prynne, J. H., Review of Charles Olson, *Maximus Poems IV, V, VI, The Park*, Nos. 4-5 (Summer 1969), pp. 64-6.

Raban, Jonathan, *The Society of the Poem* (London: Harrap, 1971).

Read, Herbert, *Poetry and Anarchism* (London: Faber & Faber, 1938).

Reed, Henry, 'The End of an Impulse', *New Writing and Daylight*, No. 3 (June 1943), pp. 111-23.

Rexroth, Kenneth, *American Poetry in the Twentieth Century* (New

York: Herder & Herder, 1971).

—'Disengagement: The Art of the Beat Generation', *New World Writing,* No. 11 (1957), pp. 28-41.

Rickword, Edgell, 'Poetry and Two Wars', *Our Time,* I, No. 2 (April 1941), pp. 1-6.

Roache, Joel, *Richard Eberhart: The Progress of an American Poet* (New York: Oxford University Press, 1971).

Rosenfeld, Isaac, *An Age of Enormity: Life and Writing in the Forties And Fifties,* ed. Theodore Solotaroff (Cleveland and New York: World Publishing Co., 1962).

Rosenthal, M. L., *The New Poets: American and British Poetry Since World War II* (New York: Oxford University Press, 1967).

—*Poetry and the Common Life* (New York: Oxford University Press, 1974).

Ross, Alan, *Poetry 1945-1950* (London: Longman for the British Council, 1951).

—*The Forties: A Period Piece* (London: Weidenfeld & Nicolson, 1950).

Rothenberg, Jerome, ed., *Revolution of the Word: A New Gathering of American Avant Garde Poetry 1914-1945* (New York: The Seabury Press, 1974).

Sagar, Keith, *The Art of Ted Hughes* (Cambridge: Cambridge University Press, 1975).

Salmagundi, I, No. 4 (1966-7). Robert Lowell Issue.

Salzman, Jack, ed., *The Survival Years: A Collection of American Writing of the 1940's* (New York: Pegasus, 1969).

Savage, D. S., *The Personal Principle: Studies in Modern Poetry* (London: Routledge, 1944).

Scannell, Vernon, *Not Without Glory: Poets of the Second World War* (London: Woburn Press, 1976).

Schmidt, Michael and Lindop, Grevel, eds., *British Poetry Since 1960: A Critical Survey* (South Hinksey: Carcanet Press, 1972).

Scully, James, ed., *Modern Poetics* (New York: McGraw-Hill, 1965).

Sergeant, Howard, ed., *Poetry of the 1940s* (London: Longman, 1970).

Sexton, Anne, 'Classroom at Boston University', *The Harvard Advocate,* CXLV (November 1961), pp. 13-14.

Shapiro, Karl, *The Poetry Wreck: Selected Essays 1950-1970* (New York: Random House, 1975).

Shaw, Robert B., ed., *American Poetry Since 1960 — Some Critical Perspectives* (Cheadle Hulme: Carcanet Press, 1973).

Simpson, Louis, 'On Being a Poet in America', *The Noble Savage,* No. 5 (October 1962), pp. 24-33.

—'Poetry in the Sixties — Long Live Blake! Down with Donne', *The New York Times Book Review,* 28 December 1969, pp. 1-2, 18.

—*Air with Armed Men* (London: London Magazine Editions, 1972).

Sissons, Michael and French, Philip, eds., *Age of Austerity 1945-1951* (London: Hodder & Stoughton, 1963).

Snyder, Gary, *Earth House Hold* (New York: New Directions, 1969).

Solotaroff, Theodore, *The Red Hot Vacuum and Other Pieces on the Writing of the Sixties* (New York: Atheneum, 1970).

Spears, Monroe K., *Dionysus and the City: Modernism in Twentieth-Century Poetry* (New York: Oxford University Press, 1970).

Spender, Stephen, *Love-Hate Relations: A Study of Anglo-American Sensibilities* (London: Hamish Hamilton, 1974).

—'On Literary Movements', *Encounter*, I, No. 2 (November 1953), pp. 66-8.

—*Poetry Since 1939* (London: Longman for the British Council, 1946).

—'War and the Writer', *Partisan Review*, IX, No. 1 (January-February 1942), pp. 63-6.

—ed., *W. H. Auden: A Tribute* (London: Weidenfeld & Nicolson, 1975).

—*World Within World* (London: Hamish Hamilton, 1951).

Stauffer, Donald Barlow, *A Short History of American Poetry* (New York: E. P. Dutton, 1974).

Stanford, Derek, *The Freedom of Poetry* (London: Falcon Press, 1947).

Stein, Arnold, ed., *Theodore Roethke: Essays on the Poetry* (Seattle and London: University of Washington Press, 1965).

Stepanchev, Stephen, *American Poetry Since 1945: A Critical Survey* (New York: Harper & Row, 1965).

Sutton, Walter, *American Free Verse: The Modern Revolution in Poetry* (New York: New Directions, 1973).

Symons, Julian, 'A Poet in Society', *Now*, No. 1 (1943), pp. 68-73.

—*Notes from Another Country* (London: Alan Ross, 1972).

—'The End of a War: 8 Notes on the Objective of Writing in our Time', *Now*, No. 5 (1945), pp. 5-13.

—'Writing and Society', *Now*, No. 3 (1944), pp. 14-21.

—'Writing in the Desert', *Partisan Review*, X, No. 5 (September-October 1943, pp. 421-8.

Tennessee Poetry Journal, II, No. 2 (Winter 1969). Robert Bly Special Number.

Thompson, E. P., ed., *Out of Apathy* (London: Stevens & Sons for New Left Books, 1960).

Thurley, Geoffrey, *The Ironic Harvest: English Poetry in the Twentieth Century* (London: Edward Arnold, 1974).

Thwaite, Anthony, *Contemporary English Poetry: An Introduction* (London: Heinemann, 1959).

—*Poetry Today 1960-73* (London: Longman for the British Council, 1973).

Timms, David, *Philip Larkin* (Edinburgh: Oliver & Boyd, 1973).

Tolley, A. T., *The Poetry of the Thirties* (London: Gollancz, 1975).

Tomlinson, Charles, 'The Middlebrow Muse', *Essays in Criticism*, VII, No. 2 (April 1957), pp. 208-17.

—'Poetry Today', *The Pelican Guide to English Literature, VII: The Modern Age*, ed. Boris Ford (Harmondsworth: Penguin Books, 1961), pp. 458-74.

—'Poets and Mushrooms: A Retrospect of British Poetry in 1961',

Poetry, C, No. 2 (May 1962), pp. 104-21.
—ed., *William Carlos Williams: A Critical Anthology* (Harmondsworth: Penguin Books, 1972).
Trilling, Lionel, 'The Situation of the American Intellectual at the Present Time', *Perspectives*, No. 3 (Spring 1953), pp. 24-42.
Tytell, John, 'The Beat Generation and the Continuing American Revolution', *American Scholar*, XLII, No. 2 (Spring 1973), pp. 308-17.
Vaughan, Keith, *Journal & Drawings 1939-1965* (London: Alan Ross, 1966).
Waggoner, Hyatt H., *The Heel of Elohim: Science and Values in Modern American Poetry* (Norman, Okla.: University of Oklahoma Press, 1950).
Wain, John, 'Ambiguous Gifts: Notes on a Twentieth-Century Poet' *Pengiun New Writing*, No. 40 (1950), pp. 116-28.
Weatherhead, A. Kingsley, 'Philip Larkin of England', *ELH*, XXXVIII, No. 4 (December 1971), pp. 616-30.
Wilson, Edmund, 'Marxism at the End of the Thirties', *The Shores of Light* (New York: Vintage Books, 1961), pp. 732-43.
Woolf, Virginia, 'The Leaning Tower', *Folios of New Writing*, No. 2 (Autumn 1940), pp. 11-29.
Zukofsky, Louis, *Prepositions: The Collected Critical Essays of Louis Zukofsky* (London: Rapp & Carroll, 1967).

Acknowledgments

The author and publisher wish to thank the following for permission to reproduce copyright material:

A. ALVAREZ: to the author for an excerpt from a conversation in *The Review*.

W. H. AUDEN: to Faber & Faber Ltd and Alfred A. Knopf Inc. for excerpts from the *Collected Poetry of W. H. Auden,* copyright 1945 by W. H. Auden and from the *Collected Longer Poems* © 1968 by W. H. Auden.

JOHN BERRYMAN: to Faber & Faber Ltd for excerpts from *77 Dream Songs* and *His Toy, His Dream, His Rest*; and to Farrar, Straus & Giroux for excerpts from *The Dream Songs* © 1959, 1962, 1964, 1965, 1966, 1967, 1968, 1969 by John Berryman.

R. E. BRAUN: to the author, and to Jonathan Williams and the Jargon Society Inc.

BASIL BUNTING: to the author.

DONALD DAVIE: to Routledge & Kegan Paul Ltd for excerpts from *Collected Poems 1950–1970, The Shires,* and *Thomas Hardy and British Poetry*; to Oxford University Press Inc. for excerpts from *Collected Poems 1950–1970* by Donald Davie, copyright © 1972 by Donald Davie.

ALAN DUGAN: to Yale University Press and Faber & Faber Ltd for a passage from *Collected Poems.*

T. S. ELIOT: to Faber & Faber Ltd and Harcourt Brace Jovanovich Inc., publishers of *Collected Poems 1909–1962* by T. S. Eliot.

ROY FULLER: to Andre Deutsch Ltd.

GEOFFREY HILL: to Andre Deutsch Ltd for excerpts from *Mercian Hymns*; and to Houghton Mifflin Company Inc. for excerpts from *Somewhere is Such a Kingdom.*

SANDRA HOCHMAN: to Martin Secker & Warburg Ltd and to Curtis Brown Inc. for an excerpt from *Earthworks.*

TED HUGHES: to Faber & Faber Ltd and Harper & Row Inc. for excerpts from *Crow.*

RANDALL JARRELL: to Alfred A. Knopf Inc. for an extract from *Poetry and the Age*; and to Faber & Faber Ltd and Farrar, Straus & Giroux Inc. for excerpts from *The Complete Poems of Randall Jarrell,* copyright © 1941, 1942, 1945, 1946, 1949, 1950, 1955 by Randall Jarrell, copyright renewed 1969, 1973, 1974 by Mrs Randall Jarrell.

DAVID JONES: to Faber & Faber Ltd and to the Chilmark Press Inc. for an excerpt from *Anathemata* and *Epoch and Artist.*

SIDNEY KEYES: to Routledge & Kegan Paul Ltd for an excerpt from *Minos of Crete.*

GALWAY KINNELL: to Houghton Mifflin Company Inc. and to the author.

PHILIP LARKIN: to Faber & Faber Ltd for excerpts from *The Whitsun Weddings*; to Faber & Faber Ltd and Farrar, Straus & Giroux Inc. for excerpts from *High Windows* © 1974 by Philip Larkin; to Faber & Faber Ltd for excerpts from *The North Ship.*

ALUN LEWIS: to George Allen & Unwin Ltd for excerpts from *Ha! Ha! Among the Trumpets* and from *Raiders Dawn.*

ROBERT LOWELL: to Faber & Faber Ltd and Farrar, Straus & Giroux Inc. for excerpts from *Life Studies,* copyright © 1956, 1959 by Robert Lowell, *For the Union Dead* copyright © 1964 by Robert Lowell, and *Notebook* copyright © 1967, 1968, 1970 by Robert Lowell; and to Faber & Faber Ltd and

Harcourt Brace Jovanovich Inc. for excerpts from *The Mills of the Kavanaughs.*

LOUIS MACNEICE: to Faber & Faber Ltd and Oxford University Press Inc. for excerpts from *The Collected Poems of Louis MacNeice,* edited by E. R. Dodds. Copyright © the Estate of Louis MacNeice 1966.

CHARLES OLSON: to the Estate of Charles Olson, Cape Goliard Press, and Corinth Books Inc. for an excerpt from *The Maximus Poems* © 1960 by Charles Olson.

SYLVIA PLATH: to Miss Olwyn Hughes for the Estate of Sylvia Plath; and to Alfred A. Knopf Inc. for excerpts from *The Colossus and Other Poems,* copyright © 1957, 1958, 1959, 1960, 1961, 1962 by Sylvia Plath; and to Faber & Faber Ltd for excerpts from *Ariel* © 1965 by Ted Hughes; *Crossing the Water* © 1971 by Ted Hughes; *Winter Trees* © 1971 by Ted Hughes; for 'Letter to a Purist' copyright 1957 and 1969 by Ted Hughes; and for an extract of prose, copyright 1977.

EZRA POUND: to Faber & Faber Ltd and New Directions for an excerpt from *The Cantos,* copyright 1948 by Ezra Pound. Reprinted by permission of New Directions Publishing Corporation.

ANNE RIDLER: to Faber & Faber Ltd for an excerpt from *Nine Bright Shiners.*

THEODORE ROETHKE: to Faber & Faber Ltd and Doubleday & Company for excerpts from *The Collected Poems of Theodore Roethke.* 'Open House' and 'The Signals' copyright 1941 by Theodore Roethke, 'I Cry Love! Love!', 'Praise to the End' copyright 1950 by Theodore Roethke, 'Feud' copyright 1935 by Theodore Roethke, 'Cuttings' copyright 1948 by Theodore Roethke, 'Root Cellar' copyright 1943 by Theodore Roethke, 'Forcing House' copyright 1946 by Theodore Roethke, 'Cuttings (later)' copyright 1948 by the Modern Poetry Association, 'A Field of Light' copyright 1948 by The Tiger's Eye, 'The Long Alley' copyright 1947 by Theodore Roethke, 'O Thou Opening O' copyright 1952 by Theodore Roethke. Reprinted by permission of Doubleday & Company Inc.

W. D. SNODGRASS: to Alfred A. Knopf Inc. and to The Marvell Press for quotations from *Heart's Needle,* © 1959.

GARY SNYDER: to New Directions Publishing Corporation for an excerpt from *Turtle Island,* copyright © 1974 by Gary Snyder. Reprinted by permission of New Directions Publishing Corporation.

JULIAN SYMONS: to London Magazine Editions for an excerpt from *Notes from Another Country.*

ANTHONY THWAITE: to the author and The Marvell Press for excerpts from *Home Truths*; to the author and Oxford University Press for *New Confessions* © Oxford University Press 1974, and *The Owl in the Tree* © Oxford University Press 1963.

TIMES LITERARY SUPPLEMENT: for an excerpt from an editorial of 8 August 1942.

CHARLES TOMLINSON: to the author for an excerpt from *Relations and Contraries*; to Oxford University Press for an excerpt from *Written on Water* © Oxford University Press 1972, and for an excerpt from *The Necklace* © Oxford University Press 1966.

PETER URE: to Liverpool University Press for an excerpt from *Yeats and Anglo-Irish Literature.*

KEITH VAUGHAN: to London Magazine Editions for an excerpt from *Journals and Drawings.*

JOHN WAIN: to the author for an excerpt from a review in *Outposts.*

RICHARD WILBUR: to Faber & Faber Ltd for excerpts from *Poems 1943–1956*; and to Harcourt Brace Jovanovich Inc. for excerpts from *The Poems of Richard Wilbur.*

WILLIAM CARLOS WILLIAMS: to New Directions Publishing Company for excerpts from *Paterson,* copyright © 1946, 1948, 1949, 1951, 1958 by William Carlos Williams. Reprinted by permission of New Directions Publishing Corporation.

241

Index

Extended reference is indicated by numerals in bold face.